THE YEAR
THEY WALKED

THE YEAR THEY WALKED

Rosa Parks and the Montgomery Bus Boycott

BEATRICE SIEGEL

FOUR WINDS PRESS ❖ NEW YORK
MAXWELL MACMILLAN CANADA TORONTO
MAXWELL MACMILLAN INTERNATIONAL
NEW YORK OXFORD SINGAPORE SYDNEY

Four Winds Press
Macmillan Publishing Company
866 Third Avenue
New York, NY 10022

Maxwell Macmillan Canada, Inc.
1200 Eglinton Avenue East
Suite 200
Don Mills, Ontario M3C 3N1

Macmillan Publishing Company is part of the Maxwell Communication Group of Companies.

Printed and bound in the United States of America

10 9 8 7 6 5 4 3

The text of this book is set in 11 point Joanna. Book design by Christy Hale

Library of Congress Cataloging-in-Publication Data
Siegel, Beatrice. The Day They Walked: Rosa Parks and the Montgomery Bus Boycott /Beatrice Siegel. — 1st ed.
     p.   cm. Includes bibliographical references and index.
Summary: Examines the life of Rosa Parks, focusing on her role in the Montgomery bus boycott.
ISBN 0-02-782631-7
1. Parks, Rosa, 1913– —Juvenile literature. 2. Afro-Americans—Alabama—Montgomery—Biography—Juvenile literature. 3. Civil rights workers—Alabama—Montgomery—Biography—Juvenile literature. 4. Montgomery (Ala.)—Biography—Juvenile literature. 5. Montgomery (Ala.)—Race relations—Juvenile literature. 6. Afro-Americans—Civil rights—Alabama—Montgomery—Juvenile literature. 7. Segregation in transportation—Alabama—Montgomery—History—20th century—Juvenile literature. [1. Parks, Rosa, 1913– . 2. Afro-Americans—Biography. 3. Afro-Americans—Civil rights.] I. Title.
F334.M753P387   1992 323′.092—dc20 [B] 91-14078

For Constance Berkley,
my good friend
and patient teacher

CONTENTS

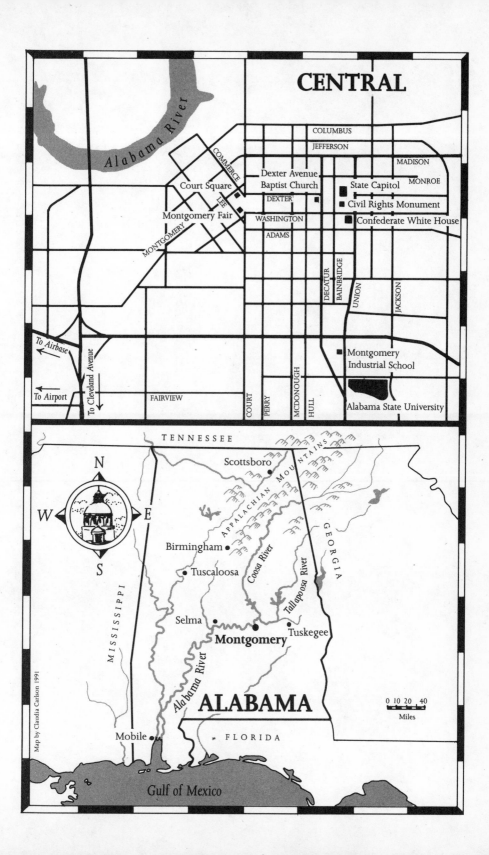

1

AN ARREST

For the third day in a row cold winds roared through the South, driving the temperature down to below freezing. In Montgomery, Alabama, the extraordinary weather made front-page newspaper headlines. Except for that, the city went about its business of preparing for the Christmas season. Twinkling red and green lights and cheerful signs announcing preholiday sales made the city look festive. In the center of Court Square, a busy intersection in the heart of the business district, stood the magnificent old bronze fountain, graceful figures of goddesses perched around its edges. On a corner opposite the fountain, people were lined up for the buses to take them home at the end of the day.

It was not unusual for those waiting for a bus to hurry to the stores across the street to do some last-minute shopping. That was what Mrs. Rosa Parks did. She was a slim, attractive, forty-two-year-old woman dressed in a winter hat and coat and wearing rimless eyeglasses. December 1, 1955, had been an ordinary enough day for Mrs. Parks, though she was a bit tired that evening and bothered by a touch of bursitis in her shoulder. She had finished her day's work as a tailor's assistant at the Montgomery Fair, the town's leading department store. The hot, stuffy room in which she worked had been busy with the holiday rush. Before she lined up for the Cleveland Avenue bus, she did some shopping at Lee's Cut Rate Drug Store for items she needed at home.

When the Cleveland Avenue bus arrived, Mrs. Parks entered the front of the bus, dropped her ten-cent coin into a box, and found a seat. Often Mrs. Parks had to pay her coin, return to the street, and reboard the bus through the rear door. Mrs. Parks had to do that because she was black. In Montgomery, Alabama, only white people could always enter a bus through the front door.

That evening Mrs. Parks was lucky, for she found a seat in the crowded bus, an aisle seat in the first row of the colored section. The first ten seats in the front of the bus were reserved for whites, while blacks filled the back. If seats were vacant in the white section, blacks could not occupy them. Sometimes hardworking black people, their arms full of packages, would have to stand over an empty place in the white section. When whites were standing, however, blacks had to give up their seats. That was the law in Montgomery, and bus drivers, all of them white, had the power to enforce the rules.

Mrs. Parks was comfortable, her packages in her lap, as the bus rumbled on toward Cleveland Court, the housing complex where she lived. In fifteen minutes she would be home with her husband, Raymond, a barber, and her mother, who lived with them. Next to her sat a black man, and black women occupied the two seats across the aisle. Two stops later, near the Empire Theater, the bus was filled and a white man was stand-

12

ing. The back of the bus was packed with black people, many standing in the aisle.

The bus driver, James Blake, looked at the four black people sitting in the first row after the white section and called out that he wanted those seats. All four would have to give up their seats, for it was against the law for a black person to sit in the same row as a white.

No one moved. Blake called out again, "You all better make it light on yourselves and let me have those seats."

At that rebuke, the three people seated with Mrs. Parks moved to the rear of the bus. Mrs. Parks remained seated.

The bus driver came up to her and said, "Look, woman, I told you I wanted the seat. Are you going to stand up?"

"No, I'm not," said Mrs. Parks.

"Well, if you don't stand up, I'm going to have to call the police and have you arrested," said Blake.

Mrs. Parks would not move. "Go ahead and call them," she told the bus driver.

Blake got off the bus to call the police. A few minutes later two police officers were standing in front of Mrs. Parks. After confirming that she had understood the driver's request, one of the officers asked, "Why didn't you get up?"

"I didn't think I should have to," answered Mrs. Parks. And she added, "Why do you push us around?"

"I don't know, but the law is the law and you are under arrest," replied the officer.

The police put Mrs. Parks into a patrol car and drove her to city hall, where she was charged with breaking the law. From there she was taken to the city jail to be fingerprinted and photographed.

Witnessing the arrest was Mrs. Pratt, a neighbor of Mrs. Parks. Shocked by what had happened, she rushed home and phoned

Mrs. Bertha Butler. Mrs. Butler knew Mrs. Parks well, and she immediately phoned Mr. E. D. Nixon, a longtime civil rights leader and head of the local branch of the National Association for the Advancement of Colored People (NAACP).

While phones were ringing throughout the neighborhood, Mrs. Parks was in the city jail. She thought no one knew where she was. After a while she was permitted to phone home. Her mother asked immediately, "Did they beat you?"

Rosa Parks was in danger, and the black community knew it.

2

SOUTHERN BEGINNINGS

She did not see herself as heroic, Mrs. Parks would say, but simply as a woman who spoke up against segregation. Where did she find the courage to do it? What was her life like before that day in December 1955?

She was born to James and Leona McCauley in Tuskegee, Alabama, on February 4, 1913. They named her Rosa Louise. Her father was a carpenter and her mother a teacher. When Rosa was two, her father moved away. She, her mother, and her younger brother, Sylvester, moved in with her maternal grandparents, who had a small farm on the outskirts of Montgomery in a town called Pine Level.

Her early school education did not amount to much. Like most southern rural schools for blacks, hers in Pine Level was overcrowded and poorly equipped. Instead of windows, the room was fitted with wooden shutters through which light filtered. When the shutters were closed on cold days, the room was dark. No amount of hard work on the part of one teacher for all grades could brighten the barren room that had no heat, no water, and no indoor toilets.

A new school in the neighborhood was for white children only, and Rosa saw them driven back and forth each day in a bus. She had to walk miles to her school. That bus made an everlasting impression. In later years Mrs. Parks would say, "The bus was among the first ways I realized there was a black world and a white world."

Nor did Rosa's school run the full eight or nine months of a school year. Hers was let out after six or seven months so that children could work on the farms. That was what Rosa did, working alongside her grandparents in the fields, planting and picking cotton, peanuts, and seasonal crops that she helped sell at the markets.

Her childhood was helped along by the church, which became the backbone of her life. With her family she regularly attended services at the African Methodist Episcopal Church. It was more than a place of worship, more than a place where Rosa learned music and sang her favorite spirituals, "Oh Freedom, Let It Ring" and "Before I'd Be a Slave I'd Be Buried in My Grave." It was where people exchanged news in the absence of a local black newspaper. It was where you could get a loan if you needed one; where you felt safe, less threatened by the surrounding white community. The church was also the center for organizations such as mutual aid societies and social and political clubs. The church and its connected organizations created a sense of community, kept people closely knit, and fostered a feeling of solidarity.

In those growing years, Rosa thought only about getting through the dreadful pattern of the days. She was six years old when she learned about the Ku Klux Klan, or KKK, the nightriders cloaked in white sheets and hoods who terrorized the black neighborhoods. She heard the grown-ups talk of homes and churches burned to the ground, of people dragged from their beds and savagely whipped or killed. The talk among neighbors was not about integration, or politics, or of dreams for the future. They talked about how to survive the persecution, how to stay away from white people who battered their lives. Though her grandfather kept an old gun for protection, it did not reassure Rosa. She remained gripped by fear, tossing in her bed through sleepless nights.

Both her grandparents had been born into slavery, and Rosa learned from them about the terrible conditions in which they had lived. Her grandmother would describe how little slave children were fed. The food was poured from one huge pot in the yard, the way chickens and pigs were fed. Rosa's grandfather, a son of the slaveowner, was treated cruelly after his father died. Crippled early in life, he was beaten by the overseer and often went without shoes and clothing.

Rosa was ten when her grandfather died and again the family moved. This time they settled in with an aunt in Montgomery. Mrs. McCauley, who could not get a job as a teacher, worked in a beauty parlor and took in sewing to add to her income.

Living through those nightmarish days, Rosa tried hard to improve herself. She credits her mother with giving her the strength to endure, building up her sense of self-worth, helping her understand that she was as good as anyone else.

Mrs. McCauley, patient and nurturing, knew the importance of education. She saved up money to pay the small admission fee to a special school so that Rosa could take advantage of a better educational opportunity at the Montgomery Industrial School.

Rosa was eleven when she entered the fifth grade there. She became one of a student body of 325 black girls. The school building itself was impressive, a large brick structure with two floors of schoolrooms and facilities for children from kindergarten to the ninth grade. The school had been founded in 1886 by two northern white women, Miss H. Margaret Beard and Miss Alice L. White. They had been helped and supported by the American Missionary Society of New York and by other northern whites who wanted to do good deeds for southern blacks. At its peak the school had ten white women teachers, who, for daring to work with black children, were isolated by Montgomery's white population.

At the school Rosa received a solid education that included classes in literature. But the curriculum emphasized practical work, teaching the children a vocation: how to be homemakers. Rosa took courses in cooking, sewing, basketry, and embroidery, and she attended lectures on cleanliness and discipline. An emphasis on "Christian values" meant chapel meetings every Friday morning, filled with sermons and singing.

Schoolmates remember Rosa as a quiet, genial sort of young girl. Everyone was fond of her and thought she was easy to get along with. Many of the youngsters who attended the school would become women active in the community, in church work, civil rights, and voter registration.

When the school closed down in 1927, Rosa was in the seventh grade. She continued her education at the Booker T. Washington Junior High School, from which she graduated at age fifteen. From there she went on to Alabama State High School, an all-black school on the campus of the Alabama State College, which was also all black. Before graduation she had to drop out of school to help the family, especially to nurse her ailing mother and grandmother. She was nineteen when she married Raymond Parks in December 1932.

By trade Mr. Parks was a barber. He was also a courageous civil rights activist deeply involved in the Scottsboro case. In the North the case had become a crusade for justice. Mass meetings, picket lines, and letter-writing campaigns called for freedom for the nine black men, aged thirteen to twenty, accused of raping two white women in a freight car traveling through Alabama. The trial was held in the town of Scottsboro, in the northeast corner of Alabama. Despite evidence proving the young men innocent, a few were found guilty and sentenced to death. Others were sentenced to seventy-five to ninety-nine years in prison.

In racist Alabama, it was dangerous for Raymond Parks to be involved in the Scottsboro case. The state legal system was determined to put the men to death. Rosa would later recall secret meetings in their apartment when her husband was trying to raise money for the cause. Equally dangerous were Mr. Parks's work for the local branch of the National Association for the Advancement of Colored People, of which he was a charter member, and his work in voter registration. People had been killed in the South for helping black citizens exercise their right to vote.

The government made special efforts to prevent blacks from casting a ballot. Registrants had to answer a series of twenty-one questions, questions so difficult that highly educated people had trouble with them. Once that hurdle was passed, registrants had to pay all the poll taxes back to their twenty-first birthday. For poor people the sum was often considerable.

Soon after she was married, Rosa returned to high school, receiving her diploma in 1933. The thirties were the years of the Great Depression, and she had a hard time finding work, going from one low-paying job to another. For a while she was a clerk in an insurance company; for a while she was a domestic worker. After work hours she did sewing at home for private customers. Several years were spent at the Crittenden Tailor Shop before she went on to the Montgomery Fair as a tailor's assistant.

Throughout these years of hard work she was involved in civil rights. In 1943 she joined the NAACP and became secretary of the Montgomery chapter, where she met Edgar Daniel Nixon, president of the state branch. Mrs. Parks knew Mr. Nixon as the most militant person in Montgomery. He spoke to her about registering to vote, and in 1945—after her third try and after paying the total poll tax of eighteen dollars—she cast her first ballot.

The cases fought by the NAACP got no publicity. They were as invisible to the public and to history as if they had never occurred. But those who, like Rosa and Raymond Parks and Mr. Nixon, were fighting against the oppression of African-Americans saw brutal crimes against their people. There were cases dealing with "flogging, peonage, murder, and rape," as Mrs. Parks described them in an interview in Ebony magazine.

From the very beginning of her social and political work, Mrs. Parks was drawn to young people. She wanted to make their lives easier, to help them along. To do so she organized a youth council within the NAACP. At first the council had only five members, who attended meetings as much to eat Mrs. Parks's cookies as to learn community values. "She was a doer, not a bragger," said E. D. Nixon.

But her work with youth expanded and became central to her activism. She tutored youngsters and saw to it that they had the proper books and clothes for school. She helped them move forward and get on with their lives.

By the 1950s Mrs. Rosa Parks was well known in the community for her dedication to children and her work in civil rights and in the church. She had become an attractive woman with a deep sense of quiet. Within that quietude was enormous strength.

A rural Alabama school for black children in 1965 (*Bruce Davidson/Magnum Photos, Inc.*)

The Ku Klux Klan burning a cross to intimidate a community (*Bruce Roberts*)

Segregation of public toilets (Bruce Roberts)

Rosa Parks in 1954 (Photo by Ida Berman, courtesy Highlander Research and Education Center)

A school desegregation workshop at the Highlander Folk School. Septima Clark is second from left; Rosa Parks is second from right. (*Courtesy Highlander Research and Education Center*)

3

THE CRADLE OF THE CONFEDERACY

S he needed that strength to live in Alabama. The state was called the "heart of Dixie" because it had played a key role in southern history.

Montgomery, located in the east-central part of the state, became the capital of Alabama in 1846. It was a beautiful city, leaning on a bend in the Alabama River. Rolling hills led from the town to the surrounding rich farmland known as the Black Belt, a region that stretched clear across the central part of Alabama into the neighboring states of Georgia on the east and Mississippi on the west.

The rich black soil grew cotton. The crop was so successful in the years before the Civil War that it became the basis of the economy and was said to rule the South. It also ruled the lives of over two million black people under the system of slavery that made its production possible.

In those long-ago years, Montgomery was a booming cotton port. Barges and steamers drew up to the town piers to be loaded with bales of cotton and sent majestically sailing down the swift-running Alabama River through wide channels into the port of Mobile, on the Gulf of Mexico. From there cotton was shipped to other U.S. ports and on to Europe for the rapidly developing textile trade.

In the fight against slavery during the Civil War, Montgomery became the first capital of the Confederacy, as the southern states that seceded from the Union were called. Jefferson Davis was inaugurated as its first president on the steps of the white-pillared state house, over which the Confederate flag was unfurled.

Though slavery was abolished during the Civil War, racism was not abolished. It remained deeply embedded in southern life. In many ways it was another form of slavery. Millions of African-Americans continued to be the victims of a web of laws, rules, and customs that trapped them mercilessly in racial inequality. No matter what amendments were added to the Constitution or what new laws were adopted, the system of racism in the South remained untouched. "It was a struggle—just to be human," Rosa Parks would say, "to be a citizen, to have the rights and privileges of any other person."

In the face of continuous hardship, the black community had to define itself and the importance of its own culture, its humanity, its kindness. It had its own history and its daily struggles, rich with the beat of many voices saying things their own way. It had courageous citizens like E. D. Nixon and Raymond and Rosa Parks; young, articulate leadership in social and civic clubs; and strong clergymen in the many black churches.

Rosa Parks would recall those days and years in segregated Alabama as a time of "meager education, meager opportunities, economic deprivation, [and] rigid racial segregation" of all walks of life. In a newspaper interview in the *Chicago Tribune*, she would say that life was "just a matter of survival . . . of existing from one day to the next."

She hated it all the time, the inequality of her way of life—an inequality without reason. She dreamed "what it should be like to be a human being," she would tell an interviewer. So much was brutal and mean, she was often tired in body and soul. It would have been easier to fall apart than to care about what was going on. She would get "upset, angry many times, probably most of the time and many times discouraged," but she carried on. She would call it taking "one more step."

Along the hard road some events gave her courage and pushed her along. She saw black soldiers returning to the South after World War II and the Korean War put up a fight for the right to vote, seeking equal rights they felt they had won on the battlefields. Their struggle was crushed by white opposition, but it left its mark. People were aroused, increasingly angry and bitter.

In May 1954 came a stunning victory. In the case of Brown v. *the Board of Education of Topeka*, the U.S. Supreme Court ruled that school segregation was illegal. The victory brought wild rejoicing in the black communities. For many it was the first sign that the federal government was responding to their needs, that the promises of democracy might be realized. But 80 percent of the white people in the South opposed the ruling and vowed not to permit desegregation of schools. Alabama's governor sent in state troopers to enforce the segregation of schools, breaking the federal law.

Out of the backlash against the Brown decision, a new white hate group took root. Called the White Citizens Council, it was formed specifically to fight integration at every level and to terrorize black and white activists. The idea of mixing the races outraged these extremists. United States Senator James O. Eastland of Mississippi became a prominent figure in the organization, giving it national prominence. By the end of 1954 four Alabama counties had sprouted branches of the White Citizens

Council. In their newsletter they printed statements such as the following: "When in the course of human events it becomes necessary to abolish the Negro race, proper methods should be used. Among them are guns, bows and arrows, slingshots, and knives."

Desegregation of schools was now the law, but it would take a tremendous struggle to put the law into effect. Black people knew that there was no progress without struggle.

In July 1955, Mrs. Parks had a personal experience that helped her to overcome other barriers and added to her inner peace. On the recommendation of her friend Virginia Durr, a white woman whom Mrs. Parks knew well, she attended a school desegregation workshop at the Highlander Folk School in the hill country of Monteagle, Tennessee. The school was an independent adult-education center dealing with problems of social change. Founded by Myles Horton, it brought together black and white activists in trade unions and civil rights to discuss ways of reshaping southern life to achieve equality and justice for all races and classes.

Recalling her visit at a later date, Mrs. Parks would say that she had not been able to laugh for a long time. But Highlander changed all that. For the first time she experienced interracial living. It seemed natural for people, regardless of race, to live and work together. The thought came to her that there could be a unified society, "one of differing races and backgrounds meeting together . . . and living together in peace and harmony." She would say that at Highlander she gained the strength to persevere in her work for freedom, not just for blacks but for all oppressed people.

She also met Septima Clark at Highlander. Clark was a remarkable woman, clear in her vision and her struggles for equality. Parks was impressed with the ability of this black educator and teacher to organize and hold things together in an interracial setting. She admired Septima Clark for the very things she herself was not. "I was tense, and I was nervous, and I was upset most of the time. . . . I felt that I had been destroyed long ago. But I had the hope that young people could be benefited by equal education," she said in her remarks to the folksinger Pete Seeger for his book *Everybody Says Freedom.*

She was reluctant to leave Highlander. Where was she to go but back to segregated Montgomery and daily humiliation? Humiliation over something she could not control: the color of her skin.

A month after her return home, the brutal slaying of Emmett Till added to the terror in black communities. The fourteen-year-old youngster had come from Chicago to visit relatives in a small town in the neighboring state of Mississippi. On the evening of August 28, 1955, a gang of white men pulled the youngster from his bed, shot him through the head, and dumped his body into the Tallahatchie River. Why? Because, it was said, he dared address a white woman in the general store in a friendly way. The two men accused of and tried for the kidnapping and murder were found innocent.

By 1955 little had changed in Montgomery, Alabama, since the end of the 1880s, the period called Reconstruction that followed the Civil War. Other businesses had replaced the cotton trade, making Montgomery a center for small clothing factories, glass products, food products, and lumber mills. But in other ways, the town seemed to have been in a long sleep. It was still the Cradle of the Confederacy. Its favorite landmark was the white wooden house where Jefferson Davis lived while president.

The state of Alabama ranked as one of the worst—forty-seventh—in its system of education. It ranked high in poverty and infant deaths. Thousands of homes did not have running water. Schools for blacks remained ill-equipped one-room shacks. Schools for whites were better, though still below the national standards. Few funds were available for education, welfare, or any of the social services. Those who suffered most were the poor blacks and the poor whites. Nevertheless even the poor whites had a sense of power through the system of segregation, which told them they were better than the black people in town.

The division between black and white was still basic to the city's structure in 1955. Of Montgomery's population of some 140,000, about 50,000—36 percent—were black. They were confined to low-paying jobs. Men worked as ditch diggers, janitors, carpenters, gardeners, parking-lot attendants, or mechanics' assistants; or they worked in sawmills and lumber camps. The majority of black women who worked held jobs as cooks and maids in white homes, whereas the majority of white women who worked held jobs as clerical workers, a higher-paying category.

Though the majority of black people were poor, there was a small black middle and upper class. It was made up of businesspeople, store owners, insurance agents, and a handful of professionals: three physicians, one dentist, two lawyers, a pharmacist, and ninety-two clergymen. There were schoolteachers and college professors. In this class were many forceful people developing leadership skills. They were the ones who organized church and social clubs. They were the ones who formed committees to visit city officials to protest against injustice.

The upper class did not escape the laws of segregation. The color of a person's skin cut across all class lines, presenting the community with common problems and common handicaps.

Though they faced common problems, the black population was not united but separated by class differences. And in the small upper class there were also factions, organizations competing with each other for power in the community.

In his book *Stride Toward Freedom*, Martin Luther King, Jr., described how the city of Montgomery appeared to him when he settled there in 1954. He found a "threefold malady—factionalism among the leaders, indifference in the educated group, and passivity in the uneducated." The quiet acceptance of the way things were bothered him, though he understood that the passivity stemmed from fear: The black community was economically dependent on whites, and when an employee spoke up against segregation, that person often lost his or her job. He also understood the indifference as resulting from years of humiliation, a shattering of self-esteem brought about by a system that continuously told blacks they were inferior. On the surface the system of segregation was seldom challenged, making Montgomery appear as if it had solved the race question.

To an outside observer in the mid-1950s, the city would have looked calm and sunny, with breezes blowing off the river over the broad, tree-lined streets. The white-marble state capitol building gleamed on top of the hill, surrounded by administrative buildings. Montgomery was also the center of state and county governments, attracting lawyers and businesspeople attending to official business. Along the quiet upper-middle-class streets were spacious mansions and well-kept lawns and gardens. Two air-force bases on the outskirts of the city contributed to its economy.

White people were proud of Montgomery, proud of its historic tradition as the Cradle of the Confederacy. Steeped in custom and southern culture, they led genteel lives filled with old-fashioned courtesies. It pleased them that the Confederate flag still flew over the state capitol.

Underneath the surface of this glistening town, however, discontent simmered in the black community from years of repressed anger and bitterness. People vented their rage at the Montgomery City Lines bus company in particular, for that is where they experienced daily humiliation. Of the total black population of fifty thousand, about seventeen thousand rode the bus twice daily, to and from work. All the drivers were white, even though the majority of riders were blacks traveling through black neighborhoods. Among those drivers were nasty men who called black passengers offensive names. Riders were angry at the system of having to pay at the front of the bus and reboard at the rear, especially when some abusive drivers then rode off before passengers could reboard. They were also fed up with having to stand over empty seats in the white section.

Rosa Parks had had humiliating experiences on the buses before her arrest, and she did not like using them. Twelve years earlier, she had gotten on the bus, and after she paid her fare the driver, the same James Blake, insisted that she get off and reboard in the rear. When she refused to do so, Blake took her by the arm and escorted her off the vehicle. Rather than get back on that bus, she waited for another. She found bus transportation so degrading that she walked whenever possible.

The bus was only one part of the whole system, a system of segregation in every walk of life. It was the way white people held on to their power, and it was protected by law. To maintain the system, there were police beatings, the terror of the White Citizens Councils, the KKK burnings of homes and churches, and lynchings. Between the years 1889 and 1941, close to four thousand lynchings took place in the South. Black parents taught their children not to challenge the laws of white society, for death lay in that direction.

The simple word "no" uttered by Mrs. Parks on December 1 threatened the whole rigid social structure of segregation. Mrs. Parks was saying that she was equal to the white man, that she had as much right to the bus seat as he did.

She had not known the exact moment or place she would choose to assert her sense of equality. Nor was it her intention at that moment to integrate the buses. All she wanted was to get home, be with her family, and carry on with the evening's plans.

She had fought a daily battle to maintain a sense of self, to value herself. The family, the church, the community, and her experiences at Highlander had helped her along the way. So had courageous leaders like E. D. Nixon and others fighting lonely battles.

4

"STAY OFF THE BUSES ON MONDAY"

Phones rang, neighbors gathered, and the community came alive with the news: Rosa Parks was arrested.

"They arrested the wrong person," said E. D. Nixon. He knew Rosa Parks well. He knew the depth of her strength and her commitment to justice.

Nixon himself was fearless. A tall, impressive man, well over six feet, he was born and raised in Montgomery. In the poor family of seventeen children in which he grew up, his education ended at the seventh grade. Still, he became the civil rights leader of the black community. When others were afraid to speak up, he spoke for them, making use of special connections he had developed with people in power.

His job as a Pullman porter on overnight trains often took him out of town on runs to Chicago. The neighborhood knew him as a devoted member of the Brotherhood of Sleeping Car Porters, the trade union to which he belonged. Nixon would credit A. Philip Randolph, the national head of the Brotherhood, with giving him the strength to stand up as a trade unionist and as a leader in the fight against injustice. The community also knew Nixon as an NAACP leader and as president of the Progressive Democratic Association.

When he heard the news of Rosa Parks's arrest, he phoned the police station. He was unable to get a reply. In effect, he was told that it was none of his business. Fred Gray, one of the two black Montgomery lawyers, was out of town, so Nixon phoned a liberal white lawyer he knew well, Clifford Durr. Both Durr and his wife, Virginia, were outspoken in their opposition to segregation and were active in the Council on Human Relations, an interracial organization in Montgomery.

Durr reported back to Nixon that Rosa Parks had been arrested for refusing to give up her seat on the bus, a violation of a city ordinance giving drivers the right to decide seating on a city bus. Durr offered to go with Nixon to the police station, and Virginia Durr insisted on going along too. It was "a terrible sight," said Mrs. Durr, "to see this gentle, lovely, sweet woman, whom I knew and was so fond of, being brought down by a matron."

When Raymond Parks arrived to take his wife home, Nixon and the Durrs accompanied them. Over coffee at the Parks's apartment, they all discussed the arrest. Mrs. Parks had not only broken a segregation law but was almost guilty of another violation when she became thirsty in jail and wanted to drink out of the water fountain. It was for whites only, she was told.

That evening Nixon carefully suggested that the Parks arrest could be the case to challenge the seating arrangements in buses—with a boycott of the bus line! The idea was explosive. Who knew where a boycott would lead? Mrs. Parks's family, fearing for Rosa's safety, was upset. As the center of a case challenging state and city segregation laws, she could be lynched. But Mrs. Parks calmed her husband and her mother and agreed that her arrest could be used as a test case. Fred

Gray, who had returned to Montgomery that evening, would represent her in the appeal to the state courts. At Gray's side throughout the complicated process would be Clifford Durr and a group of experienced black lawyers from other cities.

That same Thursday evening, a different scene was being acted out in another part of town. Mrs. Jo Ann Robinson heard of the arrest through a late-night phone call from Fred Gray. A bright, energetic English professor at Alabama State College, she was an acknowledged leader in town. At the time of the Rosa Parks arrest, she was president of the Women's Political Council. The organization had been formed in 1946 by Alabama State professor Mary Fair Burks to work on voter registration and, in general, to try to maintain self-esteem in the black community in the face of daily insults.

Like many other women, Mrs. Robinson had had her own humiliating experiences on Montgomery City Line buses. In her memoirs she tells of an incident during one Christmas vacation when she boarded a bus to the local airport. Her arms were filled with packages, gifts she was taking to friends in Cleveland. Deep in thought, she forgot for a moment where she was and sat down in the front of the bus. In an instant, before she could collect her thoughts, she heard the booming voice of the bus driver shouting at her: "Get up from there! Get up from there!" Shaken by the angry voice and the menacing gestures of the driver, who looked as if he were ready to strike her, she fled from the bus, dropping her packages.

"I felt like a dog," she said. "And I got mad, after this was over, and I realized that I was a human being, and just as intelligent and far more trained than that bus driver. . . . I cried all the way to Cleveland."

At that time Mrs. Robinson vowed she would do everything possible to end the abuses on the buses. On several occasions the Women's Political Council had met with city officials to protest the behavior of the bus drivers and the needless indignity of having to pay at the front of the bus and reboard at the rear. The council also protested the regulation requiring blacks to stand over empty seats in the white section. Their protests were to no avail.

Several times in 1955 women had been forced to give up their seats on the buses. When they refused to do so they were arrested. Women usually paid the fine and did nothing more. But high-school student Claudette Colvin was different. She said she was tired of standing for white folks every morning. When she refused to give up her seat one day, police officers tried to arrest her. In resisting the arrest, she scratched the face of a policeman. She was handcuffed, taken off to jail, and kept there until the middle of the night. Not even her family knew where she was.

The incident caused an uproar in the community. The Women's Political Council was ready to make a test case of the arrest when it was discovered that Colvin was pregnant.

"Women were ready to explode" at the accumulation of insults, said Mrs. Robinson. More than once they had thought of boycotting the bus line. When Mrs. Robinson heard of the Parks arrest, she immediately got busy. She knew Mrs. Parks to be the right person: She was respected, hard-working, and she could stand up under pressure. Mrs. Robinson and Mr. Nixon readily agreed that Mrs. Parks could well be the one around whom they might bring about a change in the community. They decided to call a one-day boycott to take place on Monday, the day of the trial. But how to get the news around? Mrs. Robinson said she would get a flier out to the public. Mr. Nixon said he would arrange a meeting of black ministers and other leaders for the next day.

Mrs. Robinson called on her colleagues in the council, and a committee of women drew up a leaflet. It asked "every Negro to stay off the buses Monday in protest of the arrest and trial of Rosa Parks. Don't ride the buses to work, to town, to school, or anywhere on Monday," the leaflet urged.

Through a network of council members in all the schools, students helped distribute some 35,000 leaflets. They rang door-bells and visited homes, schools, shops, bars, and restaurants in the black community.

In the meantime, Nixon contacted black ministers with the assistance of Ralph D. Abernathy, the twenty-nine-year-old pas-tor of the First Baptist Church and secretary of the Baptist Min-isters Alliance. Through the alliance, Abernathy could reach all the Baptist leaders in town. He himself was a forceful man and an effective public speaker. After serving in the U.S. Army in World War II, he became an educator and then studied for the ministry. Bright and vigorous, he used his talents in the crusade for progress for African-Americans.

Abernathy suggested the fashionable Dexter Avenue Baptist Church as a meeting place. It had a new pastor named Martin Luther King, Jr. At first the Reverend King hesitated about hav-ing the meeting there. He was new to the pastorate and felt pressured by many responsibilities. But he quickly realized the emergency nature of the boycott and agreed to let his church be used for the meeting.

Fifty community leaders were present Friday evening, De-cember 2. Among them were ministers, heads of social and political clubs, businessmen, and teachers, making up a basic network for spreading the news. By the time of the meeting, leaflets calling for a boycott of buses on Monday, December 5, had already blanketed numerous neighborhoods. Faced with an accomplished fact, the group moved forward with plans to put out another 7,000 leaflets to be sure that every part of the city was covered. They also laid plans for alternate methods of transportation, setting up car pools and arranging for pickup stations. They called on the eighteen Negro taxicab companies, with two hundred cabs available. Plans were also made to hold a mass meeting Monday night after the day's boycott to decide on a future course of action. The mass meeting would be held in the community's largest hall, the Holt Street Baptist Church, which could hold hundreds of people.

Mrs. Parks attended the Friday-evening meeting. Though her friend E. D. Nixon was out of town on a trip to Chicago, she was warmly received and made comfortable. She spoke before the group, telling of her bus experience. That morning, the day after the arrest, she had shown up for work at the Montgomery Fair to the surprise of the other employees. They had seen the news item tucked away on page nine of the *Montgomery Advertiser*, the city's leading newspaper:

Negro Jailed Here
for 'Overlooking'
Bus Segregation

The article went on to tell about the arrest and pointed directly to "the woman, Rosa Parks, [of] 634 Cleveland Ave. . . ." A letter appeared in the *Advertiser* in response to the story. "Bring back the Klan," that was what Alabama needed, it said.

Tensions were rising in the black community. People were edgy working out alternate ways of getting to work. Rallying behind them were the wealthy people who owned their own cars. Those cars, needed for transportation, would become an important factor in the day's outcome.

On Sunday, December 4, news of the boycott was announced from every pulpit in every black church. The ministers explained that this radical step was a way of protesting the system of transportation that brutalized and humiliated Montgomery's black citizens every day. More than any other institution, the bus system was a reminder of their "inferiority," an attack on their dignity. The boycott was called, explained the ministers, not only to protest the arrest of Mrs. Rosa Parks but to make a statement for freedom. They were demanding their basic human rights.

Those who did not attend church would learn about the boycott in an unexpected way: through the pages of the *Montgomery Advertiser*. E. D. Nixon had leaked the story to Joe Azbell, the city editor. Azbell ran a front-page news item:

Negro Groups
Ready Boycott
of City Lines

The article referred to the leaflets flooding the streets and also announced the meeting set for Monday night at the Holt Street Baptist Church.

From pulpits, street corners, newspapers, telephones, and word of mouth, the call went out to the entire black community of 50,000: STAY OFF THE BUSES ON MONDAY IN PROTEST OF THE ARREST AND TRIAL OF ROSA PARKS.

5

"NOW IS THE TIME"

A cold, bitter wind blew through the city on Monday, December 5. Rosa Parks, Martin Luther King, Jr., Jo Ann Robinson, and E. D. Nixon peered through their windows or stood on street corners, watching the big yellow buses roll down the streets. They were empty—empty of black riders, except for a few here and there. It was a miracle, said Dr. King. "The once dormant and quiescent Negro community was now fully awake." It was "the beginning of a new age for an oppressed people," said another black minister.

The city, to keep the buses full, had arranged for two motorcycle policemen to follow each bus to be sure that black "goons" were not intimidating riders. Other policemen guarded bus stops. But these ruses did not work. The boycott was a success.

At Court Square, where Rosa Parks had boarded the bus on the fateful evening of December 1, a handwritten sign was tacked onto the wall of the bus shed: PEOPLE, DON'T RIDE THE BUS TODAY. DON'T RIDE IT FOR FREEDOM.

42

In the downtown area of the city, black people were waiting on street corners for rides. Bundled up in winter coats and sweaters against the cold, wet day, many jammed into cars with volunteer drivers who stopped to pick them up. Or they piled into black-owned taxis at an agreed-upon fare of ten cents, the same fare paid on buses. They climbed onto pickup trucks. Thousands walked, lunch bags in their hands. Schoolchildren accompanied by parents walked the mile or more to school. High-school and college students walked or thumbed a ride. A few horsedrawn carriages and muledrawn carts appeared on the streets. The long walk had begun in Montgomery.

At eight o'clock that same morning, fifty black people gathered near the Recorder's Court, where the Rosa Parks trial was to take place. By the time court opened, the crowd had swelled to over five hundred, overflowing from the courtroom into hallways and streets. Accompanied by E. D. Nixon and her lawyer, Fred Gray, Mrs. Parks entered the court. Within five minutes the proceedings took place and ended. Tried on an old city code provision regulating bus segregation, she was found guilty, fined ten dollars and court costs of four dollars, and freed on a $100 bond. Her lawyer announced that he would appeal the case.

On Monday afternoon, the leaders of the boycott met to prepare the agenda for the mass meeting to be held that evening at the Holt Street Baptist Church. Exuberant over the success of the boycott, they saw the need for a new organization, one that would unite the black community and confront city officials with their demands. They called the new organization the Montgomery Improvement Association (MIA) and elected Martin Luther King, Jr., as the first president. An executive committee would carry on the work.

The Reverend King was not only new to the community and an inexperienced minister; he had been married only two years before, to the talented and beautiful Coretta Scott, and he was a new father. Baby Yolanda Denise had been born on November 17.

The twenty-six-year-old pastor had come from a background of strong family figures and religious leaders. His grandfather had been a Baptist minister, as was his father. Young Martin—or Mike, as he was called—grew up in an upper-middle-class family in Atlanta, Georgia, and had the advantages of a superior education. After graduating from Morehouse College, he went on to Crozer Theological Seminary, where he was class valedictorian and was awarded his bachelor of divinity degree in 1951. Given a scholarship for further education, he entered the Boston University School of Theology for a doctorate in philosophy.

In physical appearance, the young minister was a short, solemn-faced man. His many years of education and philosophical discussions gave him a thoughtful air during his first year in Montgomery, as if he had to ponder every aspect of a question. At all times his manner was unassuming, for he himself did not appreciate his power.

He was appointed to his first position in September 1954, when he became pastor of the Dexter Avenue Baptist Church in Montgomery. It was an old church built eighty years before during the Reconstruction period. The simple red-brick building stood on the corner of Montgomery's busiest thoroughfare. Dexter Avenue stretched from Court Square, with the fountain in its center, up the hill to the state capitol building on top of the slope. One block below the capitol, the Dexter Avenue Church stood in full view of the Confederate flag flying over the white-marble State House. The church was an enclave for the black elite, for college professors, businesspeople, professionals, and others prominent in the black community.

During his first year as minister, Dr. King had won over his parishioners. He was patient, persuasive, and responsible in caring for the needs of his congregation. He was an extraordinary orator, his words sparkling with knowledge that came from hundreds of books and philosophical discussions. His sermons, too, rolled with the voices of biblical figures and with the ancient history of his people. His deep passion for social issues had not yet been tapped, but he knew some things for certain. He wanted freedom and justice for all African-Americans. He also knew that violence was not an answer to their problems, not an answer to the violence visited on them by whites through history. Violence was not the way of God.

His first leadership role, as president of the Montgomery Improvement Association, would change the Reverend Martin Luther King, Jr. The movement would force him to grow in unexpected ways. And though at first people were not sure of him—who was he?—he had behind him the aura of the prestigious Dexter Avenue Church. And because he was a newcomer to the community, his slate was clean. He had not taken sides in local controversies.

' The ministers at the Monday-afternoon meeting were uncertain about whether to continue the boycott. They would let those attending the mass meeting that night decide. In the upheaval over the Rosa Parks arrest, the community was experiencing growing pains, working together for the first time. If nothing else happened, the successful boycott that day would write a glorious chapter to history.

The day had been so busy that Dr. King did not have time to prepare his talk for the evening. He was deep in thought as he approached the Holt Street Baptist Church and at first could not understand why traffic and dense crowds of people were blocking the streets. Rosa Parks, too, had difficulty getting into the church, and Virginia and Clifford Durr could not get through the crowds at all. They had to turn back.

Over five thousand people had spilled from the church and overflowed into the streets. They stood jammed together, a diverse crowd, people of different religious beliefs, social values, and classes: the laborer and the professional, the domestic worker and the upper-class lady. Through them ran a current of energy, strength, and good cheer. They felt a kinship to each other through their concern for Rosa Parks and their elation over the success of the day's boycott.

The mass meeting started with the audience standing to sing the hymn "Onward, Christian Soldiers." They sang in rapturous choral voices, the massive sounds coming from both within and outside the church. After prayers, E. D. Nixon said a few words from the podium, urging everyone to be strong, to "stand on our feet and take our rightful place in society."

The Reverend Martin Luther King, Jr., was called on to give the main talk. He stood at the pulpit of the church, facing the intent audience, aware of the thousands who would hear him over the loudspeakers. "We are here because we are American citizens," he said in his opening sentences, "and we are determined to apply our citizenship to the fullness of its means." He went on to talk about the practical situation before them: the arrest of Rosa Parks. "I'm happy that it happened to a person like Mrs. Parks," he said, "for nobody can doubt the boundless outreach of her integrity. Nobody can doubt the height of her character. Nobody can doubt the depth of her Christian commitment. . . ."

The words began to flow. They pulsed with the man's eloquence. "There comes a time," he said, "when people get tired of being trampled over by the iron feet of oppression." Excitement surged through the crowd, enthusiasm breaking out in a chorus of "Yes! Yes!" and "Amen!" As Dr. King continued to speak, he looped his words together into a new beat. The thousands listening to him cheered him on with their shouts of

"Amen!" And while the cheering and shouting were going on, King's voice continued to ring out. "There comes a time, my friends, when people get tired of being flung across the abyss of humiliation where they experience the bleakness of nagging despair," he said. "There comes a time when people get tired of being pushed out of the glittering sunlight of life's July and left standing amidst the piercing chill of an alpine November." He called for dignity, for staying united as they stood up for their rights. "We must stick together and work together," he cautioned, "if we are to win . . . our rights as Americans."

Speaking from the depths of his own soul, he touched his listeners' terrible pain and heartache. He spoke against the use of violence, maintaining that the only weapon they had was the "weapon of protest." He quoted from the Bible, saying that they were determined in Montgomery to work and fight "until justice rolls down like waters and righteousness like a mighty stream."

At that first mass meeting, King introduced a new approach to the civil rights struggle. In his vision, love was the guiding star. Blacks must not hate their white opponents while they sought justice. Instead, he urged his listeners to have compassion and good will toward whites. This approach was known as nonviolent resistance, and it would develop into a social force and a powerful weapon of protest.

King also emphasized the need for unity, the need to work together. "Right here in Montgomery when the history books are written in the future, somebody will have to say, 'There lived a race of people, of black people, . . . of people who had the moral courage to stand up for their rights.' "

After the young pastor's forceful talk, the evening reached another emotional peak with the introduction of Rosa Parks, to thunderous applause and a standing ovation. People saw in Mrs. Parks a symbol of their hopes and aspirations. This shy-looking woman had put up a fight—could they do less?

In describing the Holt Street mass meeting, city editor Joe Azbell reported in the *Montgomery Advertiser* that he had never heard such singing. "They were on fire for freedom. There was a spirit there that no one could capture again . . . it was so powerful."

Jo Ann Robinson (*Courtesy Booker T. Lee*)

The Reverend Martin Luther King, Jr., addressing a meeting of the MIA. The Reverend Ralph Abernathy is in the first row on the left; Rosa Parks is seated next to him. (*Don Cravens*)

Motorcycle police watch a black-owned parking lot where people gathered
for rides (*Don Cravens*)

Fred Gray (*left*), the Reverend Ralph Abernathy (*center*), and the Reverend Robert Graetz (*right*) discuss boycott business (*AP/Wide World Photos*)

Rosa Parks fingerprinted by a deputy sheriff in February 1956, at time of arrest
of over one hundred in boycott case (*AP/Wide World Photos*)

E. D. Nixon and Rosa Parks entering the courthouse in bus boycott case
(*AP/Wide World Photos*)

The Reverend Martin Luther King, Jr., addressing a mass meeting (*Collection of Bayard Rustin*)

6

THE YEAR THEY WALKED

The thousands gathered in the Holt Street Baptist Church and on the streets gave the leadership its answer: Continue the boycott!

Resolutions passed at the meeting called on all citizens to stay off the buses owned by the City Lines bus company until demands were met. Those demands were announced by the Reverend Ralph Abernathy. They had been drawn up in the afternoon by members of the Montgomery Improvement Association and asked for the following changes:

1. Blacks were to sit in buses from the back forward, whites from the front backward. No one would have to give up a seat, and no one would have to stand while seats were empty.
2. Bus drivers were to be courteous to all riders.
3. Blacks, who represented 75 percent of all riders, should be able to apply for jobs as drivers.

The demands were so modest that they did not even include a call to end segregated seating on the buses. Further resolutions enlisted car owners to help people get to work; asked employers to help transport their employees; and called for a delegation to try to meet with the bus company to discuss the demands.

The movement was in the hands of the MIA and its executive board of forty-six people, over half of whom were ministers. They had always provided a network that knit the community together. But now, instead of ministering to a troubled congregation, they were dealing with a rebellious people.

On the board were several women, among them Mrs. Jo Ann Robinson, who would be the publicist for the movement. There was also Mrs. A. W. West, a dynamic leader and wife of the only black dentist in town. Others on the board included physicians, college professors, labor leaders, and one white, the Reverend Robert Graetz.

But the success or failure of the movement rested on some seventeen thousand black people who rode the buses twice a day. They were ordinary people, people who would never become famous, people who could not afford to miss a day's work. They were the ones who would face employers who insulted them and motorcycle cops who threatened and harassed them as they filed into cars and taxis. They were the disciplined ones who would attend mass meetings twice a week, patiently listening to talks advising them not to be violent, to turn the other cheek. They would convert the boycott into a mass movement, filling it out with their anger and bitterness over years of racial incidents. As they took charge of their own lives, their strength would sweep like a tide over everyone. They had waited a long time for change.

The struggle exploding around Mrs. Parks had become larger

than the single person, though the movement would not forget that she had led the way and cast a spotlight on the city of Montgomery.

Within a few days of the Holt Street mass meeting, Montgomery became known as the "walking city." Thousands were seen hurrying along to their jobs on foot. Some walked as far as twelve miles a day to their places of work and back home.

To make the boycott a success took more than determination and help from a few white employers. It took practical planning, which evolved with time. It took the daily, plodding work of a small staff paid by church collections and groups of volunteers. Together, they put into operation a smooth-running system of alternate methods of transportation.

The most important job was that of chair of the transportation committee. For the first few months Rufus Lewis, a wealthy businessman, took on the work. Dedicated to the community, active in voter registration, he owned his own business and could not be affected by the white power structure. He was replaced after several months by the Reverend B. J. Simms, an ordained Baptist minister and professor of history and philosophy at Alabama State College.

A downtown parking lot owned by a black man became the central command post for a fleet of cars that operated like shared taxicabs. Within weeks some three hundred vehicles were in the car pool. Financial recordkeeping was tightened so that the few who tried to abuse the system by collecting fares twice or getting more gas than needed were disciplined. In the tight organization, certified shops were designated to handle all repairs, and careful records were kept.

Black churches became shelters for thirty-two morning dispatch stations and forty-one afternoon and evening pickup stations. People could wait indoors in bad weather. Street corners were also designated as pickups as the system expanded. Three dispatchers were put on the staff. Their goal was for all black workers and their families to be able to get from one place to another without using a city bus.

Committees of volunteers sprang into action: volunteers who used their cars for transportation; volunteers who cooked for the boycotters; women who staffed the office, or acted as dispatchers, secretaries, and clerks. Among the active women were Mrs. Ann Pratt, chief assistant to Professor Simms. Mrs. A. W. West drove her green Cadillac through the neighborhoods in the car pool. Mrs. Johnnie Carr, an energetic woman, also drove her car through the streets, giving people lifts. Black soldiers and three white ones from the nearby Maxwell Air Force Base helped out in the car pool.

The huge, orderly plan surprised the white community. Here was a new movement, led and staffed by black people, providing an effective alternate system of transportation for thousands. White support was minimal, coming from those who privately contributed money. In the first months the financial needs were met by the small contributions from the mass of blacks. Months later funds would come from all over the state and, finally, from the entire country.

Through the changing seasons, through the winter, spring, summer, and fall of 1956, the black population of Montgomery thumbed a ride, or used a car pool or station wagon, or walked to and from their jobs. Through it all, people acted and moved together, filled with high spirits and self-respect as they saw their actions turning the city around. The empty buses rolling by told them the boycott was a success.

"My feet are tired," said one woman, "but my soul is rested." Another woman, rejecting the offer of a ride, explained, "I'm walking for my children and my grandchildren."

BACKLASH

Not until the fourth day of the boycott, Thursday, December 8, did a meeting take place between the delegates of the MIA and city officials. Representing the MIA at the meeting were the Reverends King and Abernathy, lawyer Fred Gray, Mrs. Robinson, and eight others. Present for the city were Mayor W. A. Gayle and two city commissioners. Acting for the bus company were James H. Bagley and Jack Crenshaw, the company lawyer.

Dr. King, speaking for the MIA, explained that the demands were moderate, since they were asking only for a more just system and not for the end of segregation. He placed before them demands similar to those approved at the Holt Street meeting: that blacks were to take seats in the bus from the back to the front, while whites occupied seats from the front to the back; the last to come would occupy whatever seats were available between the two. He also asked for better treatment by bus drivers and the hiring of black drivers on buses covering black neighborhoods.

After days of negotiation, the MIA won a minor concession. Crenshaw agreed that abusive bus drivers would be reprimanded. He would introduce no further changes, however. The time was not ripe, he said. City officials were afraid that if they made any concessions, no matter how small, black people would want everything changed. "Give them an inch and they'll take a mile" was the general attitude.

The MIA leaders began to see that they would have to forge ahead to a new level and challenge the segregation laws themselves in order to win new seating arrangements on city buses. In the first weeks of the boycott they were not ready for such a step. The whole situation was new—would it hold together?

Empty buses were rolling along the streets. Seventy-five percent of their former riders were black and were involved in the boycott. The company reported a loss of sixty-five percent of its income, which came to thousands of dollars. Still the whites were uncompromising, though increasingly frustrated by the strength of the boycott. To crush it became their goal.

They started off by spreading rumors. They said the boycott leadership was getting rich, making money from the protest movement. Then they said there was infighting among the leaders, with young ones pushing the older ones out.

When rumors did not work, police began to arrest black drivers of taxis and autos and charge them with speeding. They targeted drivers going thirty miles per hour in a twenty-five-mile zone. They also stopped overloaded cars. Jo Ann Robinson was given seventeen tickets in a few months.

They also began to harass black cab drivers who were charging passengers ten cents a ride, demanding that taxis charge the minimum rate of forty-five cents a fare. Boycotters could not pay that. To get around the new ruling, the MIA made a special plea to owners of private automobiles, asking them to chauffeur people to their jobs. There were hundreds of volunteers. Some white women drove their maids to and from their jobs rather than do the heavy household work themselves.

As the boycott went on, the business district and the economy of white Montgomery began to feel the economic pinch. Black people not only stopped taking buses, they stopped shopping in downtown stores. Despite the serious downward slide in the city's finances, white officials would make no concessions. The Reverend King, however, made a concession on behalf of the MIA. He proposed to postpone the demand for the employment of black drivers until a later date.

The Monday- and Thursday-night meetings became the rallying ground for boycotters and their leadership. They increasingly took on the form of a combination protest rally and church service. Crowds arrived early in order to get a seat. They sang, prayed, talked to each other, or read a book or newspaper until the meeting started. After hymn singing and scripture reading, Dr. King would give an update on the boycott's progress. He would be followed by the Reverend Abernathy, who discussed future strategies. People spoke up, giving their opinions. The meeting ended with a pep talk, exhorting everyone to remain disciplined and united. Boycotters were asked not to be violent, and to resist all provocations by whites.

While blacks were developing a nonviolent philosophy, whites were moving in the opposite direction. The boycott was in its fourth week on January 6 when the White Citizens Council held a meeting in Montgomery. Twelve hundred people jammed the hall. At the meeting, Police Commissioner Clyde Sellers announced to a standing ovation that he was joining the council. Two weeks later, on January 24, Mayor Gayle and City Commissioner Frank Parks also announced that they had joined the White Citizens Council. In making public their membership in a coercive, segregationist organization, city officials were warning the black community that they would stop at nothing to break the boycott.

Though many in the protest movement were frightened by this turn of events, unity remained strong even when the council began to exert economic pressure. Blacks could no longer get bank loans, and many lost their jobs, among them Rosa Parks, who was fired from the Montgomery Fair.

Hardships increased, for many black people were dependent on whites for their livelihood. Those few whites who were friendly to boycotters were isolated and harassed. The Reverend Graetz, the young white pastor of the Negro Trinity Lutheran Church, had his car vandalized. Prowlers broke windows in his home. Violence escalated, with threatening phone calls to the leaders. The Reverend King was a favorite target, as was Rosa Parks.

In the face of the stepped-up harassment, the MIA announced additional mass meetings. At the same time, Police Commissioner Sellers, addressing a meeting of businessmen, vowed that it was important to maintain their way of life. "What they [black people] are after is the destruction of our social fabric," he announced to the white population, and he vowed to pursue every means to stop them.

Police dispersed groups of blacks waiting for car rides on street corners. Mayor Gayle singled out for criticism the white women who continued to give rides to black domestic workers despite his plea that they stop doing so. He wanted to be sure that absolutely nothing was done to aid the "Negro radicals," as he called the leadership directing the boycott.

Police began to trail taxis and cars filled with black people, giving them traffic tickets for nonexistent or trivial violations. One victim was the Reverend King, stopped by a police car and given a summons for speeding though he was going only thirty miles per hour. He was put into a patrol car and driven through lonely streets to a distant jail. Placed in a filthy cell, he was treated like a common criminal, taken out and fingerprinted. Word spread quickly, and a group of colleagues hurried to the jail to bail him out.

When these forms of harassment failed to halt the boycott, violence exploded with the bombing of the Kings' house on the evening of January 30. Dr. King was away at the time, speaking at a church meeting. But Coretta Scott King and a friend, Mrs. Mary Lucy Williams, were home, and two-month-old baby Yolanda was asleep in a back room. The two women heard a loud thud, as if something heavy had landed on the porch, and they heard footsteps. Alarmed, they both rushed to the back of the house. They had barely retreated to the other room when an explosion shattered the glass in the living room, sending fragments shooting in all directions and filling the house with smoke. After making sure the baby was safe, Mrs. King phoned the church to alert Dr. King of the bombing. A neighbor phoned the police.

When he got the news, Dr. King rushed home to find hundreds of neighbors and supporters gathered in front of the house, wanting to make sure the family was not hurt. The mayor, police commissioner, and fire chief were all there, examining the damage of the blast, but they could not restrain the anger of the crowd, enraged at the violence against the King family.

Only Dr. King could calm them. Standing on the porch of the parsonage, the mayor and police chief on either side of him, he assured his supporters that his family was unharmed. He urged that they do nothing violent to the white community. "If you have weapons, take them home. . . . We must meet violence with nonviolence," he said. He ended his talk saying, "I want it to be known the length and breadth of this land that if I am stopped this movement will not stop. If I am stopped our work will not stop. For what we are doing is right. What we are doing is just. And God is with us."

"God bless you, Brother King," the crowd shouted.

8

FRIENDS AND ALLIES

After eight weeks of increasing violence, the MIA and its lawyers, Fred Gray and Charles Langford, decided to attack the matter from a different angle. On February 1, they filed suit in U.S. district court seeking an injunction, or order, against segregated bus seating. In their suit, they asked specifically that the Montgomery city code of 1952 requiring racial segregation on transportation facilities be declared unconstitutional.

On the same day the brief was filed, the home of E. D. Nixon was bombed, in spite of promises by the mayor to find and punish those who had bombed the King home just two days before. Nixon was away, but his wife, Arlet, and a neighbor's seven-year-old child were in the house. They escaped injury.

In the increasing violence, Dr. King and Mrs. Parks were singled out for a flood of hate mail and nasty phone calls. Each day the King family received thirty to forty calls from unidentified persons who cursed and insulted them. Postcards filled with brief messages and signed "KKK" threatened their lives. "Get out of town, or else" was the gist of the messages. The family, shaken by the hate mail and threats, could get neither sleep nor rest. But they did not give in, despite the urgent pleading of both Dr. King's and Mrs. King's parents. Both fathers had rushed to Montgomery when they heard of the bombing and insisted that the young family return to Atlanta, where they would be safe. Dr. King explained that he could not do that; his place was among his people.

As the threats grew more frequent, Dr. King experienced a terrible fear that either he or some family member would be killed. One night he was not sure he had the strength to go on. During hours of personal anguish and prayer, he overcame his fears and knew that thereafter, no matter what happened, his life belonged to the struggle for justice.

For Mrs. Parks and her family it was a costly victory. When she was fired from her job at the Montgomery Fair, she was told she was being laid off because the Christmas rush was over. Her husband, too, lost his job as a barber at the Maxwell Air Force Base. Not only was the Parks family experiencing the awful economic pinch of unemployment, but they were besieged by hate-filled phone calls. Night and day the phone rang. Callers threatened to kill Mrs. Parks. The family was wracked by tension, bringing about the complete physical breakdown of Mr. Parks.

For a while the MIA employed Mrs. Parks, sending her out to speak at schools and churches in order to raise money for the boycott. At other times she worked in the MIA office as a clerk, and she then became head of the welfare committee. She also took on odd jobs as a seamstress. To her brother's repeated pleas that the family join him in Detroit, where he lived and worked, she said no. Montgomery was her hometown, and that was where she wanted to be.

It became clear in those first few months of the movement

that the educated and articulate Reverend Martin Luther King, Jr., had emerged as the leader. Surrounding him was a group of skilled young aides, among them many ministers. These natural leaders continued their role in the community, acting like strong patriarchs, directing, advising, preaching.

The role of women in the boycott was not always appreciated. The male leadership simply assumed that women could not be leaders, though they were valued as assistants, secretaries, and clerks.

Women made up 56 percent of the total black population, and they were, in a way, the backbone of the movement. They not only trudged back and forth to work, but they ran their homes, shopped, and took care of the children, all without the advantage of bus transportation. They attended weekly meetings, always cheerful and committed to the struggle.

Women had also been the trailblazers of the movement. The protest was rooted in the bold "no" to segregated bus seating uttered by Mrs. Rosa Parks. Mrs. Jo Ann Robinson set the boycott into immediate motion. She was helped by her friends and colleagues in the Women's Political Council. Women were on the MIA executive board and active on the finance committee and in the car pool. And four hard-working, dedicated women were the paid staffers of the MIA. Women like Mrs. Georgia Gilmore, the mother of six children and a domestic worker, enlivened the weekly meetings with reports about their success in raising money for the boycott. Mrs. Gilmore, who had once been arrested for refusing to get off the front of a bus and reboard in the rear, organized a group of neighbors into the Club from Nowhere. Mrs. Inez Ricks organized the Friendly Club. Both women baked and sold cakes and pies to workers and cafeterias to raise money.

Everyone could see that something precious and miraculous

was emerging out of the protest movement. Montgomery's black citizens, once without hope, had bonded together and could feel their power. Changes were slowly taking place on other fronts. Backed by the Supreme Court decision desegregating schools, a student named Autherine Lucy made the first attempt to integrate Alabama schools when she entered the campus of the University of Alabama in Tuscaloosa. On her first day she was confronted with the mob violence of over one thousand white students who marched to the house of the university's president to demand that the university stay white.

Extremists got a boost from Senator James Eastland, the main speaker at the prosegregation rally held at Montgomery's largest arena, the state coliseum. Under a show of waving Confederate flags, and red, white, and blue colors, the Mississippi senator urged resistance to desegregation.

As blacks nevertheless made progress, racist terror continued to increase. To break the dangerous tug of war, white businessmen stepped in. Calling themselves the "Men of Montgomery," they tried to restore peace to the city. They sent delegations to meet with representatives of the MIA, but the two groups could not resolve their differences. For instance, the MIA suggested that only five seats be reserved for white riders, but the Men of Montgomery insisted on ten.

In the continuing struggle, a handful of white people remained staunch supporters of the boycott movement. Others fell by the wayside, unable to cope with the criticism of the white community. Two white women made known their early support in letters to the *Advertiser*. Frances P. McLeod suggested that Montgomery follow the lead of southern cities such as Nashville and Richmond that had a first-come seating arrangement on their buses. Mrs I. B. Rutledge, in her letter, wrote that many agreed with her that Negroes had as much right to bus seats as white people. The Reverend Thomas Thrasher, who voiced such ideas, found his white congregation staying away from his church.

Clifford and Virginia Durr made a stir in Montgomery by their outspoken support of integration and their friendship with black people. These two whites, born and raised in the Deep South of what was called "aristocratic stock," had resettled in Alabama after years in Washington, D.C., where Mr. Durr had held important posts in Roosevelt's New Deal administration. Through their work in interracial organizations and their friendship with Mrs. Parks, E. D. Nixon, and others, they were accepted in the black community. The white community could not completely isolate them because the Durr family was too steeped in the white upper class. Though Lucy Judkins Durr did not endorse her son's racial beliefs, neither did she cut him off from the family.

Both Virginia and Clifford Durr well knew the price that had to be paid for outspoken liberal ideas. Like others who suffered business losses as a result of white pressure, Mr. Durr's legal practice barely survived on the low-paying cases he handled. But he was helped by his brother, a successful Montgomery businessman; and to cut expenses in his law office, Virginia Durr became her husband's secretary.

Another unique person was the slender, blond Reverend Robert S. Graetz. A former missionary, he became minister of the all-black Trinity Lutheran Church on Cleveland Avenue in Montgomery. Dedicated and hardworking, he was the only white member of the MIA executive board. From the first days of the boycott, he was active as a volunteer, chauffeuring forty to fifty people a day to and from their jobs. As a member of the transportation committee, he helped organize the hundreds of vehicles that became the backbone of the car pool. Targeted by the police, he was arrested one day for running a taxi service but released after half an hour. He, his wife, and their two small children lived in the parsonage next door to the church. Asked why he put his life in danger to support the boycott, he replied, "I know that I shall be criticized for my stand. I may even suffer violence. But I cannot minister to souls alone. My people have bodies."

For his support of the boycott, angry whites twice slashed the tires on his car and poured sugar into the gasoline tank. Both his church and his home would bear the violence of the white community.

A tragic victim of persecution was a young white librarian, Juliette Morgan, the daughter of an old southern family. A brilliant young woman, she was elected to the honor society of Phi Beta Kappa during her studies at the University of Alabama. In letters to newspaper editors, she made known her firm convictions that segregation was an evil. In one such letter to the *Advertiser* she wrote, "One feels history is being made in Montgomery these days. It is hard to imagine a soul so dead, a heart so hard, a vision so blinded and provincial as not to be awed with admiration at the quiet dignity, discipline, and dedication with which Negroes have conducted the boycott." She compared the movement to Mahatma Gandhi's struggle against British rule in India, in which he used nonviolent resistance. In another letter she wrote, "I think that segregation is an evil that has limited our horizons and dwarfed our souls."

For her daring and outspoken support of the boycott, she became the target of segregationist hate groups, among them the White Citizens Council. They hounded her and demanded that she be fired from her job as reference librarian at the Montgomery Public Library. To put pressure on the city, white people boycotted the branch library where she worked. She received threatening phone calls both at her home and in the library. Rocks were thrown through the windows and she was insulted on the streets.

She refused to stand by and do nothing, but unfortunately she was not surrounded by a network of support. Hers was a lonely battle in a sea of hate. Bereft of friends, frail, and sensitive to the abuse, she suffered untold anguish . No one came to her defense. She took a leave of absence from her job and became increasingly a recluse. She died in the summer of 1957— apparently a suicide, for she left a note saying, "I can't go on."

In her memory her mother placed volumes of her letters and writings in the state archives in Montgomery, Alabama. As teacher, writer, and educator, she expressed her idealism and hope that "equal rights and respect for all people" would prevail.

9

"A GREAT MOMENT OF HISTORY"

Whits officials tried a new tactic: mass arrests. In the eleventh week of the boycott, they pulled out a seldom-used state law against illegal organized boycotts, and on February 21 they rounded up 115 MIA leaders and members. Eighty-nine of these were indicted, charged with committing a crime. Though attention centered on Rosa Parks and the Reverend King, the assemblage included twenty-four ministers, among them Ralph B. Abernathy. Also in the group were Mrs. Jo Ann Robinson and the elderly Mrs. West. They were all fingerprinted and photographed with large numbers hung around their necks. As soon as the procedures were over, lawyers freed the prisoners on bond.

The boycott had been like a train chugging along, gradually picking up steam. The mass arrests acted like rocket fuel, shooting the movement forward. During the first months only black newspapers informed the country about the boycott, but after the arrests, newspaper reporters and television and radio commentators descended on Montgomery. They saw the drama of the boycott and the personal heroism of those involved. They wanted to know about leaders such as E. D. Nixon and Rufus Lewis, and they were drawn to the magnetic Dr. Martin Luther King, Jr., whom they wrote up as the man of the hour.

What's going on? they asked. They ferreted out background material and sent the news around the world—to Rome, London, Tokyo, South Africa, Australia. In India people eagerly read about Dr. King, who, like their leader Gandhi, was taking up the cause of nonviolent resistance. Television and radio began to transmit regular up-to-date news of the boycott. Thousands of pieces of mail were delivered to the MIA office as letters and money poured in. Montgomery had won worldwide attention.

Black organizations throughout the country—professional groups, sororities and fraternities, church groups—sent thousands of dollars. Trade unions announced their support. The International Longshoremen's and Warehousemen's Union in San Francisco sent in a $1,500 contribution, and one of its locals pledged a $99.99 weekly contribution for ten weeks. They were acting, they said, "in the true spirit of brotherhood, and knowing that an injury to one is an injury to all." A woman in Switzerland sent in a $500 contribution with a letter, saying, "I feel deeply ashamed for the white people to which I belong [sic]." Tourists visited Montgomery to see for themselves what was going on, considering the boycott a historic event. Five inmates in a prison in Pennsylvania sent a dollar each to the MIA. And the literary community made its support felt in contributions, articles, interviews, and books.

The world learned about Rosa Parks, Martin Luther King, Jr., and the spirit of some fifty thousand people who, in the fourth month of a bus boycott, remained strong and united. The mass arrests pulled them still closer together and inspired them anew. Five thousand showed up for the meeting the night of the arrests. As usual, they began to arrive long before the hour.

They talked to each other and sang their favorite hymns, "On-ward, Christian Soldiers" and "Leaning on Everlasting Arms." Elegiac voices filled the church, filtering through the stained-glass windows to merge with the singing of the crowds out-doors.

After the prayer and scripture reading, Dr. King sounded a note of encouragement, reminding people how important it was to love rather than to hate. He talked in the special cadence he was developing, his voice deep, lyrical, repeating key phrases: "We have known humiliation, we have known abusive language. . . . And we decided to rise up only with the weapon of protest. . . . If we are arrested every day, if we are exploited every day, if we are trampled every day, don't let anyone pull you so low as to hate them. . . . This is not a war between the white and the Negro but a conflict between justice and injus-tice. We are not trying to improve the Negro of Montgomery, but the whole of Montgomery."

Changes had taken place within the city, and no one knew that better than Rosa Parks. In March 1956, she returned to the Highlander Folk School to give a talk at the second annual lecture series. The bus boycott was four months old, and Mrs. Parks opened her talk by saying that "Montgomery today is nothing at all like it was as you knew it last year." She stressed the unique unity among the black people. That unity was hold-ing firm, she said, in the face of months of difficulties and ha-rassment. It ruffled white officials to see that black people could be disciplined and could struggle to improve their conditions. Furthermore, she pointed out, Montgomery had become the center of worldwide attention. From all corners of the globe, money was coming in to support the boycott.

As the boycott became front-page news, northern organiza-tions sent delegates down to try to make the struggle national in scope and broaden its goals. Dr. King, too, had a sense of the widening impact of the movement. "We are caught in a great moment of history," he said at a mass meeting. "It is bigger than Montgomery.... The vast majority of the people of the world are colored.... We are part of that great movement" to be free, he said.

On Monday, March 19, the Reverend King was the first of those who had been indicted in the mass arrests to be brought to trial. Three days later, on March 22, he was found guilty as charged and fined $500 and $500 in court costs. He was freed on $1,000 bond; his lawyers planned to appeal the case. The others who were indicted would not be brought to trial until the appeal decision was handed down, a procedure that usually took a year.

The young minister, now twenty-seven, appeared to onlookers to be an older man. At first unprepared for the role into which he had been thrust, he had gone through periods of self-doubt. He had questioned his abilities and his courage. As the struggle wore on he became a strong and self-confident national leader, carrying his message of equality and justice to the church groups and political and social clubs before whom he spoke. He sounded the catchwords for the spirit of the boycott: unity, discipline, and nonviolent resistance.

The MIA itself had developed into an extremely efficient organization. By mid-April it had bought over fifteen station wagons for the car pool, making transportation more stable. Each one was registered in the name of a black church. The work of volunteers was slowly replaced by a paid staff of twenty full-time drivers and seventy-four part-time ones. Dispatchers were also put on salary, making procedures more reliable. The MIA tried to get a license from the city to operate a jitney, or small bus service. But the city rejected the application.

In April the movement was cheered by an unexpected piece of good news: The U.S. Supreme Court upheld a lower court ruling that segregated bus seating on city buses in Columbia, South Carolina, was unconstitutional. Though the South Carolina decision raised the morale of the boycotters, it split white officialdom in two. The Montgomery City Lines, owners of the buses, made a dramatic concession: Their drivers would no longer enforce segregated seating on city buses. But Mayor Gayle, on behalf of the city, declared that the segregation laws must be upheld.

The MIA began to understand the need for political power through the use of the ballot and it undertook a voter-registration campaign. "The chief weapon in our fight for civil rights is the vote," said Dr. King.

Finally, the Montgomery bus boycott movement won a stunning victory. In June the federal district court, before which the MIA had challenged segregated bus seating, declared segregated seating in Montgomery unconstitutional. While the black population celebrated the triumph, the city commissioners vowed to take the case to the United States Supreme Court, a slow, complex procedure.

In October, with the boycott in its tenth month, the city again tried to break the car-pool system. With no advance notice, officials cancelled the insurance policies on the station wagons. Without insurance, the cars could not operate. Again the black leadership outwitted city officials. Through the assistance of a black insurance agent in Atlanta, Georgia, arrangements were made for new policies.

In response to that victory, the segregationists moved on to another tactic. They got a court order from the state preventing blacks from gathering on street corners while waiting for a pickup, claiming that the congregation of people was a public nuisance.

Violence continued, this time directed at the home of the Reverend Graetz. Fortunately, neither he, his pregnant wife, nor their two small children were at home when the bomb struck, destroying part of the house. But the strain of nasty phone calls and threatening notes was taking its toll on the young family. They moved around so much to avoid danger that they no longer had a home.

When all else failed, the city took legal action against the car-pool system itself, asking the court to declare it illegal.

City lawyers were in the midst of arguing this case in court when word reached Dr. King that the United States Supreme Court had reached a decision in the case of the Montgomery bus boycott: It had declared Alabama state and city laws requiring segregation on buses unconstitutional.

Rosa Parks sits in the front of a Montgomery bus integrated by a federal court order (*Courtesy the* Montgomery Advertiser)

Rosa Parks with the Eleanor Roosevelt Woman of Courage Award (*Courtesy the Montgomery Advertiser*)

Virginia Durr, Fred Gray, and Rosa Parks singing "We Shall Overcome" at the twenty-fifth anniversary celebration of the bus boycott (*Courtesy the Montgomery Advertiser*)

Coretta Scott King kissing Rosa Parks after giving her the Martin Luther King, Jr., Nonviolent Peace Prize (*Courtesy the* Montgomery Advertiser)

The Civil Rights Monument in Montgomery, Alabama (*Courtesy the Alabama Bureau of Tourism and Travel*)

10

"WHEN I WAS A
CHILD . . ."

People wept at the news. They stood in the streets—women, men, and children—and wept. "We felt that we were somebody," was the way Jo Ann Robinson put it, "that we had forced the white man to give what we knew [was] our own citizenship." They wept not only at the victory but at the pain they had suffered: the bombings, the arrests, the harassment.

Rosa Parks would say years later, "I don't recall that I felt anything great about it. It didn't feel like a victory, actually. There still had to be a great deal to do."

The Reverend Graetz read the scriptures that evening at two mass meetings held in churches at either end of town. Quoting from the Bible, he said, "When I was a child, I spoke as a child, I understood as a child, I thought as a child; but when I became a man I put away childish things." The words brought a loud outburst of cheers from the congregation. People recognized how much they had changed, how much they had grown in the struggle.

But the struggle was not yet over, for the leadership had decided to call off the official protest immediately but to delay the return to the buses until the written order on desegregation arrived in the city of Montgomery. On the same day the desegregation ruling was handed down, Circuit Court Judge Eugene Carter announced his ruling putting an end to the car-pool system. He did so on the grounds that it was a "public nuisance" and a "private enterprise." With the car-pool system declared illegal, people took to the streets by the thousands.

Nor did city officials accept the desegregation order quietly. They immediately issued a statement saying, "[We] will not yield one inch, but will do all in our power to oppose the integration of the Negro race with the white race in Montgomery, and will forever stand like a rock against social equality, intermarriage, and mixing of the races under God's creation and plan."

That night forty carloads of hooded KKK members rode through the black community. Their plans to demonstrate were announced over the radio, and threats of bombings and violence were rampant. Dr. King's mail was unusually threatening, announcing that the KKK would "burn down fifty houses in one night, including yours."

The spirit of victory was not dimmed. Black people knew they had won the battle in the Supreme Court decision. When the Klan rode through the back streets of their neighborhoods, blacks defied them, standing quietly on their porches and on the streets as the Klan went by. Klan power had weakened that day, like dead leaves scattering in the wind.

To prepare for desegregation, the MIA launched several programs in churches and schools. In wide-ranging discussions, the point was made that desegregation was not a victory of blacks over whites but a victory for justice and democracy. It was a victory for all Montgomery, as Dr. King had hoped.

Fliers were distributed throughout the neighborhoods suggesting ways to integrate the buses. Among the suggestions was this one: "Do not deliberately sit by a white person, unless there is no other seat." And: "If cursed, do not curse back. If pushed, do not push back. If struck, do not strike back but evidence love and goodwill at all times."

No one prepared the white community for bus integration. On the contrary, a leader of the White Citizens Council threatened that any "attempt to enforce this decision will lead to riot and bloodshed."

On December 20, 1956, the written order for desegregation of buses reached Montgomery. One year and fifteen days had passed since the boycott had started. For a total of 381 days, 50,000 black people had waged a great rebellion. They won a battle not only over a social system but over their own fear of facing white power.

To pave the way for integrated seating, the ministers agreed that they would ride the buses for a few days. At 5:45 A.M. on the morning of December 21, Martin Luther King, Jr., Ralph Abernathy, E. D. Nixon, and a white friend, Glen Smiley, a representative of the Fellowship for Reconciliation, boarded a bus. Television crews and newspaper reporters recorded the event for history. It took place peacefully, as if nothing special were happening.

Rosa Parks, at the urging of a group of reporters, also integrated the bus that day. She took a seat in the front of the bus. What was she thinking? That it had taken a painful thirteen months of struggle and protest to make this simple event possible? That she could at last take any seat in a bus where she rightfully belonged as a citizen and as a human being?

The calm lasted a few days before random violence broke out. Snipers fired at buses; a fifteen-year-old teenager was beaten by five white men as she waited at a bus stop; a twenty-two-year-old pregnant black woman riding a bus, Mrs. Rosa

Jordan, was shot in both legs. A new round of bombings shattered neighborhoods, beginning with an attack on the home and church of Ralph Abernathy. Within a few hours bombs had destroyed the front of the Graetz home and also hit his church. This was the second bombing for Graetz in six months. In the series of attacks two more Baptist churches were destroyed. Though no one was hurt in the attacks, the damage was extensive and the effect was frightening.

For the first time groups of white people spoke out against the bombings. The *Montgomery Advertiser* asked the question, "Is it safe to live in Montgomery?" Several white ministers condemned the bombings as "un-Christian and uncivilized."

The city of Montgomery ordered the buses off the streets and established a midnight curfew for teenagers until the bombings stopped. In taking this step, the city was also punishing the bus company for accepting the order to desegregate seating. Despite this drastic order, the bombings continued. This time bombers struck at a black-owned taxi stand and at the home of a boycotter, a black hospital worker. Another attempt was made to bomb the Kings' home. Fortunately the family was away at the time, and the sticks of dynamite were discovered before they could explode.

Montgomery was in turmoil. To quiet both black and white residents, the city finally launched an investigation into the bombings, offering rewards for the arrest of the perpetrators. Seven men were arrested and two were brought to trial. Though evidence presented at the trial in January 1958 linked the men to the violence, the jury returned a verdict of not guilty.

The arrests resulted in the end of the bombings, and desegregated buses now rolled along the streets.

11

"... UNTIL JUSTICE ROLLS DOWN LIKE WATERS ..."

Looking back at the experience of her arrest years later, Rosa Parks would describe it to a group of college students as a trauma that she suffered both mentally and physically. She had always avoided becoming a public figure, but that evening's courageous act had thrust her into the spotlight. The shy woman had to speak before large audiences, meet with reporters and interviewers, and travel as a fund-raiser for the boycott movement.

Martin Luther King, Jr., called the boycott a "social revolution." No one in the movement remained the same. Dr. King would become the head of the Southern Christian Leadership Conference, a new organization headquartered in Atlanta, Georgia. Remaining in the forefront of the struggle, he would become the leader of the militant civil rights movement until his death from an assassin's bullet in 1968. He would take his place as a leading figure in United States history.

Both black and white residents of Montgomery were affected by the upheaval. A shift in social and economic values took place. Black people learned that from their unity came strength, and that they had purchasing power vital to the economy of the city. White merchants, banks, and businesses learned to respect that economic power and to treat it carefully. No longer were black customers shunted aside, treated rudely, and ignored. They were addressed by name and waited on, and their purchases were encouraged. It would take militant struggles before blacks could share in other public facilities such as water fountains, bathrooms, and lunch counters, but a beginning had been made.

And if the boycott was so successful in Montgomery, why not do the same in Birmingham and in Mobile? Other cities in the South used the boycott and other methods of nonviolent resistance to win changes in their regions.

Rosa Parks remained the great hero of the movement. The MIA honored her when it held its first annual Institute on Nonviolence and Social Changes in December 1957. The Reverend Abernathy, chair of the occasion, called the institute "Gandhi in America." Black and white social scientists and religious leaders read their papers before an audience of 1,500. Emerging from the conference was the fact that blacks had become leaders and that continued unity was essential to win new victories in the fight against segregation.

For Rosa Parks the Montgomery bus boycott brought a great upheaval in her way of life. In 1957 she, her husband, and her mother moved to Detroit, Michigan, to be near her brother. She had agreed to resettle when she found it difficult to find a job after being fired from the Montgomery Fair. It was a sad leavetaking, and one that E. D. Nixon regarded as most unfortunate. It seemed to him that she was a victim of the courageous act that had changed the city. She had stood up for the black community, he told an interviewer, but the community did not stand up for her. When the whites did not give her a job, the

MIA should have found steady employment for her. But Mrs. Parks did not share Mr. Nixon's feelings. As long as she was well, she commented, it was her "responsibility to do whatever I could for myself." At a farewell party, the community raised $800 to help her resettle.

The first few years in Detroit were also difficult for Mrs. Parks. Jobs were scarce for both her and her husband. For one year she left Detroit to work at the Hampton Institute in Virginia, sending home what she could from her salary. Not wanting to be separated from her family any longer, she returned to Detroit in 1958. That year her husband was hospitalized with pneumonia. The following year she was hospitalized with stomach ulcers.

Mrs. Parks had finally found work in a small tailoring shop when in 1965 she came to the attention of Congressman John Conyers, Jr., a newly elected Democratic member of the House of Representatives. He offered her employment in his Detroit office, where she worked first as a receptionist and then as a special aide.

Throughout her years in Detroit, Mrs. Parks has continued her activism: in the church as a deaconess of St. Matthew African Methodist Episcopal Church, in the NAACP, and also in the Southern Christian Leadership Conference, the organization first headed by Dr. Martin Luther King, Jr. And once again she committed herself to helping young people, counseling them about their rights and urging them to take advantage of every opportunity, no matter how small. Her own experience had taught her the importance of pushing on, of not falling by the wayside.

In the years when Mrs. Parks was finding it difficult to find a decent job, the public was acclaiming her a national hero. The story of the shy black woman who stood up to the rigid racist laws of the South, thereby starting a bus boycott and a crusade for justice, was being turned into legend. Reflecting the broad range of public appreciation for her unbroken record of civil rights activism, a long list of tributes and awards were bestowed on her. Here are a few of them.

In 1979 Mrs. Parks received the Spingarn Medal, the most prestigious award given by the National Association for the Advancement of Colored People. In making the award, Judge Damon J. Keith of the U.S. Sixth Circuit Court of Appeals, said, "Your courageous act on that quiet and cloudy day in Montgomery has secured your claim to immortality."

In 1980, at the twenty-fifth anniversary celebration of the bus boycott, a sixty-five-year-old Rosa Parks received the Martin Luther King, Jr., Nonviolent Peace Prize, the first woman recipient of the award. "It is so extraordinarily painful to look back on some of the things we went through," she said on that occasion. Mrs. Coretta Scott King, Dr. King's widow, in honoring Mrs. Parks called her "a woman whose courage and commitment have shaken the conscience of America."

A special tribute to Rosa Parks was held in New York City at a Broadway theater in June 1982, and in 1984 she was given the Eleanor Roosevelt Woman of Courage Award at a ceremony in New York's Plaza Hotel.

In 1985 she returned to Montgomery to celebrate the thirtieth anniversary of her arrest. She made it clear in her talk, as she has throughout her life, that she did not see herself as heroic but simply as a woman who took a stand against segregation. She could see the changes that had taken place in Montgomery over the years. It was no longer outwardly segregated. Signs separating the races had been removed. Hotels, bus stations, and public drinking fountains were integrated. Schools had both whites and blacks in attendance. Nevertheless the struggle to win full equality continues.

And the awards go on. In 1987 Mrs. Parks was given the Roger

E. Joseph Prize of the Jewish Institute of Religion for being the "mother of the modern Freedom Movement." More than two thousand people attended the services at Temple Emanu-El in New York City, at which she was given a cash award of $10,000. It would go toward the founding of the Rosa and Raymond Parks Institute for Self-Development, which Mrs. Parks was planning in Detroit. The institute would offer guidance to black youths in preparation for leadership and careers.

In 1987, after more than twenty years, Mrs. Parks retired from her job in Representative Conyers's office. The congressman was at her side in February 1990 when her seventy-seventh birthday was celebrated in Washington, D.C. She was hailed as a pioneer of the Civil Rights Movement. The 3,000 people in the Kennedy Center and the several hundred at a pregala dinner raised funds for her institute in Detroit.

The Rosa Parks story has also found its way into dance, theater, music, film, and literature. A Philadelphia dance group, Philadanco, performed in New York City in April 1990. On the program was a dance called "Rosa" that dealt with the "courage of those who dare to be different." The dance communicated the loneliness of the fight against the established order.

Now on view at the National Portrait Gallery in Washington, D.C., is a bronze sculpture of Mrs. Parks unveiled at the end of February 1991. The bust, by Artis Lane, places Mrs. Parks among the country's most famous and accomplished citizens.

The country needs to see and hear Mrs. Parks. She stands out as a symbol of courage and of the continuing fight to make democracy work in the United States. While Mrs. Parks tries to fulfill some of the many demands made on her, she links her name with struggles worldwide, such as the fight against apartheid in South Africa.

Three flags now fly over the state capitol in Montgomery, Alabama. On the top of the flagpole flies the Stars and Stripes.

Below it is the Confederate flag, and below that the state flag.

The Confederate flag is a continuous reminder of the laws and customs of the old South, a reminder that Montgomery was the Cradle of the Confederacy. But Montgomery has also become known as the cradle of the modern Civil Rights Movement. Built to commemorate that movement and its heroes and martyrs is a simple but powerful sculpture. It stands in a plaza in front of the Southern Poverty Law Center, a nonprofit, public-interest organization located just below the state capitol and close to the Dexter Avenue Baptist Church.

Every week hundreds of schoolchildren and other visitors come to see the memorial. Etched on a large, black disk are key events of the Civil Rights Movement and the names of forty men and women who died in the struggle. Rosa Parks is listed as a leader of the Montgomery bus boycott. Over the disk perpetually flows a thin sheet of water. In back of the disk is a nine-foot-high curved black granite wall. Engraved onto the wall, beneath a sheet of water also perpetually flowing, are Dr. King's words chosen from the Bible and first spoken at the mass meeting at the Holt Street Baptist Church on December 5, 1955. "We will not be satisfied," he said,

> ". . . until justice rolls down like waters and
> righteousness like a mighty stream."

ACKNOWLEDGMENTS

I am grateful to Virginia Foster Durr for facilitating my research during my visit to Montgomery, Alabama. I would also like to thank several of the women in Montgomery who shared their experiences with me, among them Mrs. Jewette Anderson, Mrs. Bertha Butler, Mrs. Johnnie Carr, Mrs. Mattie Lee Langford, and Mrs. Mary Jo Smiley.

My special thanks to Keeta Kendall, state librarian of Montgomery's Department of Archives and History, for making archival material accessible.

As always, I am dependent on the cooperation of librarians for my research, and I would like to thank the staff of the Schomburg Center for Research in Black Culture in New York City.

BIBLIOGRAPHY

An extensive literature exists on the subject of the Montgomery bus boycott, ranging from scholarly texts to popular articles. These are a few selected sources from my research:

Juan Williams, *Eyes on the Prize* (New York: Viking, 1987) and the film by the same title are invaluable overviews of the civil rights years.

Dealing with the role of Martin Luther King, Jr., are two essential books: *Bearing the Cross*, by David J. Garrow (New York: William Morrow and Co., 1986), and Taylor Branch's *Parting the Waters* (New York: Simon and Schuster, 1988).

Personal memoirs and autobiographies give special insights, and I here mention three distinguished books: the memoir of Jo Ann Gibson Robinson, *The Montgomery Bus Boycott and the Women Who Started It* (Knoxville: University of Tennessee Press, 1987); Martin Luther King, Jr.'s *Stride Toward Freedom* (New York: Harper and Row, 1958); and Virginia Foster Durr's *Outside the Magic Circle* (Tuscaloosa: University of Alabama Press, 1985).

Important material was found in Lamont H. Yeakey's unpublished Ph.D. dissertation, "The Montgomery, Alabama, Bus Boycott, 1955–56" (Columbia University, 1979).

Invaluable to my research were the many interviews granted by Mrs. Parks that have appeared in newspapers, periodicals, and books. Here are a few of them: Lerone Bennett, Jr., writes about "The Day the Black Revolution Began" in *Ebony* magazine (vol. 32, September 1977). Vernon Jarrett, in a series in the *Chicago Tribune* (November 30 to December 4, 1975) deals with "The Forgotten Heroes of the Montgomery Bus Boycott." Howell Raines has an interview with Mrs. Parks in *My Soul Is Rested* (New York: G. P. Putnam's Sons, 1977). Arthur E. Thomas in *Like It Is*, edited by Emily Rovetch (New York: E. P. Dutton, 1981), interviewed leaders in black America. Also interesting were the comments made by Mrs. Parks to Earl and Miriam Selby for their book, *Odyssey, Journey Through Black America* (New York: G. P. Putnam's Sons, 1971).

Adding a personal dimension to my research were the visuals that can be viewed at the Schomburg Center for Research in Black Culture. In addition to the film "Eyes on the Prize," there are, among others, Gil Noble's "An Amazing Grace" and a film called "Martin Luther King, Jr.: From Montgomery to Memphis," put out by Bailey Film Associates.

SUGGESTED TITLES FOR YOUNG READERS

Cook, Fred J. *The Ku Klux Klan, America's Recurring Nightmare.* New York: Julian Messner, 1980.

Harris, Janet. *The Long Freedom Road: The Civil Rights Story.* New York: McGraw-Hill Book Co., 1967.

Jakoubek, Robert. *Martin Luther King, Jr.* New York: Chelsea House, 1989.

Schulke, Flip, editor. *Martin Luther King, Jr.: A Documentary . . . Montgomery to Memphis.* New York: W. W. Norton & Co., 1976.

Severn, Bill. *The Right to Vote.* New York: Ives, Washburn, Inc., 1972.

Sterling, Dorothy. *Tear Down the Walls: A History of the American Civil Rights Movement.* New York: Doubleday and Company, 1968.

Stevenson, Janet. *The Montgomery Bus Boycott, December, 1955.* New York: Franklin Watts, Inc., 1971.

INDEX

Page numbers in *italics* refer to illustrations.

Quarantined!!

"Then, of course, the disease could have been spread intentionally, considering the ease of access to your facilities. I would think that because of the speed in which the infection has moved through your herd, such a scenario is a distinct possibility. Apparently, the virus is readily available in several of the Mid-Eastern countries which have been experimenting in biological warfare. Someone could have obtained the virus and added it to the cattle's drinking water.

"I hate to even breathe the thought," Dr. Mosely continued, "But we all know that Saddam Hussein has been experimenting in biological warfare in Iraq for many years. And since his embarrassment in Desert Storm, he could be seeking revenge. He, or any of the international terrorist organizations, could be responsible for just such an experiment as this, if in fact it is determined that this is an intentional contamination. I am certain that the FBI, the FDA, the CIA or USDA will be called in to conduct a thorough evaluation and investigation. That, however, is not a part of my jurisdiction. My job is to see that this contamination is confined to as small an area as possible and to see that it is cleaned up and eradicated in a most timely manner. That, I intend to do!"

With that statement, he forced the door open and left the office. The white van carrying the TDCDC personnel stopped at the gate, as it was leaving the feed yard, and one of the men stepped out and nailed a huge orange sign to the gate.

"QUARANTINED — FOOT AND MOUTH DISEASE — NO LIVESTOCK MAY ENTER OR LEAVE THESE PREMISES UNTIL FURTHER NOTICE —TEXAS DEPARTMENT OF CONTAGIOUS DISEASE CONTROL. "

Quarantine!

QUARANTINE!

Gerald McCathern

This is a work of fiction--all characters and events portrayed in this book are fictitious.

Library of Congress Catalog No. 97-093257
ISBN - 0-9656946-1-5

Food for Thought Publishers
419 Centre Street
Hereford, Tx 79045
806-364-2838

Other Books by Gerald McCathern

Horns
A western historical novel circa 1865-1875
270 Pages Hardcover

From the White House to the Hoosegow
Personal account of the great farmer
protest movement of 1977-1978
282 Pages Paperback

Gentle Rebels
Farmer's protest and great tractorcade
to Washington, D.C. 1977-1979
504 Pages Hardcover

To Kill the Goose
Is the U.S heading for food shortages?
Why and how to prevent it.
248 Pages Hardcover

Order from
Gerald McCathern
419 Centre Street
Hereford, Tx 79045
Ph. 806-364-2838
888-583-9408
FAX 806-364-5522

The question is not "*if it will happen ----*"

The question is "*when will it happen?*"

Author's Statement

Terrorism has become an act of undeclared war against the United States by members of groups representing several Middle-eastern countries. Since 1982, when Pan Am Flight 830 was crippled by a bomb over Hawaii, there have been several acts of terrorism against the United States.

April, 1983, the U.S. Embassy in Beirut, Lebanon was bombed.

October, 1983, the U.S. Marine Barracks in Beirut was bombed.

June, 1985, TWA Flight 847 was hijacked en route from Athens to Rome and forced to land in Beirut.

October, 1985, the Italian cruise ship, Achille Lauro, was hijacked off the Egyptian coast.

December, 1988, Pan Am Flight 103 was bombed over Lockerbie, Scotland.

January, 1993, a shooting outside CIA Headquarters building in Langley, Virginia.

February, 1993, World Trade Center in New York City was bombed.

November, 1995, American military training center in Riyadh, Saudi Arabia was bombed.

June, 1996, Khobar Towers, an Air Force barracks in Dharan, Saudi Arabia was bombed.

August, 1998, U.S. Embassy in Tanzania and Kenya was bombed.

All of these actions have resulted in tremendous loss of life and property, but are minor in comparison to what could happen if terrorists, either domestic or foreign, were to make a concerted effort to spread lethal viruses on the American people.

In a recent test in New York City, it was determined by federal officials that a pound of highly concentrated anthrax virus released in the air from a ship in the harbor, could contaminate the entire city and infect a majority of the city's population. Sadly, no one would be aware of the contamination until most of the population had been infected.

Just as great a danger is the possibility that terrorists would attack our food producing industry with lethal viruses, an industry with little or no security in the production, processing or distribution of those products.

Who knows whether or not some of the recent outbreaks of ecoli and botulism bacteria in the beef, poultry, and vegetable industries were accidental or perpetrated by groups who are experimenting with biological warfare?

Since the end of Desert Storm, the United States and the United Nations have been trying to seek out and destroy stockpiles of lethal viruses in Iraq, with little success. Apparently, the technology of growing and storing these viruses: anthrax, ebolla, ecoli, smallpox, and hundreds of others, is fairly simple and is being practiced by several of the Middle Eastern nations. And many of those nations are not on the best political terms with the United States.

It is known that Iraq, the major manufacturer of these viruses, has grown and used them against its own people, the Kurds, as well as against the Iranians in a border conflict. There is no reason to believe they would hesitate to use that knowledge and ability against the United States and its people, whom they blame for actions taken against them in the Desert Storm conflict.

Biological warfare has been the term coined to describe these activities. However, such a description is misleading. Our nation does not have to be involved in a war to suffer tremendous damage from terrorists, who might opt to spread lethal viruses anywhere within the continental United States.

The U.S. Department of Agriculture, the Food and Drug Administration, the Federal Bureau of Investigation, and the Central Intelligence Agency are aware of this danger and have been conducting research on how these viruses might be released on the American public, as well as actions that might be taken to prevent it from happening--or how to combat it after it happens.

Recent worldwide trade treaties such as NAFTA and the World Trade Agreement have made such scenarios more of a possibility because of the lowering of trade barriers and the ease of shipping and traveling across international borders.

Quarantine is a fictitious story of what could happen if terrorists were to target one of our important food producing industries. It is not meant to panic the general public, but hopefully, to make them understand and be aware of the danger--and possibly take steps to make our food production, storage, and transportation facilities more secure against such actions.

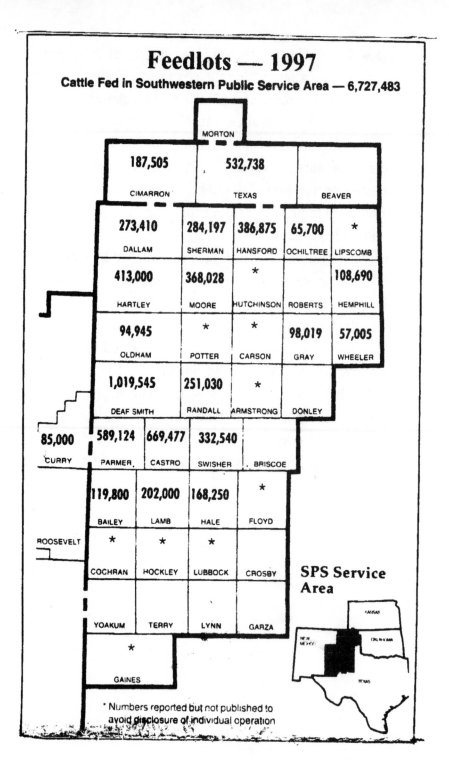

Feedlots — 1997

Cattle Fed in Southwestern Public Service Area — 6,727,483

MORTON				
187,505	532,738			
CIMARRON	TEXAS		BEAVER	
273,410	284,197	386,875	65,700	*
DALLAM	SHERMAN	HANSFORD	OCHILTREE	LIPSCOMB
413,000	368,028	*		108,690
HARTLEY	MOORE	HUTCHINSON	ROBERTS	HEMPHILL
94,945	*	*	98,019	57,005
OLDHAM	POTTER	CARSON	GRAY	WHEELER
1,019,545	251,030	*		
DEAF SMITH	RANDALL	ARMSTRONG	DONLEY	
85,000 — CURRY	589,124 — PARMER	669,477 — CASTRO	332,540 — SWISHER	BRISCOE
	119,800	202,000	168,250	*
	BAILEY	LAMB	HALE	FLOYD
ROOSEVELT	*	*	*	
	COCHRAN	HOCKLEY	LUBBOCK	CROSBY
	YOAKUM	TERRY	LYNN	GARZA
	*			
	GAINES			

SPS Service Area

* Numbers reported but not published to avoid disclosure of individual operation

IV

Foreword

The eagle soared lazily on the warm updrafts, high above the flat plain of the Texas Panhandle, a mere speck in the sky. His telescopic eyesight was scanning the flat prairie below for his noonday meal, a fat jackrabbit or maybe a smaller field mouse.

Below him, the patchwork shape of a large cattle feedlot appeared, as the breeze moved him slowly to the east. He could see the thousands of cattle— forty thousand in this particular yard—leisurely eating the ration of corn and silage which cowboys had placed in the feed bunks for their fattening process. The feed yard was enclosed around its perimeter by steel corrals, with the interior divided into more than two hundred smaller pens, each housing two hundred head of the fattening cattle. There was much activity taking place inside the perimeter of the feedlot. Cowboys on horses, trucks carrying feed to the pens, tractors with huge buckets mounted on the front which were loading the trucks, and pickup trucks rushing to and fro carrying out the duties required to keep the cattle content and fed.

The cattle would gain three to four pounds a day in the confined area, eating the high protein ration and receiving little exercise. Within one hundred days, a seven hundred pound steer would gain enough weight to be ready for market. Then would be slaughtered in one of the numerous packing plants, and shipped throughout the nation, supplying prime beef for the nation's dinner table.

As the eagle's gaze moved towards the horizon, he could see numerous facilities such as the one below, some containing as many as one hundred thousand head of cattle in feedlots, covering no more than a square mile of the area.

In the area between the feedlots, dust clouds swirled where farmers were operating huge tractors, preparing the land for growing the corn which would be used to feed the cattle.

Now the winds had carried the eagle over the small, rural community where fifteen thousand people, many of them workers in the feedlots, resided. Huge grain storage facilities rose from the town, reaching into the eagle's skies, where millions of bushels of grain were stored for future use in the cattle feeding industry.

A shift in the breeze moved the soaring eagle farther north, and below he could see a group of pickup trucks with horse trailers hooked to their rears, parked near another steel enclosed pen. Looking closely, he could see several mounted cowboys taking turns pursuing smaller cattle down the center of the enclosure. As they reached the center, one cowboy would throw his lariat and snag the steer's horns, another cowboy would then throw his lariat under the steer's belly and snag his hind legs. The steer, caught between the two horses, would fall to the ground, held snugly by the two trained horses.

Although the eagle could not know, the pen below was a rodeo arena and the cowboys were practicing the art of a sport known as *team roping,* a favorite pastime for the feed-lot cowboys.

No more than three miles from the rodeo arena, the eagle's sharp eyesight picked up the shapes of two boys approaching the edge of a small, dry playa lake bed, and a large, fat jackrabbit rushing from its hiding place near the edge of the dry, weed covered lake floor.

The eagle made a pass at the running rabbit and would liked to have grabbed it with its sharp talons, but he had learned from experience that it was best not to get to close to those two-legged animals, who sometimes carried sticks that made loud noises and threw pellets at him.

Circling high above the two boys, the eagle could see another two-legged person, lying in the weeds in the center of the dry lake bed. A black dog was circling this person, barking excitedly at his find. The boys abandoned their pursuit of the rabbit and rushed through the weeds towards the sound of the dog's barking.

The eagle abandoned thoughts of seeking its dinner in the area where the boys were hunting and sailed off to the east, directing his hunt in an area more isolated from human habitation.

Dedicated to my friend, Donald Kimball, who has fought the battle of MS for many years--and who has encouraged me to be faithful to my literary pursuits.

1

The body was lying face down in the middle of the dry playa lake bed, hidden by the knee-high cochia weeds covering the playa's floor. The black dog, however, had found it and was barking to tell the two boys that he had found something which they should investigate.

This small playa lake was not unlike the thousands of playas which dotted the flat High Plains of Texas, holding water when it rained. But since it seldom rained, they were usually dry and covered with tall weeds and grass and were a favorite habitat for rabbits, raccoons, skunks, possums and pheasants.

The boys, ages ten and eleven, were rabbit hunting with their new .22 caliber rifles, that had been Christmas gifts only two months before, and had followed a large jackrabbit into the lake's weed-covered floor. They heard the dogs frantic barking and rushed through the weeds towards the sound.

"Old Max got him a skunk cornered!" Cody, the ten year

old, shouted as they pushed through the weeds a couple of hundred yards away from the sound.

They knew it was no rabbit because a rabbit would not set in one place and allow Max to pester it with his barking. This must be something mean enough to keep the dog at bay.

"Ain't no skunk bark," Joey, the eleven year old responded as he pushed an exceptionally tall cochia aside. "Betcha he's got hisself a rattler cornered this time--leastwise I hope so. I sure ain't wanting to smell no skunk on his hide for the next two weeks. You know how Mom is, when old Max comes in smelling like a skunk. She'll make us take him down to the windmill and wash him with lye soap."

"Might be a coon," Cody replied, " 'member we seen them coon tracks up by the water trough. Betcha it's a coon!"

As the boys approached closer, the breeze, blowing from the direction of the dog, became permeated with an odor which was unpleasant to their smell, but was not the sharp, pungent odor of an upset skunk. It was something neither of them had ever smelled before. They could see the tip of the dog's tail as he darted around and around the varmint but were unable to see exactly what he had cornered because of the height and thickness of the lake-bottom weeds.

As they approached cautiously, with their rifles held in both hands, ready to fire if the varmint attacked, Joey said softly, "You watch yourself, Cody, if that's a big old rattler we sure don't want to get too close, 'member what Dad said about staying away from rattlesnakes!"

"Ain't no rattlesnake, Joey. Rattlesnakes don't stink like that," Cody replied.

2

The boys had found several rattlesnakes while exploring the boundaries of their father's farm. The south forty of the farm was the location of a large prairie dog town and the burrows, which were the homes of the prairie dogs, were a prime nesting ground for the rattlesnakes. Wes Tinsley, their father, had cautioned them to stay well away from that area of the farm while on their hunting forays.

They were now within twenty feet of the varmint, and the dog seeing them approaching, increased his barking as if to say, "I've got him cornered, boys, but be careful, he's dangerous!"

Joey, being the taller of the two, was first to see through the weeds that it wasn't a skunk and it wasn't a rattler. Whatever it was had on blue jeans and cowboy boots!

"Lordy, Cody," he shouted, "It's a man and looks to me like he's deader'n a doornail!"

Although he didn't know how dead a doornail might be, Joey had heard the phrase used by his dad in describing the condition of one of their bulls that had gotten into the grain bin, overeaten and died.

Cody, still unable to see the body and not hankering to see a stinking dead man, began backing away from the spot where the dog was indicating danger lay. Sometimes, when he became excited or scared, he was prone to stutter. "L-l-let's get out'ta here, Joey!", he stammered. "W-w-we ain't got no b-b-business messing around with no d-d-dead man."

But Joey, being the older of the two and not wanting to appear cowardly to his younger brother, cautiously moved forward a couple more steps where he could see the entire form of the corpse stretched out face down. His hands were taped together behind his back, his ankles taped tightly together, and two bullet holes showed plainly in the back of his head!

The dog, seeing that he was now backed up by his two young masters, calmed down and slowly crept up to the dead man, cautiously smelling the bloated body.

Cody, not anxious to look at a dead man but scared to move too far away from his older brother, slipped silently up to Joey's side and took hold of his belt for protection as he peered through the weeds at their discovery.

"G-g-gawd d-d-dang!", he stammered, forgetting that his mother would wash his mouth out with soap if she ever heard him using profanity.

The two boys slowly circled the body, with Cody squeezing tighter to Joey's belt. "Let's get the hell out of here and go tell Dad," Joey said, also forgetting the soap threat.

This was farm and ranch country where a boy learned to be a man by watching and listening to those who had already reached manhood. The small ears of the two boys had soaked up most of the fine prose and curse words, attributed to manhood, by listening to their father and his friends discuss cattle, farming and the world's political situation. They had also learned other fine arts, growing up in this High Plains country of Texas such as riding, roping and dipping snuff. Their mom, Clariss, a gracious church-going and God-fearing woman, was continually trying to break them of these manly habits.

Turning their backs to the corpse, they began running through the weeds towards their house, a half mile to the east, and now that they could no longer see the dead man, their imaginations ran amuck! He probably had gotten up from the ground, someway untied his arms and legs and was breathing down their collars, trying to stop them from reporting their find. They were not about to stop their retreat and turn their rifles onto the pursuing dead man. Everybody knew that bullets did no good against ghosts and dead men. The best thing for them to do was to reach the protection of their father as soon as possible.

They ran faster and faster, and both began to scream at the top of their lungs, afraid of the sight they might see if they looked back. The two new rifles were a hindrance to their speed, and were discarded on the hillside as they streaked towards the safety of their home. The black dog ran at their heels with his hair bristling in fear, wanting no part of his discovery now that the boys were not backing him up.

Their father was in the corral putting out hay for the cattle when he heard their screams. He dropped the hay fork, vaulted the fence and ran towards the two frightened boys, knowing by their actions that they surely must both be bitten by rattlesnakes. Hadn't he warned them over and over about watching where they walked when rabbit hunting?

Seeing their dad running towards them, they screamed all the louder. Tears were rolling down their cheeks and they were totally winded when they fell into the protection of his arms, unable to say a word.

Wes, of course, was trying to see where they had been bitten, pulling up their jean's legs and searching for the telltale marks of the rattler's fangs. "Where'd he bite you?" he screamed as he held Joey at arm's length and looked into his frightened eyes.

Through his sobs, Joey finally blurted, "Weren't no snake, Dad. It's a dead man!"

"A dead man! What you mean a dead man, boy?"

"W-w-we found a d-d-dead man, Dad," Cody stammered. Then both boys began to talk a mile a minute.

"There's a dead man down in the middle of the lake. Old Max found him and he's all tied up and been shot right in the back of his head," they cried.

Had it not been for their tears, Wes would have thought it was just another one of the wild stories they were prone to fabricate. They had seen something, he was certain, and asked, "What makes you think it was a dead man?"

"Cause we got real close to him, Dad. He's all swelled up and stinks and we could see two holes in the back of his head," Cody said.

"That's right, Dad," Joey agreed, then added, "Deader'n a doornail!"

"Get in the pickup and show me," Wes instructed as he headed for the truck which was parked next to the barn.

Wes stopped the truck on the hillside and retrieved the two rifles the boys had discarded, then followed their directions through the weeds to the middle of the dry lake bottom. However, he was unable to find the body until the dog pointed it out by once again barking frantically next to the body.

Wes could not believe his eyes when he stopped the truck twenty feet from the body. As he stepped out of the truck, he instructed the boys to stay inside as he walked slowly towards the barking dog. It was as the boys had described, the man was lying face down with his feet and hands tightly bound with duct tape and with two neat holes in the back of his head.

Wes walked slowly around the body, being careful where he stepped so as not to disturb any evidence that might be on the ground, since it was evident that the man had been murdered. Not only was it evident that he had been murdered, it was evident that he had been murdered elsewhere and dumped in the weeds of the lake bed, because there was no blood at the scene. Wes wanted to turn him over and look in his face because there was something vaguely familiar about the body. Someone he felt he should know but couldn't identify from the back. He decided it best not to disturb the body, however, before notifying the authorities.

Probably not much left of his face, anyway, he mused, as he thought about the damage caused by the two exiting bullets.

He returned to the pickup truck and dialed 911 on his cellular phone. A female voice came crisply through the receiver, "This is 911 emergency, how can I help you?"

"Give me Sheriff Blackwell," Wes replied, "this is Wes Tinsley and there's been a murder."

The female voice responded, "I am paging the sheriff, Mr. Tinsley, please give me the information. Who has been murdered and where?"

"I don't know who, ma'am, but it's a man all tied up and shot and he's laying in weeds in a dry playa lake bed about a half mile west of my house."

"Just give me directions from town, Mr. Tinsley, we may have a deputy in your area."

"It's eight miles north on 385 and two miles east. My house is on the south side of the road and you'll see my pick-up parked in the lake bed just a half mile west of my barn."

"Thank you, Mr. Tinsley, there will be an officer there shortly."

Wes Tinsley, a thirty-five year old farmer, had lived in Deaf Smith County, Texas, all his life and could not remember ever hearing about a murder in the county before. Seeing the murdered man in the middle of his farm was hard to believe, but there he was, bound and tied and *dead as a doornail* as Joey had so aptly described him.

This was not a country where people went around murdering other people. Deaf Smith County was basically a peaceful, law-abiding county in the Texas Panhandle. It certainly had it's share of petty robberies, stealing, small-time drug peddlers and assaults— but not murders. It was still old-west cow country, with over four hundred thousand head of cattle filling the numerous cattle feed yards, and a few thousand cowboys who worked in the feed yards, tending the cattle. Cowboys didn't run away from a good, old-fashioned rough-and-tumble brawl; but they knew when to stop before something like this took place.

Old Erasmus "Deaf" Smith, the county's namesake, had been a Texas Revolutionary War hero, who was deaf and had fought beside General Sam Houston in 1836. Speaking fluent Spanish and able to read lips. Smith would slip close to Mexican lines, train his binoculars on the Mexican officers who

8

were discussing attack plans, read their lips and carry their plans back to General Houston. This information was invaluable in helping Houston defeat the Mexican army.

Texans liked to name their towns and counties after their Revolutionary War heroes.

It had always been cow country but with developing technology and irrigation, it now boasted about eight hundred farmers. The farmers had plowed up much of the prairie grass and were growing the corn and feed grains used by the feed yards to feed the four hundred thousand head of confined cattle.

Hereford, the only town in the county, had received its name from the Hereford breed of cattle that had been brought in from England, before the turn of the century, to crossbreed with the native longhorns. It was also the county seat, and boasted a population of about fifteen thousand people. Main street was only four blocks long, and like most of the small towns across rural America, many of the main street businesses had closed because of the past twenty years of a failing agriculture economy.

Sheriff Pete Blackwell had been the county's chief law enforcement officer for over fifteen years and knew almost all of the fifteen thousand by their first names. His constituents loved him, knowing him to be fair and conscientious; but firm in upholding the duties of his office. The criminals had less favorable opinions of him but respected his authority. His staff consisted of four deputies, two jailers, two radio dispatchers and one secretary.

For the past fifteen years, the job of upholding the law in

Deaf Smith County had been relatively easy. The small county jail housed mostly drunks, petty thieves, small time drug dealers and illegal Mexican wet backs, so dubbed because they had to swim the Rio Grande River to slip into Texas illegally. However, the discovery of the murdered man in the dry playa lake bed by Wes Tinsley's two boys would turn this peaceful community upside down and Pete and his boys were going to start earning their law enforcement money!

2

On his day off, Deputy Sheriff Buster Thornton, was participating in his favorite sport, team roping seven hundred pound Mexican steers with his friend, feed yard owner and manager, George Autry. They were entered in a team roping rodeo which was to be held in a few weeks and were practicing for the event. George had just made a clean catch of their third steer's horns, when Buster pulled his horse close behind and threw his lariat under the steer's belly; catching its two hind legs as his horse slid to a stop and began backing. The steer, stretched between the two horses by the lariats, fell to its side

"Good catch, Buster," George said as they released the steer and recoiled their ropes.

"Mutual," Buster responded, smiling, as he dismounted and led his horse out the gate of the roping arena. His pickup truck and trailer were parked near the gate and as he opened the tailgate to the trailer, he heard his two-way radio squawk.

"All available sheriff's deputies, proceed eight miles north of Hereford on 385 and two miles east. Turn in at house on south side of the road and proceed to playa lake one-half mile west of house. Unidentified male reported murdered. Local farmer, Wes Tinsley waiting at body. Please respond," the crisp female voice instructed.

Buster quickly loaded his horse, latched the tailgate, shouted to George that he had a call, jumped into his truck and responded as he swung the truck onto the highway and headed south.

"Base, Unit Three here," he said as he keyed his mike. "My 1020 is ten miles north of town at the Billings roping arena, proceeding to Tinsley farm. Should be there in three or four minutes.

This is a helluva coincidence, he thought, *for me to be only four miles from a murder scene on my day off and apparently the only deputy available-- and to top it all, it's on Wes's farm!*

He and Wes had been friends for several years, almost kin. Buster's former wife, Kellie, who had died of ovarian cancer three years before, was a cousin to Wes's wife, Clariss. Buster and Kellie had been married for ten years but never had children, probably because the cancer had been eating away at her, long before it was discovered by Doc Wilson. Cody and Joey had filled in part of that void in their lives, almost like their own sons. Buster had given each of them a horse on their sixth birthday and had been teaching them the art of throwing a rope. He hoped that someday they would be top team ropers. The boys called him *"Uncle* Buster", even though he was only a cousin by marriage.

He swung his truck and trailer into the yard at the Tinsley farm, circled around to the barn and down the turn-row to the lake bottom where he could see the blue pickup truck parked. A man was standing beside the truck waving his hat to attract his attention. The two boys were inside the truck cab with their heads hanging out the window.

"Howdy, Wes, howdy boys," he said as he stepped from his truck. "Hear you've got a problem here."

"Howdy, Buster," Wes replied, his concern registered on his face. "You've damn sure got that right. My boys stumbled onto a dead feller that's been shot in the back of the head. Looks like he may have been here two or three days."

"Howdy, Uncle Buster," the boys spoke as one, "We found us a dead man!"

The deputy walked over to the body and stared in disbelief as he removed a tin of Skoal from his shirt pocket and placed a pinch of snuff between his teeth and lips. "Looks like someone was mad as hell at him," he said. "The way he's all bound up and shot. He's not only been murdered, I'd say he's been executed. Got any idea who he is?"

"Something about him looks mighty familiar but I can't place him without turning him over where I can see his face," Wes replied.

"Yeah, I see what you mean, something familiar about him but no way to tell who he is from this position. You did right by not touching him," Buster said. "We best wait until the coroner and the sheriff gets here, we certainly don't want to mess up no evidence."

Buster was a college graduate but he never did place too much emphasis on correct grammar, using words and phrases that suited him; rather than those which his English professors had insisted were proper. Double negatives and split infinities flowed from his mouth like warm molasses. He spoke with a slow, southern drawl and was prone to interject a few choice expletives to emphasize a point.

Turning, he walked by the window of Wes's pickup and handed the tin of snuff to Joey, knowing that Clariss would chew him up one side and down the other if she knew; but he always shared his snuff with the boys when she wasn't around. Wes had his eyes glued on the dead man and didn't notice the gift. The boys quickly took a pinch and placed it between their lips and gums just like Buster had taught them. Buster smiled and winked at Joey as he turned and walked to the cab of his truck, keying the mike to his radio, he spoke, "Unit Three to base."

"This is base, go ahead, Unit Three," the female voice responded.

"Irene, better get the coroner out here. We got us a homicide for damned sure. White male, five eight or nine, looks like maybe a hundred and sixty pounds, all tied up and shot in the back of the head. No blood at the scene so he musta been shot elsewhere and then dumped out here. How about the sheriff, has he been notified?"

Another male voice interrupted, "This is Sheriff Blackwell, Buster. I heard your call and I'm on my way, be there in about ten minutes."

Buster walked to the rear of the trailer, opened the tailgate and spoke to his horse. The horse backed out and stood trembling as he picked up the scent of the dead man. Horses are smart critters and recognize dead smells, becoming very nervous when their nostrils pick up the scent. It's virtually impossible to get a horse close to any kind of dead animal.

Buster mounted and began to ride slowly in the direction of the county road, looking closely at the ground covered by the weeds, searching for anything that might be evidence. His horse shied and snorted as if to clear the smell from its nostrils, as it passed close by the dead man. Buster's position, high above the weeds on the horse's back gave him a good view of the ground beneath the weeds. Many of the dry weeds had been broken over, indicating that the body had been dragged from the road to its resting place in the middle of the lake bed. He followed the trail, finding nothing until he reached the barbed wire fence separating the pasture from the roadbed. There, clinging to one of the barbs was a piece of cloth about a half inch in diameter, finely woven wool and dark in color. Whoever had dragged the body from the road to the lake bed had been wearing an expensive suit and had tangled it in the fence.

Buster dismounted and retrieved the cloth, carefully placing it in his wallet. *Sure as hell ain't no cowboy's or farmer's trousers,* he thought.

The two boys had climbed into the back of their dad's truck and the dog jumped over the tailgate and joined them. He continued to bark sporadically as Buster rode slowly back to the body, looking for other signs of evidence. Joey pointed towards the highway as flashing red and blue lights could be seen coming towards them, kicking up dust on the county road. There were three sets of lights: an ambulance, the Justice of the Peace's red Chevy, and the sheriff's white Ford bringing up the rear.

Now they could hear the wail of the sirens as the vehicles sped towards the scene, a strange sound that sent chills down the boys' spines. Living on the farm, they had never heard such loud wailing before. The three vehicles pulled up to the scene, driving in the tracks made by the two trucks. The red and blue lights continued to flash, casting colored images on the parked vehicles, on the men's faces and on the body in the weeds.

The sound of the sirens slowly faded away as the occupants of the vehicles stepped out and converged on the dead body. The boys huddled together in the back of their father's pickup, their hearts racing and their bodies shivering, at the scene unfolding before their eyes.

While the others stood back and waited, Justice of the Peace, Janey Torrington, who also acted as county coroner, approached the body--camera in hand--and took several snapshots before instructing the two emergency personnel to turn it over. There was a gasp of disbelief when the murdered man's face was disclosed. Upon exiting, the bullets had torn flesh and bone away, totally destroying the facial features.

Cody and Joey turned their eyes away and began to cry. The dog whined and licked their faces, trying to comfort them.

"Ain't no way of identifying him from his looks," Sheriff

Pete Blackwell said. Turning to Deputy Thornton, he instructed, "See if he's got any identification in his pockets, Buster."

Janey handed Buster a pair of surgical gloves, which he pulled onto his hands before beginning his search. While Buster was going about his grisly business, a dirty green Chevy turned in at the house and sped across the pasture towards the scene. A young man wearing thick horn-rimmed glasses jumped out, camera in hand, and started taking pictures.

"Howdy, Lane," Sheriff Blackwell greeted, "Be careful where you walk, we don't want any evidence messed up."

"Sheriff," the young newspaper reporter nodded seriously, as he quickly moved around the group, burning film. At nineteen years of age, this was Lane's first murder scene and he intended to make certain he caught it all on film.

After getting his photo shots, he walked over to Wes, pen and note pad in hand and started asking questions. "How did you find him, Mr. Tinsley?"

"I didn't, Lane, my boys did. Maybe you should ask them."

Lane stepped over to the pickup and placed his note pad on the edge of the truck bed, prepared to get a statement from the two boys, when the black dog growled menacingly and made a lunge at his hands. The reporter jumped back, dropping the note pad and barely saving his hands from the teeth of the snarling dog.

Joey grabbed the dog by the nap of the neck and pulled him back. "Old Max don't like for strangers to get too close to me and Cody 'till he gets acquainted," he said in a slow drawl, mimicking that of Buster, as he spit a brown stream of snuff juice over the side of the truck bed.

Joey picked up the note pad which had fallen inside the pickup bed and handed it to Lane as he spoke to Max, convincing him that the newspaper reporter could be trusted. Lane smiled nervously, trying, unsuccessfully to hide his fear as he asked, his voice breaking, "How'd you find the body, boys?" He kept well away from the truck, holding the pad in one hand and writing with the other.

The two boys, both speaking at once, told the hair-raising tale of how they had stumbled upon the dead man. Even adding a few of the expletives they had heard Buster use in describing the body, and giving Max credit for the initial find. Lane replaced the note pad with the camera and pointed it towards the boys and clicked the shutter. When the flash went off, the dog made another lunge at the reporter, thinking he was up to no good. Lane jumped away from the snarling animal and moved back into the crowd of people surrounding the body, glad to put an end to that interview.

After searching in all four pockets, Buster announced, "Picked clean, Pete. Guess whoever done it didn't want us identifying him too quickly. Another thing, Pete, I looked the place over real good before you arrived. There weren't any tire tracks other than ours coming in here. Whoever dumped him had to drag him here by hand from the road, and that's nigh onto three hundred yards. Looks like two people did the dragging. I found a piece of cloth on the fence, don't match anything on the body and I'd say it probably came from an expensive business suit."

Suddenly, Wes Tinsley who had been staring at the body, spoke. "Well I'll be damned! I knew there was something fa-

miliar about this guy when I first seen him laying there.
Look at that belt buckle, made out of gold and got a Cessna aircraft emblem right in the middle. Only person I know a-
round here got a buckle like that is Spinner Murphy, the
spray pilot out at Murphy's Spraying Service--done a lot of
spraying for me and my neighbors in the past."

* * * * * *

Douglas "Spinner" Murphy, forty year-old owner and operator of Murphy's Spraying Service, could have been one of
the world's best fighter pilots except for one thing--his age.
Born in 1956 in Dimmit just twenty miles south of Hereford
to Will and Edna Murphy, Spinner was too young for the Viet-
nam war and too old for Desert Storm. That didn't, however,
dampen his love for flying. Father Will had been a fighter
pilot in World War II, flying Corsairs from carriers in the Pa-
cific. His tales of dogfights with Japanese Zeros and torpedo
runs on enemy ships, only increased young Spinner's determination to be a flyer when he grew up.

While still in high school, he spent his time around the
airport, helping do odd jobs for spray pilots and occasionally
was given the opportunity to ride in one of the planes. One of
the companies continued to use the old bi-wing, two seat,
World War I Stearmans for spraying crops and Spinner per-
suaded the owner, Flip Bowman, to teach him to fly. It was
apparent that he was a natural with the old plane. And before
he graduated from high school had received his pilot's license and was filling in as a spray pilot when the regular pi-

lots were sick.

After graduation from high school he tried college but his love of flying took too much time away from his books. After failing most of his courses the first semester, he dropped out and took a full time job, flying for Flip.

Determined to own his own company, he worked long hours, saved his money, lived frugally and by the time he was twenty-eight, bought his own Cessna spray plane and opened up for business in Hereford. He had never married, believing that flying crop dusters was too dangerous an occupation for him to consider marriage. Besides, he just didn't have time for women--maybe later when he felt more financially secure.

It didn't take long for local farmers to recognize that Spinner was one of the best and most dependable pilots around and his business boomed. However, crop spraying was a seasonal business and there were times during the year when demand for crop spraying dropped to zero, when nothing needed spraying or dusting. During those times, Spinner's income suffered, so he borrowed the money and bought a used six passenger Cessna 210. He added charter flights to his business and began flying customers to Mexico on fishing excursions and vacationers to Las Vegas for gambling--this at a time when drug trafficking from Mexico was expanding rapidly.

While servicing his plane one weekend at the airport in Las Vegas, after delivering his charter customers, and about six months before his body was found in the lake bed, Spinner was approached by a stranger, medium build, dark hair and olive complexion who spoke with some kind of foreign accent. Spinner couldn't quite place it, but suspected it to be Middle Eastern. The stranger asked if his plane was for hire.

"Sure is," Spinner answered as he shoved the dip stick back into the engine after checking the oil, "Long as it's legal and profitable."

The stranger smiled and said his boss would like to talk to him. Spinner wiped his hands and accompanied him to a waiting black Buick, that carried them to the Strip and stopped in front of one of the major casinos, where they took the elevator to the penthouse. He was introduced to an elderly, heavyset, gray-haired gentleman, who also spoke with the same Middle Eastern accent. The huge diamond ring on the gentleman's right hand convinced Spinner that he had been introduced to a very wealthy person. His suspicions were correct, for the man informed him that he was a major stockholder in the casino.

Dinner was served in the privacy of the penthouse and before the evening was over, Spinner accepted a lucrative contract to occasionally act as courier for the casino. He was to fly employees of the casino around the country and deliver *supplies* from Vegas to Chicago.

It was almost a deal he couldn't refuse, but Spinner told the casino owner that he had worked long and hard to build his spray business; and would be unable to accept the deal unless he could work it in conjunction with his spray business.

It was agreed that Spinner would continue his spray business in Hereford and fly for the casino only during the winter months or when an emergency might arise. Smiling, the casino owner said, "Mr. Murphy, I can assure you that you will make so much more money with us than you could ever make spraying crops that you will be ready to dump the spray business and take on this job full-time by the time spring arrives."

* * * * * *

Spinner's body was loaded into the ambulance and the group entered their respective vehicles and headed towards town.

Lane was anxious to get his film developed and write his story. What a break! Only six weeks on the job and getting to cover the first murder case in Deaf Smith County, in no telling how many years. The other reporters on the paper were certainly going to be envious!

Wes and his two boys returned to their house, a half-mile from the murder scene, where the boys rushed in to explain to their mother the excitement they had just witnessed--after first spitting out the remains of the Skoal that Buster had given them.

3

Sunday's edition of the *Hereford Bull* had a large picture of Joey and Cody standing behind their black dog, Max, in the back of their father's pickup. The headlines above the picture read, "Local Boys Discover Body of Murdered Pilot."

Their graphic story filled the right-hand column while the left-hand column had a smaller picture of Spinner Murphy which related the story of his life as a spray pilot in Deaf Smith County, as well as speculation about who had murdered him and why he had been murdered. The by-line on both of the stories was *Lane Martin*.

* * * * * *

"Drugs, I'd say. Used to be bootleggers that gave us problems but now, since liquor's been made legal, this county's getting to be a hotbed for small-time drug dealers--marijuana mostly," Sheriff Blackwell said in response to Texas Ranger

Allen's question about a motive. "What I can't figure, is why would he be all taped up like that before he was shot? We've had a few knifings and shootings over drugs before but never any cold-blooded executions like this."

The group of law officers were discussing the murder in the sheriff's office, located on the ground floor in the Deaf Smith County courthouse. The Texas Rangers had been notified and Ranger Allen had come down from Amarillo to help in the investigation.

"I've seen it before down state," the Ranger replied, "in Dallas and Houston, but it's always been mob related. You know, a pay back for doublecrossing the gang, moving in on somebody's territory, squealing or something of the sort."

Buster, who had been listening to the conversation, spoke. "Sheriff, I've talked to a lot of folks since the shooting, personal friends of Spinner's and not one of them believe he was involved in any kind of criminal activity, most especially drugs. He just lived and breathed flying and had built up a good solid spray business. You know, he also did some charter flying during the off season, fishing trips and flying folks out to Las Vegas for a gambling weekend. Slim Edwards, pilot out at Pecos Spraying Service, told me that Spinner did a lot of flying for some folks out in Vegas. He kept those planes busy and was making too much money to get involved in anything illegal. It's got to be something other than drugs."

Sheriff Blackwell paced back and forth, rubbing his chin as if in deep thought, then spoke. "I knew Spinner pretty well, myself, and it's hard to believe but you've got to admit that Cessna 210 he owned would make an ideal drug trafficking plane, plenty of room to haul a big load and enough power to pull it. Those fishing trips to Mexico certainly add suspicion to the trafficking angle. A lot of honest people have been compromised when large sums of easy money are concerned. Until we find something else to go on, we're going to have to assume that drugs are behind it one way or another and conduct our investigation accordingly."

Turning to Ranger Allen, he asked. "Can we depend on your help, Chuck? This thing may get bigger than our county, in a hurry, and you know how we're limited in doing any investigations outside of county."

"I'm sure we can, Pete. I'll speak to the Captain about it and be back in touch. If it does prove to be drugs, the Drug Enforcement Agency should also be notified," he said as he retrieved his hat and stepped out the door.

Walking across the room to the coffee pot, Sheriff Blackwell poured himself another cup, dumped a couple of spoonfuls of sugar in and started stirring. He was a tall, rugged looking individual, six-three and over two hundred pounds, with a mop of unruly gray hair that kept falling across his brow. It was worrisome to him and he was continually pushing it back out of his eyes, when in deep thought. His broad shoulders and bulging biceps indicated a man of tremendous strength but his age and too much time behind the desk had influenced the growth of an oversized stomach falling over his belt. Getting shirts the proper size across the shoulders that would fit around his waist had become a problem and usually the middle button was noticeably unfastened.

His age and deteriorating physical condition hadn't affected his ability to enforce the law, however, as many of the local criminal element had found out the hard way. He could still manhandle the best of them, and knock in their heads if the situation warranted.

The three deputies smiled as he shook his head and said, "My wife says if I don't stop using so much sugar it's gonna kill me but I can't stand the damn stuff without doctoring it up." Taking a sip he turned to his chief deputy, "Since you were the first on the scene, I guess you might as well take charge of the investigation, Buster. Talk to some of our contacts and see if you can come up with any leads that might link Spinner to the drug dealers. The rest of you guys keep your eyes and ears open and give Buster any help he might need."

Turning to his young undercover deputy, he said, "Johnny, maybe you need to make a few purchases from your street people, ask some questions and see if any changes are taking place in the local delivery system. Remember, guys, election is coming up and I sure as hell don't need any unsolved murders or drug wars on my hands. Keep me posted and if you need any help outside the county, get in touch with the rangers. That'll be all, fellows. Let's get started."

* * * * * *

The airport wasn't much, an office where flight plans could be filed, a couple of gas pumps at the edge of the runway, and several small hangers where small private planes belonging to local citizens were hangered. To facilitate the huge cattle feeding industry, the runway had been extended and upgraded to handle business jets. A quarter of a mile from the office was a group of smaller buildings, belonging to several spray companies, where chemicals were stored and hoses and pumps for filling the planes with water, insecticides and herbicides were available.

Buster, having just completed an unsuccessful search of Spinner's home, pulled up to one of the buildings where a sign proclaimed it to be the operating headquarters of Murphy's Spraying Service. He stepped out of the Sheriff's Department four-wheel drive Blazer, followed by a gray, German Shepherd dog, who immediately ran to the nearest post and marked it with his urine.

"O.K., Shep," Buster said, "It's drug hunting time, see what you can find."

Shep began to slowly circle the building, nose in the air and sniffing for the familiar odor which he had been trained to detect. Buster watched, waiting for the dog to indicate he had located the scent, but nothing changed. He stopped and looked at Buster inquisitively as if to say, *You certain there's drugs here?*

Buster unlocked the door to the building and motioned for Shep to enter. The dog made a quick search of the building and once again announced that there was no scent of drugs.

Next he opened the door of the small hanger where the Cessna spray plane and the larger six place two-ten were stored. Again Shep came up empty, finding nothing that would indicate that the planes had carried any kind of drugs.

Upon examining the spray plane, Buster was impressed with the cleanliness of the plane. He had been around spray planes a lot. He had worked for one of the spray companies while he was in high school, flagging in the fields and cleaning the planes after a job was completed. He even learned to fly and earned his pilot's license while working for the spray company. Usually the planes were washed down with a high pressure water hose and the tanks were drained and flushed each time. Most pilots were not too particular in their cleaning procedures and would leave a trace of the chemical around the nozzles and in the tank. This plane was immaculate, not a speck of dried chemical showing on the spray nozzles, in the tank, or on the plane. Actually, Buster thought, *as clean as it is, it looks as if this plane has never been used to spray chemicals.* But he knew that wasn't true because he had seen it flying fields for seven or eight years. *And I know Spinner, he just wasn't that neat a person. Even his truck didn't get washed twice a year*, he said to himself.

Well, what the hell, probably don't mean nothing, he muttered under his breath as he loaded Shep and shut the car door. He started the engine and slowly circled the building and turned towards town; but braked to a stop and backed up once again to the office--something just didn't quite fit. He allowed his gaze to slowly circle the area then stop at the loading pad.

It was a flat concrete-covered pad about thirty by thirty feet, which dipped slightly from the sides to the center where a six inch drain plug was installed. The spray planes were parked on this pad when being filled with chemical and then again when they were being washed down, in order that any spilled chemicals would be caught in a buried septic tank. The EPA had gotten pretty strict with the spray boys about spilling chemicals on the ground. Buster picked up a small plastic evidence bag from the glove compartment and stepped out of the Blazer, then walked to the drain plug. Kneeling down, he looked at the drain and seeing some sediment around its edges, pulled a knife from his pocket and scraped several blade-fulls into the plastic bag.

Returning to the truck, he stepped in and once again headed for town. Out of the corner of his eye he noticed another car, Buick or Lincoln, dark in color, parked on a dirt road on the opposite side of the airport, accelerate and head north away from town. *Could be they was watching what I was doing through binoculars*, Buster mused, then shook his head *no*-- he was letting his imagination run away with itself.

* * * * * *

"Mr. Autry, I think you'd better take a look at these sicks we picked up in several pens this morning," head cowboy Hank Clements said as he leaned against the doorway of George's office.

George, looking concerned, took his hat from the hat rack, pulled it securely on his head and followed Hank out the door. He always pulled his hat firmly on his head before

29

going outside; because the incessant West Texas winds had pulled too many of the two hundred dollar Stetsons off his head and rolled them across the manure-soaked feedlot. Hank had brought two horses to the hitching rail in front of the office, and the two cowboys mounted and rode down the alley to the sick pen.

George knew that if Hank asked for advice, something terrible was wrong. Hank had been working for George for several years and had proven to be one of the best cowboys in the area. He could spot a sick animal a quarter of a mile away, and knew exactly what kind of medication would get the animal back to normal health. George had commented many times that Hank probably knew more about cattle than most of the veterinarians in the country.

Several head of cattle stood inside the pen with heads hanging low, saliva drooling from their mouths and limping as if their feet were sore.

"Beats hell out of me what's wrong with them, Boss," Hank said as he opened the gate, led his horse through and waited for George to ride into the pen before closing the gate. He remounted and they rode slowly through the cattle, looking closely at each sick animal.

There were about fifty head in the pen, all appearing to be stricken with the same sickness. "Most of them came from pens over on the west side of the feedlot but only one or two from each pen," Hank said.

"All different sizes, too," George added, "so it's apparent that they are not from the same herd."

Shaking his head, he said, "First time I've ever seen

these symptoms--better call the vet and have him take a look, maybe he can prescribe a medication that'll take care of the problem."

* * * * * *

Johnny Avila, twenty-six year old undercover deputy for the Sheriff's department, had been working the streets, searching for evidence that might tie Murphy to the drug traf- ficking that had recently increased in the county. Johnny was a small, wiry Hispanic, looking much younger than his actual age. His black hair was shoulder length and his fine facial features were covered with a scraggly beard. His uni- form was a pair of worn blue jeans, a dirty cotton shirt and scuffed Reeboks. He drove a rebuilt, black, 1971 half-ton Chevy pickup which had a souped-up 350 engine. The little truck sported a stick shift, twin exhaust pipes, cut-down springs and wide low-profile tires. It was also equipped with an expensive stereo and large boom-box speakers, mounted in the back which were usually rattling windows with a deep bass sound as he cruised around town. He always carried a large roll of bills in his shirt pocket and was known by most of the dealers as being a good market for their products.

Johnny didn't look too tough, but most of the troublemak- ers around town had found out that he could take care of him- self in a fight. He didn't seek out trouble, but association with members of several street gangs gave him ample opportunity to either fight or run. *He didn't like to run*. A stint in the army's special forces had taught him the fine art of karate and he didn't hesitate to use it when provoked.

About a mile south of town, an area known as the Labor Camp was known as a place where many small-time drug dealers hung out. The camp, several blocks of surplus army barracks converted into living quarters for Mexican field workers, was the temporary home for hundreds of migrant farm workers who hired out to local vegetable and sugar beet farmers during the growing season. Mostly legal *green card-ers* but some illegal *wet backs*. These transients made good *mules* for the transport of drugs from Mexico, and it was sus- pected by law enforcement officers that it was a distribution center for some of the more organized traffickers from the Dallas and Houston areas. Recently, a few dope-heads had been arrested with small amounts of crack in their pockets. The sheriff's department and the drug enforcement boys did their best to keep the drug trade out of the county, but it was almost an impossible task.

Johnny Avila did a lot of business in the labor camp, usu- ally buying a few joints of marijuana from the small-time dealers while playing cards and shooting dice in the back rooms. He asked very few questions but kept his ears open for information that could be used by the drug enforcement agents to put down the larger operations.

As he slowly drove through the nearly deserted camp at 10 p.m. with his boom-box blaring, he stopped next to a small group of teenagers who seemed to be passing around a joint.

"Hey, man, how ya doing, Johnny?" one of the teens shouted.

"Great, Manuel," Johnny replied as he tuned down the

32

stereo and added. "Where's the action, man?"

"L-14, in the back, man."

"Gracias," Johnny replied, holding out his left fist with his thumb extended upward as he released the clutch and depressed the accelerator, kicking up dirt and gravel as the rear wheels spun to the response of the 350 V-8. The group of teens laughed as the little Chevy slid around the corner on the dirt street and headed for L-14.

"Man," one of them said, "I need me a truck like that."

Several cars and pickups were parked along the street next to L-14. Johnny parked next to the only streetlight on the block and walked the short distance to the blacked-out door of the barracks. The streetlight would help discourage theft of his expensive stereo speakers. He gave three short raps on the door, paused, then rapped twice more. The door was slowly opened as the bright light from the room stabbed out into the outside darkness and illuminated Johnny's face. Recognition was established as a voice inside said, "Hey, man, come on in! We need some new blood."

Johnny stepped in and the door was quickly closed. The room was filled with the sweet smelling aroma of marijuana smoke as several men, on their knees, were shooting dice on a blanket in the corner. Another group across the room at a card table were playing poker while six more were laughing and talking next to the door.

Johnny glanced around and subconsciously counted fifteen to twenty people in the room, mostly men. A couple of girls who appeared to be no more than seventeen years old were being fondled in the corner by their boyfriends. He gave them only brief notice, seeing by their actions that they had been hitting the weed pretty heavy.

"Whose got the grass, man?" he asked one of his acquaintances, speaking in Spanish, as he pulled the roll of bills out of his shirt pocket and peeled off a twenty.

"Raul," the answer came as the friend nodded towards one of the men around the dice game.

Johnny walked across the room to Raul, spoke and handed him the twenty and the dealer gave him a small package of smokes, ready-rolled and stuffed in a used Marlboro pack. Johnny moved back to the group next to the door, lit one of the joints, took a drag and passed it around the group. Turning his head as if to speak to a friend across the room, he blew the smoke, without inhaling into his lungs. He needed to keep his head clear and his mind functioning as he searched for any information that might indicate a change in drug activity within the county.

If anybody knew what was going on, it was Raul. Johnny walked back across the room and stood next to the dealer who was talking sweetly to the dice as he made his first roll. "Come on baby, we need a seven," he said as he threw the dice against the baseboard. A five and a two appeared! Groans of disappointment sounded as Raul pulled his winnings aside, then pushed a twenty back on the blanket. Four onlookers each dropped a five dollar bill to cover the twenty and Raul rolled again. Eleven! More groans. The next roll was two ones and the groans turned to laughs as one of them shouted "Snake eyes!" Raul passed the dice to the next shooter, walked to the corner and pulled a beer from a cooler.

Johnny followed and helped himself to a beer.

"Hey, man," Raul said, "what's new?"

"Not much--you remember my cousin, Domingo? Cops busted him for taking some tools didn't belong to him. He's in the county jail--I went in to visit him this morning and he told me he heard two of the cops talking about that spray pilot's murder. They said he was big-timing pot and crack and maybe someone didn't like it for him to be moving in on this market and took him out. You know what I mean, man?"

"That's bull shit, man," Raul swaggered. "Ain't nobody new been peddling around. I know all the dealers--everything's cool. Maybe Murphy got to messing with somebody's lady and they didn't like it. He wasn't into no drugs."

"O.K., man, I thought you should know what they're saying, they might start making things hot for awhile."

"Thanks, man, I'll keep it in mind."

Johnny moved back to the dice blanket and lost twenty dollars before leaving for home. The next morning he called Buster and reported what he had learned.

* * * * * *

The bar on Amarillo Boulevard was busy with the usual clientele. Four Hispanics were shooting pool on the lone pool table at the back of the room, while several customers sipped beer at the scattered tables. Three Vietnamese, employees of the local beef packing plant, were arguing about something in their native tongue at the end of the bar. Three well-endowed, boulevard prostitutes were exhibiting a lot of flesh while they sat at the bar, hoping that some *john* would make a pass.

Amarillo, the largest city in the Texas Panhandle, was the trading center for the surrounding area. Before the turn of the century, it had been a major rail shipping point for the hundreds of thousands of cattle, grown on nearby ranches. Amarillo natives were proud of their western heritage, and flaunted their pride with Stetson hats and cowboy boots.

However, growth of the cattle feeding industry had influenced beef packing companies to build huge slaughter houses in the area, and with it had come a variety of ethnic races, mostly Mexican and Vietnamese aliens who sought work in the meat packing plants. *Nike* shoes and baggy clothing were now mixed with the Stetsons and boots.

The two men sitting at a table in the corner looked out of place in the seedy surroundings, dressed in expensive tailored suits with brightly shined, black alligator shoes, covering their feet. Their faces were nearly as brown as those of the four Hispanics shooting pool. They were talking quietly as the waitress approached and asked what they would like to drink. She noticed that they had a distinct brogue, unlike that of the Hispanics and definitely alien to this West Texas area.

They ordered two Michelobs and continued their discussion as the waitress turned to leave.

"We shoulda dumped the body down in the sandhills along the Canadian River, Benny. I told you someone was liable to stumble onto it that close to town," the larger of the two said as he fingered the torn spot on his trousers leg.

"Maybe so, Tony," the small man replied, "But they ain't

no way they can tie the murder to us. No one but Murphy even knew we was in the country."

"You're probably right, but we can't take any chances. The newspaper said that deputy we saw, snooping around Murphy's hanger, was in charge of the investigation; so we better keep an eye on him for a few days. We may have to take him out, too, if it looks like he might be onto something."

"O.K., but I'd feel better if we was back in Vegas. They ain't nothing to do in this one-horse town but ogle the street walkers, and if I'm going to ogle, I'd rather it'd be at them Vegas showgirls," Benny said.

Tony smiled, "Another week ain't gonna kill you. It'll make Vegas that much more enjoyable, once we get back home."

4

"How's the cattle market?" Buster asked George Autry while they were removing the saddles from their roping horses, after a good practice session at Billings arena. Buster had been so busy trying to find leads in the Murphy murder that he hadn't kept up with the markets. He usually stayed on top of cattle prices since he had an interest in four hundred head of the cattle being fed in the Autry feed pens. He had noticed that George seemed despondent and was wondering if there was something he could do to cheer him up. They were at the horse corrals on the east side of Autry's feed yard where over forty thousand head of cattle, two hundred to the pen, were leisurely eating the feed which workers had placed in the bunks.

The majority of the cattle were owned by custom feeders--ranchers, farmers, packers and speculators--and Autry was paid for the feed and labor required to fatten them for market. Forty thousand head required a lot of close supervision and the Autry Feed Yard kept fifty employees busy, from bookkeepers in the office to pen riders, truck drivers, manure pilers and mill operators in the yard. It was actually an efficient factory, manufacturing *prime beef* which was shipped from coast to coast and border to border. The cattle usually came into the feed yard weighing about seven hundred pounds and were sold to the packing houses for slaughter, after gaining three to four hundred pounds. If everything worked right, with grain prices low enough and beef market prices high enough, the cattle could turn a decent profit--sometimes as much as one hundred dollars a head. For the past few months, however, everything hadn't been working right.

The Autry feedlot was only one of several which dotted the area around Hereford, but George had the reputation of being one of the best operators in the business and his pens were full.

George and Buster had grown up in the area and had been close friends for a long time. They had roomed together at Texas Tech University in Lubbock, where they both majored in Animal Husbandry. As members of the Tech Rodeo Club, they became partners in team roping, winning the national collegiate championship their senior year. After graduation, Buster went into law enforcement, while George stayed with his college major and took a position as assistant manager of one of the largest cattle feeding operations in Texas. Later, with three years experience behind him, he borrowed the money and built his own feed yard, convincing Buster to invest in the project. They both stood to lose a lot of money if the price of cattle continued to fall.

"Not worth a Tinker's damn," responded George to Buster's question about the markets, as he led the sorrel into the horse corral. "What with NAFTA allowing all those cattle out of Mexico and Canada into the U.S., our markets are shot to hell. Steers that we gave a buck a pound for, just eight months ago, are only worth about fifty cents a pound on to-day's market. On top of that, the drought has caused the price of grain to nearly double in the last twelve months which means our cost of gain has doubled."

Shaking his head, he added, "Don't take no Einstein to figure that we're going to lose our ass if something don't change! We could easy lose a couple hundred dollars a head if the market stays steady where it is today. My bet is that we're going to see even lower prices before it's all over."

This information caused a frown to appear on Buster's face, realizing that *he* was included in that *we*, since he owned four hundred head of the cattle in George's pens.

Me and the banker, he reminded himself.

Buster removed the bridle from his horse's head and scratched him between the ears before he responded.

"Damn, George. That'll not only hurt you and the folks with cattle in these pens but it'll just about bust the economy of this county and hurt everyone who lives here. I had cof-fee with the County Agent just last week and he said that with all the feed yards that operate in our county, close to five hundred thousand head of cattle are fed at any one time. With a two and a half turnover every twelve months, over a mil-lion head are shipped out of Deaf Smith County to market each year. Taking care of that many cattle keeps a lot of people employed. It's hard to believe we could lose two hundred bucks a head. Hell's bells! That means feeders in the Hereford vicinity alone could lose over two hundred million dollars in just one year."

"That's just a drop in the bucket compared to the area losses with feedlots scattered from here all the way into Kansas and Nebraska," the feed yard owner reminded him.

George closed the gate and they walked towards Buster's truck and trailer. "Now you see why I'm so worried and upset," he added. "Not only have we got the weather and the government working against us, we don't have any control over our markets. The price of beef grown in this country is set and controlled on the Chicago Board of Trade by the big traders, packers and exporters. They jockey the markets up and down at will, and all we can do is talk to the buyers and ask them 'what'll you gimmee', and they give us whatever they darned well please and we have to take it."

Buster could tell that the subject of cattle prices had upset George, so he didn't interrupt.

Using his finger to emphasize a point as Buster made the final adjustment to the trailer jack, George continued. "And another thing that burns my ass is that while we're struggling to stay in business, because the packers say there's a surplus of beef, the government is allowing Argentina, Mexico and Australia to import into our markets over a billion pounds of deboned and boxed beef each year. Now you tell me how much horse sense that makes. If we cut back on feeders to try to bring the supply down, the buyers just increase their imports from foreign countries and cut the price some more. There just ain't no justice in that system!

"I've lost a lot of sleep trying to figure out why we allow a bunch of pencil pushers in Chicago to control our destiny by buying and selling millions of fictitious paper beeves. They probably buy and sell seventy or eighty times as many cattle on paper as we produce every year by gambling on the market, selling cattle they never owned and buying cattle that don't exist. Supply and demand, be damned! Why, they can knock forty or fifty dollars a head off the price of our cattle, just because the government statisticians say we've got one percent more cattle on feed today than we had this time last year. Maybe we have and maybe we haven't, but just the statement by some bureaucrat in Washington can cost us millions. But I'll be hanged if I know what to do about it, a fat steer is just like a tomato or banana, it's a perishable product and when it's ready for market you've got to sell it; and so we sell at their price, not ours."

As they opened the doors of the pickup and climbed in, George said, "That's not the only problem that's got me looking at my hole card. Drive down to *M* alley, pen number 109, I want to show you something."

The red Chevy kicked up a swirl of chalky dust as Buster followed George's directions. As he pulled to a stop at pen 109, George pointed to the mass of cattle in the pen and said, "That's one of our sick pens. We always have a few head with bloat and pneumonia and some chronic sicks but never as many as we have seen the last few days. We just gathered these today, one or two out of each pen around the feedlot.

42

See that black baldy there? If you'll look real close you'll see his tongue is all swollen and he can't eat. And that Charolais over there, he acts like his feet are so damned sore he can hardly walk."

Buster nodded his head in agreement and said, "Looks like they all got the same ailment. What's the matter with them?"

"Wish I knew," George said with a scowl. "They just came down sick this way a couple of days ago and it's the first time in my life I've ever seen these symptoms. The thing that's got me buffaloed, is that this sickness is not just out of one or two batches of shipped in cattle, we're finding them in pens all over the yard, some of them have been here for over three months. It's pretty obvious that whatever they've got is contagious. Usually we have to worry about shipping fever and pneumonia but not something like this. The vet was here a couple of days ago and took some tissue samples to send off to the state lab--said we should be hearing something today. I've also got my nutritionist making some tests to see if we've got a problem with our feed. The problem is, if they stay this way for very long they'll die because they can't eat or drink. What makes it worse is that some of them are almost ready for market now and the packers won't take them, if they show any sign of sickness."

"That's terrible, George, I hope you find the trouble before my steers are ready for market, Losing two hundred bucks a head because of the market price is bad enough but if one dies, that's six hundred bucks down the drain," Buster replied, as he headed the truck back towards the office building.

He also had problems in the Sheriff's Department, the Spinner Murphy murder investigation had bogged down and he was at a loss what to do next. He remembered a statement George had made immediately after Spinner's body had been found by the two boys, and asked, "You remember last week, you told me that Spinner had flown you to Vegas a couple of times on charter flights. What do you remember about those trips?"

"Concerning what?"

"You know, like what hotel did you stay in while you were there?"

"We all stayed at the Frontier, me and Spinner and a couple of my customers. That seemed to be his favorite hangout. I think he must have had a deal with the hotel and they furnished him a free room if he brought his clients there. He flew us out on Friday and we came back Sunday night."

"Notice anything strange about Spinner's time he spent there, where he went and who he might have hung around with?"

"Not really. Come to think of it, I didn't see much of him after we checked into the hotel. A couple of guys, friends of his I guess, picked him up and he didn't show back until time to come home. I thought at the time that they were pretty tough looking characters, foreigners of some kind, but I don't make a policy of judging people 'till I get to know them so I didn't say anything."

Pausing as if in deep thought, George added, "Something else that I didn't give much thought to at the time but might have some bearing on the case. I was sitting up front with Spinner on the trip and I noticed the tack time on the planes hour meter showed exactly thirty-four hundred hours, when we landed in Vegas, but when we got loaded up to come home, it was showing thirty- four hundred and thirty hours."

"Are you sure? Thirty hours on a plane could mean a lot of miles."

"Yeah, I'm certain. It was thirty hours, even."

"Sounds like Spinner was doing some flying while you guys were gambling," Buster said. "Don't guess he indicated where he might have gone?"

"Didn't say and I didn't ask."

George opened the pickup door and Buster said, as he stepped out, "See you next week. I think I might take a run up to Vegas this weekend and do a little snooping. I still can't find an answer as to why Spinner was executed the way he was unless he might have had some ties with out of state mobsters. Since he seemed to have friends out there, it's as good a place as any to start. Pete and the Rangers are pretty well convinced that he was involved in dealing drugs but I haven't found a cotton-picking thing that would tie him in with that crowd. One of our undercover agents has been poking around the streets and he says Spinner was clean and wasn't linked to any local drug dealers. I know it'll be like looking for a needle in a haystack but I've got to start somewhere."

Smiling, he added, "It might be fun, searching for a murderer in amongst all them Black Jack tables, slot machines and naked chorus girls."

* * * * * *

The rented Ford was parked a half block east of the court house in Hereford and the two men were watching closely as Buster exited the east door and walked across the parking lot to his Blazer.

"We ain't going to learn nothing just sitting and watching that deputy, Tony," Benny said, disgustedly, as Buster opened the door and stepped into the vehicle. "If the boss is so certain that he might find something, why don't we just put a slug into his back and be done with it? I'm getting tired of this crap!"

"You ain't no more tired than I am but you know what the boss said, watch him and if it looks like he's getting too hot, take him out, otherwise just leave him be. No use stirring up a hornet's nest if we don't have to. It don't look like he's found a damned clue yet, and I'm betting that a hick like him ain't going to find anything. We covered ourselves good and they ain't nothing in Texas to tie us to Murphy."

Buster pulled out of the parking lot and headed north out of town, the blue Taurus followed a half mile behind. Eight miles out, the deputy turned off the highway to the east and drove the short distance to the corner of Wes Tinsley's farm, stopped and started walking slowly along the dirt road bordering the playa lake where Spinner's body had been found, keeping his eyes on the ground.

Like looking for a needle in a haystack, he thought as his eyes roamed the roadbed and the bar ditch. *And even if there was some evidence left by the murderers, it probably would be gone by now,* his mind told him.

Reaching the spot where he found the cloth on the barbed wire fence, Buster stopped and gazed across the weed covered lake bottom to the spot where Spinner's body had been found. He watched as the southwest wind pushed and whipped at the dry weeds. His gaze slowly returned to the fence and the weeds close by and watched as they bent towards the northeast, as if pointing in that direction. Dust was whipping across the east-west roadbed and reached the north bar ditch fifty feet east of where Buster was standing. A small, white flicker at the base of a small weed along the edge of the graded roadbed caught his eye. Walking across the road to the spot where he saw the white flash, he reached under the weed and pulled out a half-used book of paper matches. Although faded from the sun, the advertisement on the matches was still legible--*Silver Dollar Casino, Las Vegas, Nevada*.

"He picked up something and is looking at it," Tony said as he adjusted the binoculars trying to focus on what Buster held in his hand. The Taurus was parked nearly a mile west of Buster's location, hidden behind a lone tree at the roads edge, and the two men were looking intently through binoculars, watching his every move.

"Too far to tell what he's looking at but it couldn't be anything too important because I made certain we didn't leave any evidence," Benny replied. "Probably a beer can someone threw out of their automobile."

"Yeah," Tony answered, "nothing to worry about. He ain't

going to find nothing out here, we better get on back to town before he spots us." But there was a note of uneasiness in his voice as he stepped back into the Taurus, closed the door and headed towards town.

Buster smiled to himself as he stuffed the match book into his shirt pocket and walked back towards his Blazer. Las Vegas — now how would a match book from Las Vegas end up not fifty feet from where Spinner's body had been pulled from an automobile and dragged across the lake bed to the spot where Joey and Cody had found it? Maybe Las Vegas had more to offer than gambling casinos and naked chorus girls!

5

On March first, three weeks after the murder of Spinner Murphy, the Southwest Airlines 737--flight 129--set down smoothly on runway 35, at McCarran International Airport in Las Vegas at 2:30 in the afternoon, taxied to the terminal building and began unloading passengers. Deputy Sheriff Buster Thornton was one of the last to leave the plane because he always took a seat in the rear. He really didn't like to fly unless he had his hands on the controls. Somewhere he had read that the rear of the plane was the safest in case of a crash. Kinda like riding a horse, he reasoned. If he got bucked off, he sure didn't want to land in front of the horse and get trampled to death. He'd rather take his chances landing behind the horse and hope the fall didn't kill him.

Thinking on it, he chuckled to himself as he stood and followed the last passenger out of the plane, *what was that old cowboy adage about getting bucked off a horse? It ain't the fall that's going to hurt you, it's that sudden stop when you hit the ground.*

He failed to notice a swarthy looking individual, seated towards the front of the airliner, who was dressed in an expensive business suit, which had an almost imperceptible repair done on the knee of one of the trouser legs, who was watching him with interest as he departed. As Buster passed, the gentleman quietly left his seat and followed him out of the plane.

As he walked down the corridor to the baggage terminal, Buster smiled, as he noticed many of the passengers had already bellied up to the one-armed bandits which were lining the walls of the hallway. They were feeding quarters into the slot machines as if there would never be another chance for them to win their fortune--*or lose it*--as luck would have it. As he passed one secretarial-type, bleached blonde, with a much too short skirt covering her well proportioned body, the slot machine she was feeding began flashing lights and sounding bells, indicating she had hit a jackpot. Quarters began filling the container and spilling onto the floor. The secretary stepped back and began laughing and jumping and clapping her hands as she watched the machine continue pouring out her good fortune onto the carpet.

"A jackpot! A jackpot! I hit a jackpot!" she screamed.

"That's for danged sure," Buster agreed, smiling, as he dropped to his knees and started gathering up quarters to help in her dilemma.

She opened her purse, an enormous thing which could have served her well as an overnight bag, and the two of them proceeded to fill it to overflowing with the fruits of her good fortune.

Still on their knees on the carpet, they each reached for the last quarter. Laughing, Buster relinquished his hold on the two bit piece and opened his palm. "Buster Thornton," he said in an informal introduction.

Reciprocating, still on her knees, she smiled sweetly and took his hand and squeezed, "Jo Willman, Mr. Thornton. And I'm pleased to meet you, I'm sure."

As they scrambled to their feet, Jo lifted the bag with the three hundred dollars in quarters bulging its sides and groaned at the unexpected weight. Buster, smiling, said, "You best let me carry that to the cashier for you and get it changed into something lighter before you come down with a mis-placed vertebra." Looking her up and down, he added, "And a very pretty vertebra if I do say so myself."

Blushing, she nodded her agreement as she handed the bag to him and stepped back to admire this stranger who had come to her rescue. Six foot-two, two hundred pounds, all muscle and a tan that gave evidence of his outdoor lifestyle. His coal-black hair and dark eyes, highlighting his chiseled face and high cheekbones, indicated an Indian heritage somewhere on his family tree. A white Stetson was pushed back on his head and a plain, but expensive, western shirt covered his chest. His well fitting blue jeans were held in place with a wide leather belt, with the name *Buster* en-graved in the back. A beautiful gold belt buckle, with an em-blem of a Cessna spray plane embossed across its center, was latched in the front. Her gaze ended at his feet which were tucked into a pair of the finest ostrich-skin cowboy boots she had ever seen.

Lord have mercy, she thought. *A knight in shining armor!*

With the twelve hundred quarters now converted to fifteen twenty dollar bills, the bag was much lighter. They walked from the cashiers desk to the baggage terminal and retrieved their bags, then stepped out into the eighty degree Nevada weather and headed for the line of taxis waiting for the incoming Southwest Airlines passengers.

"Now that we've been formally introduced, I don't see any reason why we shouldn't share a cab into town," Buster said, smiling.

"My sentiments, exactly," replied Jo, relishing her good fortune at winning the three hundred dollars and at the same time meeting such a handsome, real live cowboy. She wasn't about to let him get away by acting too hard to get.

"Where you bunking?" Buster asked as they climbed into the rear seat of the taxi.

"The Frontier," Jo replied as she tried unsuccessfully to pull the short skirt down below the embarrassing level.

"What a coincidence," Buster responded, "That's my bunkhouse."

Jo laughed as the cab driver, listening to the conversation, accelerated out of the airport entrance and said, "The Frontier it is, folks, and I hope you break the bank while you're in town."

On the ride from the airport to the hotel, Buster learned a lot from his talkative and excited companion. For instance, she had lived all her life in the small farming community of

Nazareth, just thirty miles to the south of Hereford. She had been a guard on the school's Girls State Champion basketball team in 1992. After graduating from high school, she moved to Amarillo where she lived alone and worked as a secretary for one of the oil companies She really intended to enroll in college at West Texas State someday, but was enjoying life too much to make that decision now. Her hair was not bleached at all but was the result of her parents' German heritage. She had been saving her pennies for over a year just to be able to make this one trip to Las Vegas to play the slots and see the sights. She had saved nearly a thousand dollars and, win or lose, she intended to blow it all on this one great weekend. And, although she didn't say it, she was thinking that meeting Buster was definitely a plus in her plans.

Buster was not too candid in his response to her questions about his background. He had come to Las Vegas to try to find some lead to the murder of Spinner Murphy and felt it best that no one would know what those plans were, including this lovely lady. To Jo, he was merely a spray pilot from Hereford, who enjoyed team roping as a hobby and was looking for a good time on a weekend off from work. The gold belt buckle was evidence enough for Jo that he was truly what he said he was. They agreed to have dinner together and hit the slots and blackjack tables later on in the evening.

The belt buckle, confiscated from Spinner's evidence sack in the Sheriff's office, was an afterthought on Buster's part as he prepared for his Vegas trip. It might open some doors that otherwise would remain closed, in his search for Spinner's killer.

Meanwhile Buster had some things to do. He had three hours before dinner with Jo and wasted no time after checking into the Frontier and seeing his bags safely to his room. His first stop was at the bar where he ordered a beer and spent some time visiting with the waitress, a very friendly young lady from Arkansas, who said she was trying to break into show business in one of the many chorus lines in the gambling casinos. The name tag on her skimpy uniform said she was Tanya. So far she hadn't received the big break but was still optimistic, she said. Then, spotting the gold belt buckle, Buster was wearing, she screamed with excitement.

"Hey, I know a pilot from Texas who has a belt buckle just like that one," she shrieked.

"Is his name Spinner Murphy?"

"It *damned* sure is," she answered, unbelieving. "Do you know him?"

"Yeah, I *knew* him," Buster said. "He was my best friend. Me and him had these belt buckles special made, only two like them anywhere in the world."

"What you mean you *knew* him. You talk like he might be dead or something?"

"Yeah, he's dead or something. Someone shot him in the back of the head and killed him a couple of weeks ago," Buster replied, sadly. "Really, that's why I'm here. He was doing some charter work for some folks here in Vegas. He told me before he got killed that they maybe could use another plane and I sure do need to be working mine. Only problem is, he never told me the name of these folks so I don't know where to start looking."

"That's a crying shame," Tanya said, with a trace of sadness in her voice. "I never knew him too well, but he usually came by and had a few drinks while he was waiting on his friends to pick him up. We used to talk some, when business was slow-- good tipper, too."

"Did he ever say anything to you about who he was working for or who his friends were that picked him up?"

Tanya thought awhile before replying, then brightened as if she had remembered something, "No, he never said anything about who he was working for but I know one of the girls, who deals "twenty-one" over at the Stardust, that he was dating. I think she had a pretty good crush on him. He took her out every time he was in town. Her name is Cristy Gale, leastwise that's what she goes by. I think the casino puts those girls up in rooms at the hotel if you'd like to talk to her."

"Thanks a million, Tanya, you've been a great help. I'll look her up," Buster said, as he placed a ten dollar bill in her hand. He smiled and thought to himself, *this luck beats hell out of Jo's jackpot at the airport. Don't know how this tip is going to show up on my expense account, though, guess I can put it down as political and maybe Pete can pay for it out of his reelection campaign funds.*

It was just a short ride to the Stardust and the ten buck cab fare seemed like highway robbery to Deputy Thornton; but he was in a hurry and paid it without complaint. Entering the hotel, he approached the registration desk and asked for Cristy Gale's room number.

"I'm sorry sir," the desk clerk replied, "But we can't give

out that information."

"Well, could you ring her room and ask her to meet me in the lobby? Tell her Mr. Buster Thornton from Texas would like to speak to her, and tell her I'm a friend of Spinner Murphy."

The desk clerk obliged and Cristy promised to meet him in the lobby.

He waited near the elevator hoping that she would recognize him when she stepped out. He wasn't really ready for the shock he received, when one of the loveliest ladies he had ever seen stepped from the elevator and approached him, as if he were a long lost friend. His law enforcement mind began to click off the statistics: *five-ten, 130 pounds, auburn hair, blue eyes, long natural eyelashes, oval face, lips full and blood red, long and slender fingers with nails the color of her lips, and a body that would turn the eyes of the most professional body watcher.*

"Mr. Thornton?" Cristy said as she offered her hand in introduction.

Taking her hand, Buster removed his hat with his left hand and said, "Yes ma'am, Miss Gale, but all my friends call me Buster."

"I knew it was you, Buster, the minute I saw that belt buckle, one just like Spinner wore. And you may call me Cristy," she said with a broad smile.

Buster was already feeling a little ashamed of the lies he was going to tell such a beautiful lady, but to get the information he needed, he knew he was not going to be totally truthful. As they stood admiring each other, Buster asked, "Can I buy you a drink?"

"Certainly," Cristy replied as she turned and started walking slowly towards the lounge, still holding to Buster's hand.

After taking a table in the corner of the lounge, a good distance from the only other two customers, who were sharing an intimate conversation at the opposite end of the room. Buster ordered a beer and Cristy a club soda.

"So you're a friend of Spinner's, I'm so glad you looked me up, I've been wanting to talk to someone who could tell me what happened ever since I heard he had been murdered."

"Yeah," Buster replied, "Me and Spinner go back a long ways. We both been flying planes since we were kids. Even flew crop dusters for the same aerial spray service together before we both put in our own businesses. After that, Spinner would send business that he couldn't handle my way and I'd do the same for him. That's kinda the reason I needed to look you up. Before Spinner was murdered he told me he had been doing some charter work for some folks here in Vegas and that they might could use another plane and pilot. But he never got around to telling me who those folks were and I thought maybe you could help me locate them."

Pausing, Buster noticed a distinct change in Cristy's facial expression when he mentioned the folks that Spinner had been working for--an expression that bordered on fear.

Trying to put her at ease, Buster continued. "I wish I could tell you more about Spinner's death than I can, but there's not much that I know. A couple of kids found him in a dry lake bed with his feet bound and his hands tied behind his back. He had been shot twice in the back of the head and there doesn't seem to be any clues as to who done it or why they did it."

Tears welled up in Cristy's eyes and she put her clenched fist to her mouth in shock as Buster related what he knew. It was awhile before she regained her composure and answered him.

"I'm afraid there's not much I can tell you about the people he was working for. I did meet a couple of guys that seemed to be with him a lot when he was in Vegas. A big guy named Tony--Tony Gallento, I think--and a skinny little punk named Benny something or other. I heard that they both were members of one of the Sicilian families that kinda run the gambling businesses, but I don't know that for a fact. Do you think they might have had something to do with his murder?"

"Anything's possible, I guess, but I just don't know. Anyway, that's a big help, Cristy. Maybe I can locate those guys and they can put me in touch with Spinner's boss. Did Spinner ever say just what sort of charter flying he was doing for these folks?"

"Well, a little," she said as she dabbed at her eyes with a tissue she had retrieved from her purse, then lowered her voice to almost a whisper. "Once he came back from a flight and told me he had taken a bag of one hundred dollar bills, probably over a million dollars, to a firm in Chicago. He seemed to be puzzled why the money was delivered to that particular business but said he thought it was owned by the same people that own one of the big casinos out here. That's about all I know except that he made several flights to Chicago during the last six months and every time he returned he had a roll of cash big enough to stuff an elephant. They must have been paying him well for his service."

"Did he mention the name of the firm where he delivered the money?"

"He may have, Buster, but if he did, I've forgotten who it was."

While they were talking, Buster noticed a tough-looking, but well dressed, man who had come in and was sitting at the bar. The stranger continued to cast furtive glances in their direction, when he thought they were not watching. Definitely of foreign descent, black hair and dark olive complexion; Italian or Middle-East, maybe Lebanese; probably just someone admiring her beauty, he thought. He tried to put it out of his mind; but the thought lingered that he had seen the man somewhere before and just couldn't remember where.

"I've still got some of Spinner's belongings in my room, Buster. I haven't had time to go through them but there's quite a few papers. Flight plans that he recorded and maybe even some papers from the people he was flying for. If you would like to meet me after I get off work at midnight, we could look through them and see if there's anything that would be of help," she offered.

Smiling sweetly, she added, "I'm still a working girl, and haven't time to do it now. I need to be at my Blackjack table in fifteen minutes."

"That would be great," Buster answered, then looking at his watch he said, "I've got to run anyway, Cristy, I have a dinner date with a friend and I completely lost track of time. I'll see you at midnight."

They left the lounge together and he walked her to the elevator where she gave him a piece of paper with her room number and disappeared as the elevator doors closed. As Buster turned to leave, he noticed the same well dressed man from the bar, standing almost hidden behind a huge potted plant in the lobby watching the glassed-in elevator as it ascended. He seemed to take note that it stopped on the tenth floor. Although Buster failed to notice, the faint outline of a professionally sewn patch could be seen on the knee of the man's expensive suit and a slight bulge under his coat indicated a shoulder holster and a gun.

Jo, bubbling with excitement, was waiting for him in the lobby of the Frontier when he returned and he apologized for being late.

"That's O.K., Buster, I won another fifty dollars on the slots while I was waiting. This is great fun!"

They walked out into the warmth of the desert evening just as the sun was setting behind the mountains in the West. However the beautiful sunset was overwhelmed by the gaudy lights and signs of the Las Vegas Strip proclaiming everything from craps to roulette, blackjack, poker, slots and girls, girls, girls! They noticed that the marquees in front of several of the casinos advertised that top entertainers were appearing daily: Wayne Newton, Reba McEntire, Bill Cosby, Debbie Reynolds and even old Blue Eyes himself, Frank Sinatra. Quite a sight for two West Texas country folks!

Since neither of them had ever visited Las Vegas before,

they were at a loss as to where a person was expected to eat. When a cab pulled up they stepped in and asked the driver his opinion of a good restaurant. The cabby recommended Caesar's Palace which he said was supposed to have the best steaks on the Strip as well as being one of the top gambling casinos. Buster allowed as how that would be fine and the cab carried them the short distance, stopping in front of the well known casino. As they searched for the dining room, it was difficult for Buster to keep Jo's mind on food instead of gambling.

"This one, Buster, I've got to put a quarter in this one, I know it's ready to hit!", she said excitedly as she inserted the quarter and pulled the lever on the brightly lit slot machine. However, she was not as lucky as she had been at the airport and the slot guzzled up five dollars worth of quarters before Buster could pull her away and into the dining room.

Although the steak was good, it couldn't compete with those he usually ordered at K-Bobs in Texas. But for a gambling weekend, the atmosphere was great. They could watch the gambling in the huge casino through the glass windows, separating the dining area from the gambling area.

They watched as old and young, male and female, fed nickels, dimes, quarters, and silver dollars into the brightly colored machines. They laughed when an elderly, gray-haired lady squealed with delight when her slot kicked out fifteen or twenty quarters. For the moment, it mattered not that she had fed over twenty coins into the machine before it partially repaid her for her efforts. But that was the thrill of gambling, Buster thought, like Kenny Rogers warned in his ballad, *Never count your money while you're sitting at the table.*

Behind one of the rows of slots Buster saw a familiar face, barely visible but nonetheless watching them as they ate. It was the same guy who had been watching him and Cristy in the Stardust lounge.

"Excuse me a minute, Jo, I'm going to see why that jackass is spying on us," he said as he pushed his chair back and headed for the door.

He pushed his way through the crowds; but when he reached the place in the casino where he had seen the man, he had disappeared. Buster walked down two or three aisles of slots but was unsuccessful in his search and returned to Jo at the table.

"Must have been my imagination," he said; but knew that he had not been imagining things. Someone was tailing them.

Having finished their steaks and an after dinner drink, Buster said, "What say we get busy spending some of those quarters," and guided Jo to the floor of the casino.

"I'm ready and willing," she shouted as she headed for the door. Buster, lagging behind, watched with pleasure as her rear profile, held snugly in a tight-fitting red dress, swung up to the slot machine, as she pushed in a quarter and yanked the handle.

After an hour of pulling handles and feeding quarters into Mr. Ceasar's pocket, Buster suggested they see if they couldn't have better luck at the Blackjack tables in the Stardust. He told Jo about his meeting with Cristy and allowed as how they might do a little playing at her table. Jo agreed. She was ready for a break from the one-armed bandits which had just about taken all of her airport winnings.

They searched the huge gambling hall in the Stardust, looking at nearly every Blackjack table in the place before finally locating Cristy. They sat down at her table and each bought a hundred dollars worth of chips. Cristy smiled and nodded a greeting but said nothing that would indicate she knew Buster. The cards were dealt and as beginner's luck would have it, Jo began winning big. By the time Cristy was rotated to another table, Jo had won nearly a thousand dollars and was bubbling with excitement. Buster had not done badly himself, and his stack had grown by nearly six hundred dollars.

They continued to play with another dealer but were not as successful with him, as they had been with Cristy. Buster decided they had best find other pastimes to enjoy and pulled Jo from her chair and led her to the craps table. While Jo threw the dice, Buster placed the bets. For three more hours they gambled, from craps to roulette and back to the slots. Looking at his watch, Buster determined they just had time to cash in their winnings before meeting Cristy at midnight. The Stardust came up loser by nearly fifteen hundred dollars when they cashed in their chips--a pleasant surprise for the two amateur gamblers.

Taking the glassed-in elevator, they watched the crowds below as it ascended to the tenth floor. They stepped out into the spacious hallway and walked on the lush carpet to room ten-twenty where Cristy answered their knock and they stepped into her small but luxurious apartment.

Buster was surprised at the cool reception they received, aware that Cristy seemed nervous and was anxious to cut their visit short. She walked to her dining table where she picked up a large manila envelope, turned and handed it to him, saying, "I'm sorry that this is all that Spinner left and I doubt that there is anything that will help you; but you are welcome to it."

Looking anxiously at the door and without any explanation, she said, "I think you had better leave now."

Buster realized that she was very frightened about something, so he didn't question her request, but nodded to Jo and they both moved to the open door. He took her hand, looked seriously into her eyes, and said, "I really appreciate this, Cristy, and if there is anything I can do for you--anything--just call me at the Frontier."

Cristy smiled weakly without answering and closed the door. Buster could hear the door being locked and the security chain being fastened as he turned and led Jo down the hallway to the elevator.

"That lady is really scared about something," he told Jo as they descended to the lobby. "I hope it didn't have anything to do with meeting us."

The events of the day had brought them very close together, and after returning to the Frontier, on the elevator ride to her room, Buster pulled Jo into his arms and kissed her warm and willing lips. She pressed her body against his as she responded passionately to his advances. There was no doubt that she wished him to join her as she opened the door to her room, looked up into his dark eyes and smiled mischievously. Without saying a word, Buster stepped in and pulled the door closed behind him. Immediately, she was in his arms again, pulling his head down to her level and locking her lips to his.

Morning found them sharing Jo's bed. Reluctantly, Buster left its folds to begin another day in his investigation of Spinner's murder. He picked up the telephone and called for room service to bring up a pot of coffee and the morning paper. He then stepped into the bathroom for a much needed shower. Jo continued to sleep.

He had showered and dressed when the bellhop knocked and entered with the coffee and paper. Buster thanked and tipped him, then relaxed on the sofa with coffee in one hand and the paper in the other. Unfolding the paper, he gasped and spilled coffee on the carpet as he stared at a picture of Cristy looking back at him from the front page. The caption above her picture stated, "Twenty-One Dealer Leaps to Her Death."

The story related how her nude body was found on the sidewalk below her tenth floor room in an apparent suicide leap. A spokesman, for the Stardust where she worked, stated that she had been despondent recently because she was unable to break into show business. A spokesperson for the Las Vegas police department stated that, even though her door was not locked, they had no reason to believe that any foul play was involved in the death.

Buster was visibly upset at the news, suspecting that Cristy had been murdered because of him, and in such a way that the police would close the books on it as a normal suicide.

Suicide? *How in hell could they think it was suicide! No one would jump from a tenth floor window without a stitch of clothes on their body. The most amateur investigator should recognize that. But then,* he reasoned, the *Las Vegas Chamber of Commerce would rather have a suicide reported than a murder.*

The police were cooperating with the Vegas C of C.

He remained on the sofa, trying to think rationally about the development. First Spinner and now Cristy, someone was definitely trying to cover up something, but what? And he was certain that her murder was the result of her contact with him. Perhaps, to make certain that she did not give him any information that not only would help him discover who murdered Spinner; but why he was murdered. Or maybe she was murdered because they knew she had already given him information and wouldn't disclose what it was she had given. And now his own life was in danger and his contact with Jo could possibly place her in danger.

He walked to the bed and shook Jo awake. She smiled at him through sleep filled eyes and reached to pull him down to her lips.

"No, Jo," he said sharply, "There's no time for that, wake up! There's something I must tell you."

Jo, sensing the urgency in his voice, sat up quickly, pulling the sheet up to cover her nakedness as she asked, "What's wrong, Buster? You look as if you've seen a ghost."

"Worse than that, Jo, Cristy's been murdered!"

"Murdered!" she cried, "I can't believe it!"

"I'm serious, Jo, she was murdered sometime this morning after we left her room. Here, it's splashed all over the front page," he said as he handed her the paper.

"But it says she committed suicide, not murdered," Jo sobbed as she read the story.

"I know that's what it says," Buster answered, "But I know it's not true. Jo, I need to confess something. I haven't been totally honest with you. Please understand, I'm not exactly what you think I am. I'm not a spray pilot, I'm a deputy in the Sheriff's department at Hereford and I've been investigating the murder of Spinner Murphy, who was a crop duster and a friend of Cristy's. Apparently, whoever murdered Spinner was afraid Cristy might have some information which could help me track down his killer. You remember the guy I said was tailing us last night? He apparently followed us to Cristy's room and killed her after we left. Then threw her body out the window to make it look like suicide."

"I apologize for lying to you, but I felt that it was best if no one knew my true identity and the reason for me being in Las Vegas. I hope you can forgive me."

"Of course I forgive you," Jo replied, "I understand, but what do we do now?"

"I suppose the best thing we can do at the moment is to try to convince the police that they are wrong about Cristy's death and enlist their help in finding her killer. I believe that if we can find her killer we will also find out who killed Spinner. Then perhaps we can determine why anyone would want the two of them dead."

"You get dressed and I'll go to my room and shave and

change clothes then we'll go to the police station," he said, as he opened the door and stepped into the hallway.

"Lock the door," he added as an afterthought, "and don't open it to anyone until I return."

His room was on the same floor but several doors down from Jo's. He was surprised when he reached his room and noticed the door was ajar. *I wish I had my gun*, he thought as he slowly pushed the door open and stepped silently into the room.

The room was a shambles, with his clothes scattered all over the floor, drawers pulled open and his traveling bag ripped to shreds. He walked slowly around the room, stopping at the small corner desk. There on the desk was a note, scrawled in an almost childlike cipher. The note read, "You're just a little fish in a big pond, deputy. Get back to Texas before the sharks eat you!"

So they know who I am, he thought to himself, *that means they've been in Hereford and must be the people who killed Spinner*.

Gathering an armful of clothing and toilet items, Buster rushed back to Jo's room, realizing that not only his life but her's, as well, was in danger. Jo was dressed and was just finishing her makeup when he returned.

"Jo," he said, "I'm sorry, but we've got to get out of town." Then he showed her the note.

"These people are playing for keeps and it's apparent that your association with me makes it imperative that you be silenced as well," he said as he started cramming his clothes into her bags. "I'm certain they would have paid us a visit last night after they didn't find the information Cristy gave us, but they didn't know who you were and couldn't locate your room number."

Buster picked up the phone and dialed the hotel lounge and asked to speak to Tanya.

"Tanya," he said, "this is Buster Thornton in room 617. Remember me?"

"Sure, Buster, you're Spinner's friend."

"Tanya, I've got a helluva problem. Could you slip out for a few minutes and meet me in 617. I wouldn't bother you but I don't know who else to turn to."

There was a quiet pause on the other end of the phone before Tanya answered. "Does it have anything to do with some characters I see hanging around in the lobby?"

"It probably does."

"O.K., Buster, I'll tell the bartender that I need to go powder my nose. I'll be up in a minute."

Five minutes later there was a light tap on the door and Buster opened it. Tanya quickly stepped inside the room and Buster introduced her to Jo.

"Tanya, the men you saw in the lobby may have had something to do with Spinner's murder. They're looking for me and Jo. We've got to get out of here in a hurry but we don't need to be carrying any luggage to slow us down. Would you see that it is sent to Texas and tell registration to send our bill to me in Hereford?"

"Sure, Buster, I'll take care of it--but be careful, those are pretty rough looking characters downstairs."

"Thanks, lady, you don't know how much I appreciate it,"

he said as he handed her a twenty dollar bill. "Don't do anything until later on this evening. We should be out of town by then."

Tanya slipped out of the room and returned to the lounge without arousing any suspicion.

"They'll be watching the airport so we'll catch a cab to a car rental agency, lease a car and drive to Phoenix where we'll catch a plane to Amarillo," he said as he opened the door and looked both ways in the hallway. There was no one to be seen.

Jo didn't argue or object, she knew that Buster was right, and followed him out the door.

When she turned towards the elevator, Buster grabbed her arm and said, "No Jo, we'll take the stairs, they are probably watching the elevator. There should be an exit to the outside from the stairs."

When they reached the ground floor, they stepped out into the bright sunlight at the rear of the Flamingo and were confronted by two rough looking men who were stationed by the door. When they reached for guns inside their coats, Buster swung from his belt with his right hand and caught the nearest thug on the chin with his fist, before he could pull the gun from his shoulder holster. With all his power behind the blow, the man went down, out like a light, with blood pouring from his mouth and nose.

Buster turned quickly to take on the other man but was too late. Farm girl Jo, not waiting to be told, swung her purse which was still heavy with quarters from her winnings the night before, and caught the man on the temple. The hood's knees buckled and he went down, stunned from the blow!

Looking to his left, Buster saw two more men who had been watching another exit at the opposite end of the building, running towards them. He grabbed Jo's hand and pulled her to the right, turned the corner and found himself on the sidewalk in front of the Frontier. Seizing Jo by the arm, he rushed out into the middle of the Strip traffic. Brakes screeched, horns honked and drivers cursed; but Buster and Jo threaded their way through the traffic to the other side of the street and into the entrance of the Stardust casino. The two hoods in pursuit were still trying to navigate through the traffic jam where vehicles were wedged bumper to bumper.

Jo stopped long enough to remove her high-heel shoes, then nodded to Buster she was ready. They darted through the gamblers who were waiting their turn at the Blackjack and Craps tables, threaded their way to a side door and once again stepped out into the bright desert sunlight.

Off to the right Buster spotted the huge tent of Circus-Circus and shouted to Jo to follow him. Jo, barefooted, easily kept pace with Buster's long stride. Reaching the entrance to Circus-Circus, they rushed inside where they found the Circus to be in full swing. Trapeze artists were going through their aerial routine, lion tamers were cracking their whips, elephants were lumbering around the middle ring and clowns were just entering from the wings which led to their dressing room. Buster took Jo's hand and dragged her towards the area from whence the clowns had appeared.

Spying a large trailer with a sign above the door which proclaimed "CLOWNS", he opened the door and entered.

The trailer was empty and they quickly rummaged through the clown costumes until they found large, loose fitting slip-ons and pulled them over their clothes. Red, curly wigs were slipped over their hair and paint from the dressing table was applied to their faces. Buster removed his cowboy boots and pulled on a pair of oversized clown shoes, stuffing his boots and Jo's shoes and purse into a canvas satchel. Jo found a pair of bright green tennis shoes and slipped them on her feet. Buster spied a large piece of poster board and with lipstick, painted *JUST MARRIED* on the poster board and tied it to the satchel. Their make-up completed, they stepped out of the trailer and marched boldly into the circus tent, Jo carrying the satchel. The two hoods who had been in hot pursuit were standing in the aisle, blocking their way, looking to the right and left for Buster and Jo, who had mysteriously disappeared. Buster shoved them aside and pulled Jo into the ring with the clowns. Not knowing what to do, they did the most stupid things they could think of, stumbling over the raised rim which made up the ring, bumping into other clowns, falling backwards into the sawdust --all the time hanging onto the satchel. The crowd loved it and screamed their delight at this unrehearsed routine, while the other clowns tried to keep their slapstick comedy from falling apart.

When the two hoods moved on down the aisle, Buster grabbed up an empty wheelbarrow which was used to clean up behind the elephants and horses, picked up Jo and set her in the single-wheeled contraption and pushed her down the aisle in the opposite direction. Jo, carrying out the farce to the end, waved and blew kisses to the crowd, holding up the Just Married sign as they headed for the exit at the rear-end of the tent.

Buster whistled at a passing cab which stopped and they jumped in. The confused driver said, "What the hell you clowns think you're doing?"

"Paying you fifty bucks if you get us to a car-rental agency that's nowhere near the airport or the bus station," Buster replied as he started removing the clown's costume.

"You're talking my language, buddy," the driver said, smiling as he sped away from the huge tent of Circus-Circus.

As the cab weaved in and out of traffic, Buster and Jo completed removal of the clown costumes, wiped most of the grease paint from their faces with the discarded costumes, combed their hair and made themselves as presentable as possible. The driver slid the cab to a halt in front of the downtown office of Budget Car Rental agency. Buster handed him a fifty dollar bill and they ducked into the agency as the cabby drove away.

While the mob's men were stationed at the airport and bus terminal, Buster and Jo slipped out of Vegas in a rented Honda and headed for Phoenix, hoping that they had given them the slip for the moment.

* * * * * *

"What do you mean, you lost them?" the large, white haired man at the enormous desk shouted. "Two yokels from Texas were able to escape from our city with fifteen of my people trying to catch them. That's preposterous!"

He pushed his chair away from the desk, stood and paced about the room, stopping at the huge glass windows and looked out over the skyline of the city--his city. The office was perched atop one of the largest gambling casinos, situated in the middle of the Las Vegas Strip--the same penthouse where Spinner had made his deal to act as pilot and courier for the casino.

"I'm sorry, boss, they just disappeared. They got to be here somewhere. We chased them into the big tent at Circus-Circus and they slipped by us some way. The boys are still searching--don't worry, we'll find 'em."

"You sure as hell better or your ass is mud!" the boss said as he pointed the unlit cigar at the one called Tony. "There's no telling what kind of information that broad passed to them. We should have took her out long before now, we knew she and Murphy had a thing going."

"One thing for sure," Tony replied, shifting nervously in his chair, "If we don't find them they'll head for Texas and we'll get 'em there!"

"No, that cow country is the last place I want you to screw up. We don't need to be messing around there until things calm down after Murphy's murder."

But things were not about to calm down in cow country.

6

"Foot and Mouth Disease, you can't be serious!" the feed-lot owner said, sitting at his desk as he looked at the report the veterinarian had handed him.

"I'm sorry, George, I am serious--Foot and Mouth or Hoof and Mouth as some would call it," Dr. Arnett said, looking as grim as the information warranted. "I made them run the tests on your cattle three times and the same answer came out all three times, Foot and Mouth Disease. Texas Department of Contagious Disease Control will be here within the hour and I suspect they are going to quarantine your entire feedlot. I need to warn you not to ship any more cattle for slaughter until they arrive."

The blood drained from George's face. *Quarantined! My God,* he thought, *I won't be able to sell any more cattle until the quarantine is lifted-- if it stays on too long it'll break me and most of the people who have cattle in my yard! Surely it's not true.*

But it was true, and he knew it, he just didn't want to ad-

mit it. He had suspected for the past three days that something dreadful was wrong when hundreds of the cattle in his
pens were showing the same symptoms--blisters in their
mouths, swollen tongues and feet so sore they could hardly
stand. Loss of appetite had caused extreme loss of weight and
some of the first that showed the symptoms had already died.
Each day hundreds more were coming down with the same
sickness.

"I know it will be no comfort to you, George, but you don't
need to feel alone, you're not the only one in this boat. A half
dozen lots around Hereford are showing the same symptoms
although tests have not been run on their cattle as yet."

"You're right!", George said, disgusted. "It is no comfort.
What can we do with our cattle, after we're quarantined?"

Dr. Arnett shook his head and failed to answer George's
question.

"Dammit, Doc, I want an answer!" George shouted, while
pounding his desk with his fist. "What do we do with our cattle after we're quarantined?"

Choosing his words carefully, the vet answered. "I've
never been in this situation before, George, in fact, this is the
first case of Foot and Mouth that I've ever seen, and I've been
practicing twenty-three years. It's been years since there has
been any report of Foot and Mouth in the United States, actually, not since 1929. Even though it is not a disease which is
transferable to humans, it is one of the most highly contagious
bovine diseases in the world, and may be passed to sheep and
swine as well. Even worse, there is no known cure for the
disease. It is my understanding that a vaccine has been de-

veloped, but is only active for about four months and has no positive effect after the virus has already entered a herd. Because of that, in the past it has been the policy to destroy all herds that have shown any symptoms of the disease in order to keep from spreading the sickness to other herds. Left unchecked, it could totally destroy the cattle, sheep and swine herds throughout the nation. Although the meat is safely edible for human consumption, it cannot be marketed for any use in order to stop the transport of tissues that might affect other herds. This means that the animals will likely be slaughtered and buried or burned. I know that sounds pretty drastic to you, but that's the law as I understand it."

"That's unacceptable, Doc!" George shouted, "Do you realize what you are saying? That could mean slaughtering forty thousand head in my lot alone and another quarter of a million head in the surrounding area. There must be another solution!"

Dr. Arnett paced the floor before responding, then said, "That's not the end of it George. The disease seems to be spreading from west to east which will get all of the feedlots in this part of the county. Just this morning I looked at a couple of sicks north of town and I'll bet my hat they are coming down with the same sickness. If that is true, we may be looking at the disease all the way to the Kansas line!"

George sat down at his desk and buried his face in his hands. "This is crazy," he whispered, hardly audible, "This will devastate the cattle industry in the entire United States. All the way to the Kansas line! If that is true, what is to keep it from spreading on into Kansas, Nebraska, Iowa and who knows where the hell it will stop."

With feed yard cattle being so tightly congested, with as many as a hundred thousand head being fed in pens which occupy less than a square mile, there would be no stopping the disease from spreading without acting quickly and drastically. It was almost impossible for him to fathom the tremendous job it would be to dispose of even a thousand head of these huge thousand pound animals; much less a couple of million head, if what the vet was saying was accurate. And the monetary loss which would be inflicted upon the owners of the animals would be so astronomical that it was totally unbelievable!

George returned to his desk, nervously taking a cigarette from his shirt pocket and placing it in his mouth as his mind tried to comprehend the results of this earth shaking catastrophe. *With that kind of loss of cattle,* he reasoned, *a shortage of beef will develop immediately and the price of beef will probably double or triple in the next few months. It won't do our cattlemen any good because they'll be under quarantine and won't be able to sell a damned head. This was not just a developing crisis, it was a catastrophe!*

The veterinarian looked at George with compassion, realizing what a tremendous burden had been placed on his shoulders. Drained, they both took seats and waited for the arrival of the TDCDC personnel.

George had regained his composure by the time the officials from the TDCDC arrived and agreed to carry them on a tour of his feed yard. As they examined the sick cattle closely, Dr. Mosley, head of the TDCDC shook his head in disbelief when he saw the tremendous number of infected cattle. This being his first visit to the Texas Panhandle, he was amazed that there were so many cattle held in such a confined area.

"It's a wonder that something such as this has not happened long before now, Mr. Autry," he told George. "With so many cattle being crowded into such a small area, I don't see how you have been able to keep other diseases under control."

"We are very particular with our health program, Dr. Mosely," George replied, indicating his anger and irritation. "We add antibiotics to our feed to build up the cattle's immune systems and we vaccinate every animal that comes into the lot for seven different communicable diseases. In addition, we ride every pen, every day, with mounted cowboys looking over each animal closely to see if it might show symptoms of becoming sick. Any livestock showing the least sign of sickness is removed and isolated from the healthy cattle. We are very proud of our health record. Cattle have been fed for market in this way for over thirty years and this is the first major problem that we have ever encountered."

"I understand, Mr. Autry, and I sympathize with you on this problem. However, under the circumstances, I have no option. The law states that I must place this yard under quarantine and forbid you from selling or shipping any cattle from these premises until further notice. In accordance with the law, I am ordering you to destroy those cattle which are now visibly infected with the disease. And, because the virus is present in the fluid of the blisters, in the blood, meat,

milk, saliva, urine and other secretions of the infected animal, the cattle must be burned or buried immediately and no
part of their carcasses may be sold, transported or utilized in
any way. I understand that there is a local business that uses
livestock which have died in the feed yards from normal
causes, processing the meat into dog and cat food and the
hides into leather. This will no longer be allowed until the
quarantine is lifted."

"Do you realize what you are ordering me to do, Dr. Mosely?" George asked incredulously. "When you say that none
of these cattle may be sold you have already signed my bankruptcy papers. Then asking me to destroy and bury the remains is asking the impossible. Burning the carcasses is out
of the question, the damned EPA won't even allow us to burn
our trash. Do you realize the expense involved in excavating a
pit large enough and deep enough to bury forty thousand head
of cattle? There is no way I can afford to do what you have
asked!"

"I understand that the law has provisions for financial
help in that respect, Mr. Autry, but I do not have the authority
to provide that help. You will have to take that problem to the
United States Department of Agriculture. In the past, the federal government has paid indemnities based on the appraised
value of the animals destroyed and has assisted in the destruction and burying of the carcasses. However, there has never
been a problem of this magnitude and I have no idea what the
federal government will or will not do. I wish that it could
be different but I have no alternative, I am ordering you to begin destroying those cattle which show visible signs of the

sickness immediately. In the meantime, I suggest you contact the Texas Commissioner of Agriculture and seek what state aid he can provide."

As he and the other officials turned to leave, he made a final statement. "I am leaving one of our men, Dr. Turner, to observe your progress in carrying out these orders. He will remain in close contact with me at all times. You should understand, Mr. Autry, that failure to carry out the terms of this quarantine or to break it in any way is punishable by up to fifteen years in a federal penal institution. I trust that you will allow him full access to your facilities as an observer in this very difficult project."

George, showing signs of defeat, stepped in front of Dr. Mosely as he reached for the door. "One thing, Dr. Mosely, do you have any idea how this disease could have spread so rapidly in my pens? It is my understanding that ordinarily, the disease is slow to move through a cattle herd, yet within no more than a week it has spread throughout my yard."

"In the past," Dr. Mosely replied, "The hot-bed for the disease on the North American continent has been Mexico. France has had several outbreaks in recent years but has been able to control them with a minimum of loss. It is possible, I suppose, that cattle coming from Mexico could have been infected, but not probable. There were reports of an outbreak in Mexico as late as 1953, but this was promptly controlled. I understand that over a million head of Mexican calves were imported into the United States last year and most of them ended up in feed yards here in West Texas. However, we have very strict regulations and policies on imported cattle and each herd is supposed to be tested for Foot and Mouth, as well as anthrax and other communicable diseases, before they are allowed to cross the border."

Shaking his head, he added, "But if you've ever been to the Mexican border, you know that there are not nearly enough inspectors to adequately inspect and test all of the cattle crossing into the United States."

Pausing, as if in deep thought, Dr. Mosely continued. "Then, of course, the disease could have been spread intentionally, considering the ease of access to your facilities. I would think that because of the speed in which the infection has moved through your herd, such a scenario is a distinct possibility. Apparently, the virus is readily available in several of the Mid-Eastern countries which have been experimenting in biological warfare. Someone could have obtained the virus and added it to the cattle's drinking water. I am sure you'll agree that security in your pens, as well as that in other yards, is very lax--visitors seem to come and go at will. But I am certain that if this contamination proves to cover as large an area as I suspect, there will be some federal investigators, much more capable than I, who will be assigned to the case to determine what actually caused the problem."

"What do you mean, someone much more capable than you?" George asked as he held the door and refused to allow the group to leave.

"I hate to even breathe the thought," Dr. Mosely replied, "But we all know that Saddam Hussein has been experimenting in biological warfare in Iraq for many years. And since his embarrassment in Desert Storm, he could be seeking revenge. He, or any of the international terrorist organizations, could be responsible for just such an experiment as this, if in fact it is determined that this is an intentional contamination. I am certain that the FBI, the FDA, the CIA or USDA will be called in to conduct a thorough evaluation and investigation. That, however, is not a part of my jurisdiction. My job is to see that this contamination is confined to as small an area as possible and to see that it is cleaned up and eradicated in a most timely manner. That, I intend to do!"

With that statement, he forced the door open and left the office. The white van carrying the TDCDC personnel stopped at the gate, as it was leaving the feed yard and one of the men stepped out and nailed a huge orange sign to the gate.

"QUARANTINED — FOOT AND MOUTH DISEASE — NO LIVESTOCK MAY ENTER OR LEAVE THESE PREMISES UNTIL FURTHER NOTICE —TEXAS DEPARTMENT OF CONTAGIOUS DISEASE CONTROL. "

That afternoon, with Dr. Mosely's official announcement that the Autry feedlot had been quarantined for Foot and Mouth Disease and other quarantines were imminent, the proverbial shit hit the fan. National TV anchormen arrived on the scene and all had five minute segments on their national evening news. News media personnel from Amarillo and Lubbock invaded the Autry feedlot. AP, UP, and CNN sent crews from Dallas to cover the story. The small airport at Hereford became congested with Lear jets carrying camera crews and equipment. Television screens across the nation had live action shots of sick and dying cattle and dead cattle being dragged to huge pits and covered with dirt by bulldozers.

And of course, the favorite conjecture by the news media on the cause of the outbreak of Foot and Mouth was international terrorists, in general, and Saddam Hussein in particular. That was newsworthy, a simple speculation that infected cattle had been imported was hardly mentioned.

Meanwhile, Buster and Jo were able to slip away from Las Vegas unobserved and arrived in Amarillo as the Foot and Mouth story broke the news. Buster had called ahead and a sheriff's car was waiting to pick them up at the airport. He drove Jo to her apartment, content that the Las Vegas hoods would be unable to find her since they did not know her name. He did, however, give her his mobile phone number as well as that of the sheriff's office, and instructed her to call immediately if she suspected that anyone was acting suspiciously around her apartment or office. He cautioned her to tell no one about their experiences in Las Vegas and especially their contact with Cristy.

"I'll be back to see you tomorrow," he said as he kissed her goodbye.

Buster read the story of the quarantine in the Amarillo News as his friend and fellow deputy, Mike Gonzalez, raced the white sheriff's car, siren blasting and lights flashing, the forty- five miles from Amarillo to Hereford.

Damn! he told himself as he read, *George must be out of his mind — forced to kill every head in his feed-lot and bury them — and that includes my four hundred head! I can't believe it!*

The situation at the Deaf Smith County Courthouse was pandemonium. Crowds had gathered on the steps of the courthouse and had overflowed onto the well kept lawn and the surrounding streets. Small groups of television crews were scattered throughout the crowds, interviewing local citizens and county officials. Deputy Gonzalez braked to a stop in front of the courthouse and Buster quickly climbed the stairs, where TV crews had set up cameras and were preparing to interview Sheriff Pete Blackwell. He pushed his way through the throngs and was surprised to see Pete, face to face with CBS anchorman Don Prather as the cameras rolled and Don asked his first question.

"Sheriff Blackwell, do you have any idea who or what is behind this epidemic of Foot and Mouth Disease? Do you believe, as most everyone is inclined to believe, that this is a plot by international terrorists to destroy the cattle industry in the United States?"

Buster could see that Pete, who had never been interviewed before a live television camera, was very nervous. So nervous, in fact, that the sheriff of Deaf Smith County was sweating profusely. He could stand toe to toe with politicians, such as the Governor, without blinking an eye but a television camera was something else. Pushing his Stetson to the back of his head, he wiped the sweat from his brow with his hand and answered, his voice breaking as the sound man stuck a microphone in his face. "No, Don, we--uh--don't have any clues as to how the virus was first introduced into the area." He shifted his weight and turned slightly, trying to get the microphone out of his face, then added, "We--uh--have no reason to--uh--believe that it is anything other than an infected herd being imported from some place, maybe Mexico, which spread the disease to many of the cattle in area feed yards."

"Well, sheriff, we have been informed by other reliable sources that there is no way that the virus could have spread so rapidly just by being passed from one animal to another, *they* say it had to be spread by other means. Do you agree with that viewpoint?"

Showing his irritation at the newsman's apparent brusqueness with his questioning, and with the sound man's microphone too close to his face, Pete regained his normal composure and replied, "Well, Don, I suppose you should be interviewing your other sources instead of me, since it's apparent they have more information than what I have," and turned to walk away.

Prather, seeing that he had upset the sheriff and lost control of the interview, followed Pete to the door and apologized. "Sheriff, I didn't mean to imply that you didn't know what is going on, I just wanted to know *if* you thought it *possible* that international terrorists were behind this outbreak of Foot and Mouth Disease?"

"Well, I suppose anything is possible, Don, but I believe that any conjecture on my part should be based on evidence. I see no evidence at this point which indicates that terrorists are behind this terrible tragedy," Pete answered, as he entered the courthouse and left national TV anchorman Don Prather standing on the steps with an empty microphone.

However, the five minute segment of CBS news later on in the evening, would find Don Prather saying that "Deaf Smith County Sheriff Pete Blackwell says that *it is possible* that international terrorists are behind this terrible tragedy.

If that is true, then Iraq, either directly or indirectly, must be responsible for this act, since they have been manufacturing these viruses for several years. And we know that Saddam Hussein has threatened the U.S. because of the oil embargo. If, in fact, it is proven beyond a shadow of doubt, what then should be the reaction of the United States government? In the final analysis, food is more important to our national economy than oil. Are we looking at another Desert Storm?"

Buster followed Pete into the sheriff's office and smiled as he said, "That Prather feller certainly got your dander up, didn't he, Pete?"

"I probably flew off the handle prematurely," the sheriff said, "But it always did rile me when someone inferred that I didn't know what I was talking about. Especially these news media people, they're always trying to make themselves look smarter than anyone else and damned if I don't believe they all could use a little more horse sense and a lot less gall!"

Changing the subject, he continued. "Well, did you find out anything in Las Vegas or did you just go out there and blow the county's money on slot machines and wild women?"

"That remains to be seen," Buster responded, smiling. "If the information in this envelope is what I think it is, we spent the county's money very wisely. On the other hand, if it's not, I probably didn't accomplish a thing except get a beautiful lady murdered just because she was trying to help me find the people who killed Spinner. One thing for certain, whoever murdered Spinner knew I was there and they did everything in their power to keep me from learning anything."

"What you mean, get a lady murdered?" This was the first that Pete had heard of the *suicide* of Cristy Gale.

Buster then related the events that had taken place from the time he stepped off the plane at Las Vegas until he returned to Amarillo, as Sheriff Blackwell lit a cigarette and listened carefully.

"A million bucks in hundred dollar bills! Do you think Spinner actually did that or was he just trying to impress his girlfriend?" Pete asked when Buster had finished.

"I don't doubt it, Pete," Buster replied. "Cristy certainly didn't doubt it and she thought he had probably made several of those deliveries. But why the hell would he be delivering that kind of money to Chicago?"

"Well, let's see what's in that envelope she gave you, maybe we'll find an answer there."

Buster dumped the material out on Pete's desk and began going through it. It didn't look like much, just a stack of material that any pilot might hang onto; flight plans which he had filed with the FAA during the past six months; some hotel receipts where he had checked out and paid with cash; receipts from several airports where he had serviced his two-ten and paid for fuel with cash; and a key to a locker in Chicago's O'Hare International Airport.

"One thing for certain, Spinner wasn't lying to Cristy about his trips to Chicago, here's five different receipts with different dates where he fueled up at O'Hare," Buster said, as he looked through the material.

"Wonder what he was doing with this key," the sheriff asked as he looked at the number and the name. "Suppose he may have been dealing from the bottom of the deck and skimmed a few of those hundred dollar bills off before making his delivery and stashed them in this locker? That could certainly earn him a couple of bullet holes in the back of the head if his employer were involved in organized crime. You'd think old Spinner would have more sense than that."

Thumbing through Spinner's material on Pete's desk, Buster picked up four or five gasoline credit card receipts and looked at them with a puzzled expression on his face. "There haven't been any crops sprayed around here since last summer but these all show that Spinner's crop duster was fueled up a couple of times in Hereford, once in Dalhart and once in Amarillo in the last six weeks. Wonder what he could have been using that spray plane for?"

Before Sheriff Blackwell could answer, the door swung open and two well dressed, business-like men entered without knocking.

"Sheriff Blackwell?" the older of the two asked.

"I'm Blackwell," Pete answered, irritably. Thinking they were some of the group of news media personnel, he added, "Don't you guys know how to knock before entering someone's office.?"

"Ace Belton, with the FBI," the man said as he flashed his badge without apologizing. "This is my assistant, Bill Williams, and we have been sent from Washington to take over the investigation of this outbreak of Foot and Mouth Disease in your county. We'll be needing an office, computer, telephones and all information you have put together to this point. We'll expect full cooperation on the part of all law enforcement officers under your jurisdiction."

"Just a damned minute," Pete said as he pounded his desk top with his fist to emphasize his anger! He hadn't fully re-covered his temper from the TV interview, and flew into the two FBI agents with vengeance! Ordinarily, Pete refrained from using too much profanity. He was well acquainted with all the *words* from his association with the criminal element in the county and a few that he had learned as a top sergeant in the Marines. He spouted most of these expletives as he read the riot act to the two FBI agents.

"This is my county, I'm the duly elected sheriff of this county. And unless the constitution has been revoked without my knowledge, it clearly makes me the highest law enforce-ment officer in the county, including you two sunzabitches from Washington, D.C. And unless my memory has failed me, I don't remember requesting any help from the FBI, the CIA or any other federal agency," Pete shouted as he walked to the door and opened it.

"Now, why don't you two impolite sunzabitches just step back into the hall, knock, come in politely and show a little more respect for the *High Sheriff* of Deaf Smith County. Then maybe we can discuss why for you're cluttering up my office," he said, as he casually placed his hand on the butt of the Colt revolver strapped to his belt.

Buster made a threatening move towards the two and Wil-liams stepped quickly into the hall, followed reluctantly by Chief FBI Agent Ace Belton.

Pete closed the door behind them and waited with his hand on the door knob. Buster noticed that the anger had turned Pete's face a deep shade of red and his breathing was faster than normal. Buster had never before seen him so angry.

After a short wait, there was a feeble knock, and Pete opened the door and said curtly, "Come in, gentlemen."

Directing them to be seated he continued, "Now that we've determined who's in charge of law enforcement in Deaf Smith County, why don't you gentlemen tell me how you think *you can help me* enforce that law."

"Dammit, sheriff," Ace said, trying desperately to control his temper, "I told you why we are here and what we need."

"Oh yes," Pete responded, "you're the two gentlemen who were here awhile ago requesting my help in a very demanding manner. I'm certain that we will be able to oblige, however, I feel we need to come to some understanding. My department will assist you in every way possible; but I will expect your group to reciprocate completely. You see, the voters of this county have *elected* me to protect them in all matters of crime. If this is, in fact a crime, then you need to understand that it is my business and my jurisdiction to look after their interests."

Relaxing, Ace smiled at Pete, and said, "Mr. *High Sheriff,* I apologize. I wasn't using very good etiquette and damned poor judgement. I agree, you're the law in this county and we are here to assist you, not to by-pass you. We *will* cooperate, completely."

Smiling, Pete walked to where Belton was sitting, stuck out his hand and said, "In that case, I'm glad to meet you Ace." Then turning to Williams, he shook his hand and said, "Glad to meet you Bill, this is my chief deputy, Buster Thornton. Most of my friends call me Pete."

"Well, Pete, I'll start over," FBI agent Belton said, "We have been instructed to look into the possibility that this epidemic of Foot and Mouth Disease was instigated by international terrorists--in fact, we believe that to be the case. We have known for years that some nations, who are not too friendly with us, have been experimenting with different kinds of biological warfare. We have been concerned that they might pull something similar to the poison gas attack on people in the subways of Japan, but never really suspected that they might strike in the heartland against our food production industry. After the Gulf War, the Agency put together a biological investigation team which I head. This is actually our first case and I must confess, we really don't have much more knowledge about how to proceed than you do."

"If you have any information at all, it is more than we have," Pete said. "Actually, we haven't listed it as a crime but merely as an unfortunate epidemic as a result of infected cattle being imported into some of our yards. I must admit, it seems impossible that so many feed yards could be infected in such a short period of time, but we have no evidence that would indicate otherwise. However, it is important to note that we have had no reports of a Foot and Mouth outbreak in any of the areas where feeder cattle originate, so at this point, we must accept the fact that anything is possible."

"I'll be bringing in two more members of my investigative team," Ace replied, "And we'll approach it as if it is an intentional contamination, caused by methods and persons un-

known. We will try to determine through airline records,
car rental agencies and motel registration records, if there
have been any foreign agents or known terrorists passing
through or staying in the Amarillo area, during the last three
weeks. In the meantime, your personnel should continue to
work with the health officials to try to determine if, in fact, it
is merely an accidental spread of the disease. Hell, we may
both be wrong, and find that some disgruntled cowboy who
was fired from his job may have gotten his hands on some
virus and spread it around because he was sore at his boss.
Who knows? At any rate, we need to coordinate our efforts
and keep each other fully informed so that we're not all barking up the wrong tree."

"Fine," Pete replied. "We've pretty well got our hands
full, anyway, what with the influx of all these nosy news media people and a full-fledged murder investigation underway.
We've got an empty office here in the courthouse next to
mine and the Texas Department of Public Safety is just down
the hall. If you would like, I'll have one of my deputies take
you around to some of the feed yards so you can kinda see
what we're up against."

"That's great, sheriff," Ace said, rising to leave. "Why
don't you have him pick us up at the motel in about an hour."
Stepping to Pete's desk and holding out his hand, he added,
"I'd like to apologize one more time for my bad manners. I
know we will be able to work together to the benefit of both
of our departments."

After they had left the room, Buster laughed and said,
"Pete, danged if I don't believe you've got more grit than John

Wayne, putting two FBI agents down like that and turning your back on a national television anchorman all in one day. You really know how to win friends and influence people."

Pete smiled and answered, "Well, neither one of those bastards can vote me in or out. And maybe they understand, now, that folks out here in West Texas don't cotton to being pushed around by the federal government or nosy news people with microphones in their hands."

Buster walked to the sheriff's desk, picked up the locker key and the five local gasoline credit card receipts and said, "I think I had better see what Spinner left in the airport in Chicago and why he's been flying that crop duster of his a-round when they ain't nothing to dust. There's something about this whole thing that just don't add up. Reminds me of that book I read about Watergate, *All the President's Men* or something like that. There was a guy called 'Deep Throat' that kept feeding those two reporters information and kept telling them to *follow the money*. Well, looks to me like we need to do the same thing and the money trail seems to lead to Chicago."

"You just watch your back, boy," Pete replied. "Someone don't want you finding out too much about Spinner's business and I haven't the time to be going to any deputy's funeral. When you go to Chicago, why don't you take them boots and Stetson off and leave them at home. See if the undercover drug boys have got any false mustaches and colored glasses to camouflage your danged good looks. It might save you and me a lot of trouble."

Buster smiled as he opened the door. "I'll do that, boss, I

ain't hankering to mess up your schedule by getting myself killed. See you in a few days."

* * * * * *

Before morning, the TDCDC had quarantined every feed yard in Deaf Smith County and were looking at cattle in surrounding counties.

News of the quarantine caused cattle futures' prices to lock in, limit up!

7

Before leaving Hereford for the airport in Amarillo, Buster did as sheriff Blackwell had suggested: shed his western clothes and donned a sport shirt and slacks, black loafer shoes and pasted on a large, bushy mustache, which he borrowed from one of the undercover drug enforcement boys. A pair of dark sunglasses put him in the same category as many of the news people who had invaded Hereford. Unobserved, he slipped out of town and traveled the forty-five miles to Amarillo in an unmarked police sedan which he borrowed from the sheriff's motor pool.

Thoughts of Jo had been much on his mind since returning from Las Vegas. Worried that he would not be around to protect her, should she run into trouble with the Las Vegas hoods, he called and asked her to take a couple days off work and accompany him to Chicago. "We shouldn't be gone long, I just need to pick up something at the airport. We should have plenty of free time to take in the sights before we return. Just in case we run into some of those goons from Las Vegas, why don't you see if you can find a wig and cover up that lovely blonde hair," he instructed after she had excitedly agreed to his offer. "No need for us to take chances on being recognized."

Buster was pleasantly surprised when he was greeted enthusiastically by a beautiful redhead, when he pulled up in front of Jo's apartment. The redhead kissed him lightly as he took her bag and threw it into the rear seat.

"What do you think," she asked teasingly, as she placed her hand on the red curls and twirled for Buster's approval?

"Just what the doctor ordered," Buster answered. "Even your ma wouldn't be able to recognize you, and danged if I don't believe you're just as pretty as a redhead as you were a blonde."

"You look pretty good, yourself, cowboy," she said as she laughed and plucked at the bushy mustache. "With that camouflage someone is liable to mistake you for a Hollywood movie star."

Four hours later they were retrieving their bags at the baggage terminal in Chicago's O'Hare International Airport. As they visited and waited with the crowds around the carousel for their bags to appear, Buster froze! There across the carousel, waiting for his bags at the adjoining carousel, was the familiar face of the man who had tailed them in Las Vegas. And although their eyes met, the man registered no recognition of Jo and Buster. *Wonder what the hell he's doing here in Chicago?* Buster asked himself, *it's apparent he's not following us.*

Buster's plans were to recover their luggage then search for the locker which matched Spinner's key. However, spotting the Las Vegas killer altered his plans.

The Vegas hood was still waiting for his luggage when their two bags appeared on the carousel. Buster guided Jo out the door to the waiting line of taxis, and they quickly loaded their bags and entered the privacy within one of the cabs. The driver flipped the flag on the meter and said, "Where to folks?"

"We don't know," Buster answered, "But there's an extra twenty for you if you will follow that guy with the gray suit who is just coming out of the terminal and take us wherever he is going."

"No problem, mister, following is my second nature," the cab driver responded as he pulled in behind the cab carrying the guy from Las Vegas.

The two cabs dodged in and out of traffic and sped towards downtown Chicago and finally braked to a stop in front of a tall office building located across the street from the Chicago Board of Trade.

Buster instructed Jo to wait in the cab as he followed the gray suit into the building and then into the elevator. Joining six more well dressed business men and three ladies in the elevator, Buster stood quietly in the corner and listened as the men talked excitedly about the price of cattle going up the limit on the futures' market. He heard one of them say it was because of the disease that was killing all the cattle in West Texas. Buster thought it strange to hear these men talking about the commodity markets, because he could see a familiar bulge underneath their coats indicating they were all carrying concealed weapons. Waiting until the Vegas hood and three of the other men had stepped out of the elevator on the fifteenth floor, Buster followed them into the hallway. When they turned right, he turned left so as not to be too conspicuous. He walked slowly down the hall as if searching for a specific office, while casting quick glances to the rear to see which office the four men entered. He turned, walked back to the office and noted that the gold embossed sign on the door read, *Corizentian Commodity, Inc. — Member Chicago Board of Trade.*

Buster returned to the elevator and rejoined Jo in the cab. "The guy went into a Corizentian Commodity office on the fifteenth floor," he told her as he slammed the door. Then turning to the cab driver, he asked, "Is there a good hotel near here?"

"Downtown Hilton is just a few blocks away," the driver responded.

"That'll do," Buster said and the driver turned left at the corner and drove a short distance before stopping in front of the Hilton.

After checking in as Mr. and Mrs. Thomas Allen, Buster and Jo followed the bellhop, a tall, muscular black man, about the same size as Buster, to the elevator and to their room on the fifth floor. Buster noticed the name tag on the bellboy's coat was Andrew.

"Thank you Andy," he said as he placed a five dollar tip in the bellboy's hand.

"Thank you, sir," a smiling Andrew replied as he pocketed the tip. "If you need anything else, just ask for me!"

Closing the door, Buster turned to Jo and said,"This is a stroke of luck, Babe, spotting that Vegas mobster at the airport. But what do you suppose he is doing going into an office that's a member of the Chicago Board of Trade? Do you suppose this has anything to do with those deliveries that Spinner was making?"

Jo shook her head and smiled, "You're the detective, you tell me. Remember, I just came along for the ride."

"Beat's me, but maybe Spinner's locker will turn up some reasons as to what those Las Vegas casinos and this Chicago commodity firm have in common."

Reaching into his pocket, he pulled out the key, looked at it thoughtfully and said, "Well, we're never going to know what that locker holds until we take a look. Let's take a cab back to the airport and see what we can find."

Jo, smiling seductively, replied, "Why don't you do that and let me freshen up a little. I've got a feeling that this is going to be a real big night for us, what with all this luck you've been having."

She pulled his head down to her five-foot seven height and kissed him softly on the lips, then pushed him towards the door, saying, "Don't be too long, Cowboy, you never can tell how much more luck will be waiting for you when you return."

Buster smiled.

The Windy City, Buster reflected as the weather had turned blustery and light rain had begun to fall. He hailed a cab and headed for the airport, not realizing that their first cab driver, sensing that there was more to be made than a twenty dollar tip, had returned to the office building housing the Corizentian Commodity firm. He then had taken the elevator to the fifteenth floor and entered the commodity office.

"There's a guy in a gray suit who came in here about thirty minutes ago who would be interested in some information I have," he told the receptionist.

"What kind of information?" the receptionist asked, looking at the cabby inquisitively as she chewed her gum and filed her nails?

"Important information," he answered. "Just give him the message."

Her crossed legs had pulled her skirt well above her knees and the cabby's eyes were locked on that space as she punched a button and spoke into the intercom, "Mr. Seigle, there's a cab driver here who says he has some important information for Mr. Gallento."

There was a pause before a brusque voice, reminiscent of Marlon Brando in the *Godfather*, replied, "Send him in."

The receptionist smiled at the cabby's apparent interest in her legs, casually uncrossed them without bothering to pull down the skirt. She then motioned towards a huge mahogany door and said, "Mr. Seigle will see you."

The cabby opened the door and was surprised to see several men sitting around the large office, on elegant leather upholstered chairs, apparently discussing business. Their coats were open and the butts of holstered revolvers could be seen protruding next to their armpits. One of the men, completing a sentence was heard to say, "And we've bought the next three months to the maximum in both cattle and hogs, just like you told us to do, boss."

The gray-haired man at the desk, ignoring the comment, turned to the cabby and in a distinct Middle Eastern brogue, said, "This better be important, or your ass is mud, we've got an important conference going on. What kind of information do you have?"

The cabby, realizing that these men were no ordinary businessmen, but members of one of Chicago's well known crime syndicates, became quite nervous as he looked around the room. He recognized many of them, from pictures he had seen in the *Tribune*--men who had been involved in numbers, prostitution, gambling and murder. When he spotted the man with the gray suit, he pointed to him and said, "I picked up a fare at the airport, a man and woman, who seemed to be very interested in where you were going. They had me follow your cab and then tailed you into the building to find out which office you entered."

Tony Gallento, masking his surprise, said, "And where the hell are these people now?"

"That information ought to be worth something, mister. I've missed three or four fares just to let you in on what I know," the cab driver replied, as he backed slowly towards the door.

Tony pushed his chair back, stepped forward and grabbed the cab driver by the collar and squeezed, saying, "Listen, punk! It may be worth a few pints of your blood if you don't tell me where they are."

Seigle spoke sharply to Gallento, "Calm down, Tony, this gentleman was very cooperative to let us know that you were followed." Reaching into a desk drawer, he withdrew several bills and said, "Here, this five hundred dollars should loosen his tongue some. And if his information proves to be worth nothing, you can get your blood later."

The cabby, realizing that he was in trouble, straightened his collar and, pocketing the five hundred, answered, "I carried them to the Downtown Hilton where they checked in but I don't know their room number."

"There's another bonus for you if you take Tony to the Hilton and wait around with him until you can identify them," Seigle said, then added, "Wait in the lobby, Tony will be with you in a minute."

After the cabby had closed the door behind him, Seigle turned to Gallento and asked angrily, "Who could be tailing you all the way from Vegas?"

"Honest-to-pete, Boss, I watched real close and no one got on that plane who was interested in me. I was the last one on the plane and the others were just a bunch of tourists that had lost their asses in the casinos."

"Well, apparently someone is interested in where you came from or where you were going; so you best get over to the Hilton and stick around until you find out who. I sure as hell don't want any slip-ups now," Seigle said as he indicated the door with his thumb, then added, "Maybe you didn't cover your trail nearly as well as you thought when you threw Murphy's girl friend out the window."

Gallento frowned and left quickly without protest.

* * * * * *

After searching for more than an hour, Buster was unable to find the locker at the airport. Finally, he stopped at an information desk and asked for help, explaining that he had been a little inebriated when he placed a bag in the locker and now couldn't remember where it was located. The girl at the information desk looked at the numbers on the key, punched in the numbers into her computer, smiled and said, "Here it is," she said, "It's located in the pilots' lounge where the private aircraft check in. That would be downstairs and at the end of the hallway on the right."

Buster thanked her and walked the short distance to the lounge, found the locker, opened it and retrieved a small valise with Spinner's initials on the leather zipper flap. Without opening it, he returned to the hotel and punched the elevator button. Contemplating what could be in the bag, he failed to notice the two men standing in the shadows across the lobby of the hotel. The cabby looked at Tony and nodded towards the elevator.

"That's the gent, the one with the black mustache," he said, adding, "He had a good-looking redhead with him."

Tony pulled the five one hundred dollar bills out of his pocket, handed them to the cabby and said," O.K., get lost and forget you saw anything."

The cabby took the money and laughed silently to himself at his good fortune. *A thousand bucks for just a couple hours' work! This guy must really be important for them to pay that much just for a little information.*

Buster looked down out of the glass-enclosed elevator to the atrium floor of the lobby just as Tony handed the money to the cabby. Seeing the two, his heart raced as he realized that it was the same cabby that had brought them from the airport and the Las Vegas hood whom they had followed. It was apparent that the cabby had sold them out. He rushed from the elevator when it stopped on his floor and slipped into his room unobserved.

Buster set the valise on the bed and opened it as Jo looked on. Their eyes flashed and their mouths fell open as the contents spilled out on the bed--several tightly wrapped packages of one hundred dollar bills.

"My Gosh, Buster," Jo said, taking a deep breath, "there must be a hundred thousand dollars or more!"

"At least," Buster responded as he spread the packages out and began counting the bills in one of the packages! Then he noticed a small pocket notebook laying in the bottom of the bag. He picked it up and thumbed through its pages which were filled with entries of money transactions with the notation, *Corizentian Commodity, Inc.*"

Looking no further, Buster returned the money and notebook to the bag, turned to Jo and said, "We've gotta get out of here, Jo. I saw our cabby talking to that Las Vegas hood in the lobby. I don't know what they're up to but I'll bet my hat they wouldn't stop at murder to get this valise. It'll not take them long to locate our room and then no telling what they might do!"

But how could they get out without being noticed? Even

now, they might be watching all exits. Looking at Jo who had put on a very sexy, snug fitting, black dress in anticipation of his return, Buster had a brainstorm. It was a gamble but worth a try.

"Pull that red wig off and brush out your beautiful blonde curls," he instructed Jo, smiling as he stepped to the phone. "They saw me come up with a redhead and won't be expecting me to leave with a blonde."

Speaking into the phone he said, "Room Service, would you please send up Andrew to room 512 to help with some luggage? -- and make it snappy, we're late for a flight."

Rushing into the bathroom, he removed the fake mustache, slicked down his hair then stood by the door with his revolver in his hand. He opened it to the bellboy's knock and then closed it quickly as the young man entered.

Andrew looked at the muzzle of the gun with open mouth, then looking up into Buster's eyes, said nervously, "Look, mister, I ain't got any money, what you pointing that gun at me for?"

Buster, smiling, replied softly, "Don't get excited, Andy. I'm not going to hurt you as long as you do what I ask. Keep your mouth shut and get that uniform off, we're going to make a trade."

Turning to Jo, he handed her the gun and winked, "If he doesn't do as I said, shoot him," then started removing his tie, shirt and trousers.

He quickly donned the bellhop's uniform and watched as the young man dressed in his slacks and sport shirt, then using his discarded belt, secured the man's hands behind his back. Tearing a strip from one of the bath towels, he placed it in Andrew's mouth and tied it behind his head.

Pushing the frightened bellhop into the bathroom, he instructed him to lie in the tub, and then tied his feet together and bound them to the faucet. "I'm sorry, fella, that we have to treat you this way, but we're in a helluva predicament and can't take a chance that you'd mess up our plans. You just lie quiet and I'll call the desk and tell them where you are just as soon as we get safely out of the hotel."

Removing a hundred dollar bill from his billfold, he kneeled down and placed it in the bellhop's shirt pocket and said, "This should cover your inconvenience."

Andrew grunted his approval.

"Jo," Buster said as he secured the valise under his arm and picked up their two bags, "Just smile and act natural, we're going to show these Chicago mobsters what a diversionary tactic is."

Jo opened the door and followed him into the hallway.

Stepping out of the elevator into the lobby, Buster walked casually to the front door, carrying the bags and trailed by the beautiful blonde in the sheik black dress. Tony Gallento, standing by the door, only glanced at them as they walked by, and turned his eyes back to the people milling in the lobby searching for a tall businessman with a black mustache and a beautiful redhead at his side. Buster walked up to a waiting cab and placed the bags in the trunk, then opened the door for Jo. She slipped to the other side of the seat and Buster stepped quickly inside and pulled the door closed behind him.

Jo, noticing the confusion in the eyes of the cabby, nonchalantly spoke, nodding towards Buster, "My boyfriend, and he just resigned his job with Mr. Hilton to take an extended vacation with me."

The cabby relaxed, smiled and said, "Don't blame him a bit, miss, looks like Mr. Hilton's loss and your boyfriend's gain. Where to?"

Buster answered as he pulled Jo into his arms, "O'Hare, and the quicker the better," he said as he glanced out the window to see if they were followed. He could see Tony still standing with his back to the door and looking in the direction of the elevators.

Upon reaching the airport, Buster removed the bellhop's coat with the prominent markings of the Hilton across the back. He then paid the fare, gathered their bags and headed for the nearest ticket counter, which happened to be United Airlines. Jo was close behind carrying the valise.

"What's your next flight out?" he asked the agent.

"Flight 765 to Washington National," the agent replied. "It's scheduled to depart in fifteen minutes."

"Two tickets on Flight 765," Buster said, smiling at the confused agent.

The agent wrote the ticket hurriedly, not waiting for an explanation and checked the two bags, "You'll need to hurry, gate five," she said as she handed him the tickets.

They were the last two on the plane and the door closed behind them. Reaching their seats, Jo held tightly to the valise, while Buster removed the phone from the back of the seat and dialed the Hilton. "There's a bellboy in room 537 who needs help," he told the receptionist and hung up.

* * * * * *

Hotel security had already questioned Andrew about the two who had tied him in the bathtub and stolen his clothes. The hotel manager decided that since no one was injured, the incident would not be reported to the police -- bad PR for the hotel. Andrew was quite content with a new suit of clothes and a hundred dollar bill in his pocket, which he failed to report to security.   He was certain that it was adequate reimbursement for being tied for an hour in the bathtub.

However, Tony Gallento was not so pleased. As Andrew exited the security office, Tony was waiting in the lobby and asked to speak to him for a moment, offering another bribe for information. Andrew was pleased to tell him that, "Yes, the woman was really a blonde and had been wearing a red wig and yes, the man had removed a false mustache in his presence." "No, he didn't know where they were going but assumed they had gone to the airport." One more thing, Andrew added, "I carried their bags to their room when they arrived and they only had two, but when they left they were carrying a third, a valise with a tag on it with the initials "S.M."

The boss is gonna kill me, it's that damned Texas deputy and he must have found Spinner's bag somewhere, Tony thought as he rushed from the hotel and took a cab to the airport. He too, stopped at the first airline desk, United, and asked if his friends, a tall dark haired gentleman and a lovely lady with blonde hair had already departed.

The agent looked at the schedule board on the wall and said, "Yes, sorry but you have missed them. They were the last passengers on flight 765 to Washington National and should be arriving there in about an hour."

Tony purchased a ticket on the next flight to Washington, D.C. then made a quick telephone call to a syndicate contact in Alexandria, Virginia.

"Raymond, this is Tony in Chicago. Need you to do me a favor. Get over to National and meet United flight 765-- should be arriving in about thirty minutes. You'll see a tall, good looking dark haired guy, about six-two and two hundred pounds. He probably will be wearing a pair of dark slacks with a red stripe down the leg, you know, like bellboys in hotels wear. May even have a Hilton Hotel jacket on but I bet he'll be in shirt sleeves. He's got a good looking blonde broad with him--sexy black dress. Follow them, they'll probably check in one of the hotels since it's going to be too late for them to get a flight out. Once they get settled, pick me up at the airport--I'll be in on United flight 915 at ten thirty tonight. O.K.?"

"O.K. Tony," Raymond answered, "but what's up, man? You sound worried."

"Yeah, I'm worried, I'll tell you about it when I get there. Don't screw up, man--don't let 'em know you're tailing them, just find out where they're going."

8

The spread of the disease continued to move slowly to the north and east, covering an area of nearly five thousand square miles and affecting cattle in over twenty-five feed yards. Strangely, the disease had not affected cattle which were on grass or wheat pasture, only those confined in the huge custom cattle feeding operations. The quarantine had been extended to cover ten counties in the Texas Panhandle and the situation had become so severe that orders had been given by government agents for owners to destroy every animal within those twenty-five yards, *over two million head!* This order increased tension between government agents, cowboys and feed yard managers. Many of those involved began carrying guns and there were a few incidents where shots were fired at law enforcement officers, though no injuries were reported.

Federal Food and Drug Administration, FDA, agents were dispatched to the area to monitor and enforce the quarantine.

However, the situation had become so volatile that yard operators had posted armed guards at their gates and refused to
allow the agents entry.

"If the feds are not going to allow us to market those cattle which are not infected, then we are not going to allow
them on our premises," one of the managers told CNN reporters, as he brandished a thirty-thirty Winchester rifle.

"Our constitutional rights are being violated when the
federal government denies us the right to market our products; then orders us to slaughter our cattle but refuses any
compensation for this action. It is our belief that the government should first purchase those cattle at fair market value,
then provide the resources required to kill and bury *their* animals. Why should we be required to bear the financial burden
for losses incurred by the action of foreign terrorists, when it
is the responsibility of the federal government to protect us
from those actions?"

Feed yard managers called an emergency meeting in
Amarillo to discuss plans to oppose the government order,
and drafted letters to the President of the United States and to
members of Congress stating that the government was ordering them to destroy other people's property, since the cattle
in the feed yards were owned by their customers and not by
the individual operators. The letter also addressed the problem of severe property loss and requested financial reimbursement to the owners of the cattle, which were ordered
killed. They voted to refuse to slaughter any cattle which did
not show physical signs of the disease until officials assured
them that owners would be reimbursed for their losses.

Congress was quick to react to the cattlemen's demands and passed emergency legislation appropriating an estimated *one billion dollars* to cover the losses by cattle owners based on the fair market value of those cattle which were ordered slaughtered. They sent the bill to the President for his signature.

After quarantine signs were posted, owners of several of the smaller feed yards filed bankruptcy, fired their employees and walked away--leaving the cattle unattended. With no one to feed or water those still alive, the death rate accelerated and dead cattle were piled in the lots along with thousands of live, but sick cattle. With no one to excavate pits or to bury the dead, the stink became unbearable and County Commissioners petitioned the governor for help.

"We've got to have state aid, Governor," County Judge Lev Anderson said when he finally reached him on the phone. "The situation here is totally out of control. We don't have enough law enforcement officers to keep the peace. We're sitting on a powder keg that could explode any day. Tempers are running so high that we are fortunate there has been no killings, but, that could change if you don't send us help immediately."

Texas Governor Jim Rose, concerned about civil unrest, reacted promptly and called out one unit of the Texas National Guard Military Police to help police the quarantined area. He further requested that the President send troops and heavy equipment in to help dispose of the slaughtered cattle. Road blocks were established by armed National Guardsmen and all vehicles leaving the area were stopped and checked to make certain that no contaminated meat was being shipped out.

The problem, however, was not limited to the Texas Panhandle, as consumers all over the nation became concerned that contaminated beef might be reaching the meat counters. Housewives began protest marches in New York City, Los Angeles, California, Washington, D.C. and all the major metropolitan areas, demanding that the government protect their food supply. In order to dispel the concern of the general public, that the beef could infect humans with the virus, Food and Drug officials began an educational campaign on national TV, emphasizing that this virus, unlike the Mad Cow Disease in England, affected only cloven-hoofed animals. And even though some of the meat might end up on the meat counter, it was not harmful to humans and would be just as good as any beef which did not contain the disease. The quarantine, they said, was implemented solely to protect other livestock from contamination and to contain the outbreak in as small an area as possible.

Four of the nation's major beef processing plants, with the capacity to slaughter over twenty thousand head of cattle per day, were shut down due to the lack of available cattle for slaughter. Nearly ten thousand workers were left jobless. Immediately the flow of beef from the packing plants to the grocery shelves slowed to a dribble and meat counters from California to New York became bare. Beef, pork and chicken prices began to skyrocket, as housewives quickly made a run on all meat counters and bought up all available supplies.

The "futures' pits" in the Chicago Board of Trade went

wild. Held to a maximum limit of two cents per pound for each of the first three trading days, then allowed to advance double that amount in the following days, the price of fed beef continued to move up the limit every trading day with no signs of weakness in sight.

The President declared an emergency and issued an executive order removing all quotas on imported beef. Australia and Argentina began loading additional transports with boxed beef for shipment to the United States.

USA TODAY, The Wall Street Journal, The Washington Post, Time, Newsweek, and all major magazines sent investigative reporters into the contaminated area. Reams of printed material, explaining everything from the history of Foot and Mouth Disease, to conjectures as to how this outbreak had started, were flooded into the world's news channels.

After four weeks, ABC, CBS, NBC and CNN continued to carry the story as their number one story of the day. The coverage of this national disaster was even greater than the coverage given to the O.J. Simpson murder trial. *Twenty-Twenty,* the popular Friday night investigative TV program, ran a full hour on the history of the Texas Panhandle. They explained the similarity of this slaughter to the slaughter of an estimated fifty million head of buffalo by hunters in this same West Texas area during the 1870's; an event which virtually destroyed the American bison herd. *Twenty-Twenty* reporters speculated that the disease would not be contained in the quarantined area but would spread across the nation, destroying the American beef and dairy industry. The general public flooded Congress with letters and telephone calls, demanding everything from apprehending the perpetrators to declaring all out war on Iraq and Iran. Since it was apparent that they were responsible for the epidemic.

The FBI increased its team in Hereford from four to ten and the FDA, the CIA, and the USDA sent in investigative teams to help in determining how the disease had originated and why it had spread so quickly. Federal workers from the U.S. Department of Agriculture were sent in to help dispose of the infected herds.

With the agreement by congress to reimburse the cattlemen for losses incurred by fulfilling requirements established by federal agencies, the volatile atmosphere began to subside and yard operators began to cooperate with the federal agents, allowing them access to their yards.

Several well known international terrorist groups, realizing they could capitalize on this panic, sent news releases to the media claiming responsibility for the contamination. Hamas and Hezbollah, the Middle-Eastern terrorist groups responsible for the bombing of the U.S. Marine barracks in Beirut, sent a letter to the FBI. In it they claimed responsibility and stated that it was in retaliation for the downing of the Iranian passenger jet by a U.S. missile in the Persian Gulf. The letter also threatened more attacks against environmentally sensitive industries in the U.S.

The FBI team, led by Special Agent Ace Belton, announced that two men who appeared to be Iraqi or Iranian businessmen were registered in an Amarillo motel, for a week, prior to the initial outbreak of the disease and were prime suspects in their investigation. They had purchased tickets on American Airlines to Chicago, but their trail was lost at that point, and their whereabouts was not presently known. It was speculated by the news media that they were probably in Iraq by now.

This announcement sent ripples through the Federal Government in Washington, D.C. and the President called a special meeting of his cabinet to determine if the State Department and the National Security Council should take any immediate action. State Department officials made contact with Iraqi and Iranian ambassadors and voiced U.S. concerns, as to the possibility that terrorists from one of those countries might be responsible for biological warfare on the U.S. food supply. Iraqi and Iranian officials strongly denied any involvement and suggested that CIA agents had themselves spread the virus in order to instigate bombing of Iraqi and Iranian facilities, suspected of manufacturing contagious viruses for use in biological warfare.

The investigation by the FBI seemed to change directions when it was reported that another FBI team, working out of Santa Fe, New Mexico, had received a tip linking the contamination to a pseudo- military group by the name of Patriots For Free America--PFFA--and the team was searching the New Mexico mountains for members of that group. There were rumors being spread that some members of the group were known to be employees of some of the feed yards.

Texas Rangers, not to be outdone by federal agents, began their own investigation by conducting extensive research into the background of all present and past employees of the infected feedlots; to determine if some disgruntled cowboy was seeking retaliation against the industry for some real or imagined mistreatment. A half dozen suspects were held and questioned but released for lack of evidence.

Members of the Texas Department of Contagious Disease Control were sent to Mexico to try to determine if there had been an outbreak of the disease, in the area where most of the Mexican feeder cattle were being grown. The Mexican government voiced its concern that the TDCDC was interfering in its internal affairs by pointing a finger of suspicion at Mexican cattle without any proof or evidence.

Throughout the United States, the general public was beginning to panic, believing that terrorists were planning to poison water supplies, grain reserves and food processing facilities. White House and Congressional phone lines were jammed with calls, demanding that the federal government round up all suspected members of terrorist groups. And, that army units be placed around each major water reservoir, which supplied water to the largest industrial cities. Impatient with the lack of government action, vigilante groups were formed in several of these cities and armed members were patrolling their reservoirs and power plants around the clock.

In upstate New York at one of the reservoirs that supplied water for New York City, two teenagers who were parked, necking, near the reservoir were shot and killed by one of the vigilante members who mistook them for terrorists.

Federal and state agents began fighting among themselves, arguing as to who had jurisdiction over each part of the investigation and even refusing to share information.

The Deaf Smith County Sheriff's Department was mired in the unwanted task of trying to coordinate the efforts of all these agencies in and around the major contaminated area. Sheriff Blackwell questioned his good judgement of demanding that his department head any and all investigative activities in his county. He could see that the investigation had grown far beyond the capability of his police force.

His department was understaffed and overworked and walking a tight rope trying to keep peace under these very adverse conditions. He set up a scheduled meeting between representatives of each of the governmental agencies involved in the investigation, which were based in Deaf Smith County, in an effort to establish better cooperation and to try to determine if there had been any concrete evidence uncovered.

At the meeting Don Pope, head of the CIA investigative team, presented evidence that the two Middle East businessmen, who had yet evaded capture, had definitely been seen in the area. And that they were considered prime suspects for spreading the virus, although the agency was unable to determine how they had been so successful in contaminating such a large area. He stated that arrests were imminent.

One FBI team, however, believed that more emphasis should be placed on investigating the possibility that it could be a terrorist act which had been planned and supervised by members of the radical militia group, which could have members working in area feed yards. FBI Director Friedman announced in Washington that his agency was close to wrapping up the case with the imminent arrest of leaders of that group.

Sheriff Blackwell was not satisfied that either group had enough evidence to limit the investigation to those particular areas and suggested that the federal agencies broaden their investigations. The meeting adjourned with tempers flaring between members of the two federal agencies, each believing that they were close to solving the case.

The weather only added to the stressful situation as March turned hot, dry and windy with the smell of death permeating the ordinarily clean West Texas air. There was no way to get away from the stench, even though the cattle were being bulldozed as fast as possible under tons of dirt--the smell was overbearing. To add to the stressful situation, hundreds of thousands of buzzards had descended on the area, feeding on the remains of the unburied cattle.

* * * * * *

Sheriff Blackwell had gone to the Autry feedlot to observe the slaughter, when the quarantine first began, and was still suffering nightmares from the scene. As he watched, one hundred head of the cattle were driven into a large open pit where two cowboys were waiting on the rim with high powered rifles. With deadly accuracy, they shot the cattle between the eyes, one after the other, killing them immediately. One hundred shots later, the pile of cattle lay dead in their own blood and bulldozers began pushing dirt over them, as another hundred head were herded into an adjoining pit. Pete tried to wipe the vision from his mind by convincing himself that this was no more inhumane than the daily slaughter of thousands of head of cattle in packing houses each day, but to no avail--the scene still preyed upon his mind.

Then there was the problem of the Spinner Murphy murder investigation. His Chief Deputy was off hell-knows-where, shacked up with his girlfriend, claiming he was hiding from Chicago mobsters who were trying to murder both of them.

He pulled his handkerchief from his jeans' pocket and wiped the sweat from his forehead, pushing the pile of papers aside on his desk, when the phone jarred him from his reverie.

"Pete, this is Buster," he heard a voice say.

"Buster, where the hell are you?" he shouted. "The situation here is driving me crazy and you're off gallivanting around the country with your girlfriend. You need to get your tail home, pronto!"

"Sorry, Pete," Buster replied, "You don't want me home any more than I'd like to be there. I've got a tiger by the tail and don't know how to turn it loose. I'm in Washington, D.C. hiding out at the Twin Bridges Marriott. It's too late to get a plane out tonight, we're scheduled to leave at eight in the morning and arrive in Amarillo at five. I got the news on TV and I can see you've got a helluva problem there but I've got problems, too. I'll tell you all about them when I get home."

Pausing, he continued, "You got a pen handy? Take this down, just in case something happens and I don't get home, which is a distinct possibility. I've got over a hundred thousand dollars in a valise which was in Spinner's locker in

Chicago. There's also a journal showing that he made several deliveries of a million dollars each, to The Corizentian Commodity, Inc., a member of the Chicago Board of Trade. You got that? Corizentian Commodity, Inc.--that's important. I don't know what those deliveries were all about, maybe a way to clean up some drug money or to hide it from the IRS, but I'll kiss your ass if they aren't someway responsible for Spinner's murder."

Sheriff Blackwell, regaining his composure, asked, "What in tarnation you doing in Washington, that's the wrong direction from Chicago to Texas?"

"I was chased here, Pete. I bumped into that Las Vegas hood that was tailing us in Nevada. They found out I was snooping around and I had to get out of Chicago fast and Washington was the quickest plane out," Buster answered. Then with a slight hint of impatience in his voice, added, "Pete, I'm serious. The Corizentian Commodity, Inc. is apparently a Mafia front and hooked into one of the big casinos in Vegas, and they don't want me messing around investigating Spinner's murder. They killed Spinner and that girl in Las Vegas and they wouldn't hesitate to murder me and Jo if they catch us. It's just a matter of time before they find out which plane I took out of Chicago and they'll be right on my tail. I just hope I get out of D.C. before they pick up my trail."

"Well, you take care, boy," Pete said, indicating his concern, "And watch your back. If it really is the Mafia that's after you, you need to be home where I can help you!"

Buster hung up the phone and looked around as Jo stepped from the bathroom, a large bath towel draped around her curvaceous body and a great big West Texas smile on her face. She looked at him seductively and said, "O.K. cowboy, all work and no play makes Buster a dull boy. It's play time."

Buster returned the smile, feeling a little guilty that he was about to have a very enjoyable night; while Pete was having such a tough time back in Texas. *What's that old adage,* he thought as he began removing his shirt, *eat, drink and be merry because tomorrow you die? Sorry, Pete!*

His mind was all cluttered with thoughts of hoods, murders, money and dead cattle; but Jo's warm body against his was able to erase those memories from his mind. Tonight they would make memories much more pleasant to think about.

* * * * * *

Raymond met Tony at the airport at ten thirty and led him to his car in the parking lot. "They're at the Marriott, room 334," he said as he pulled the BMW into the line of traffic heading for D.C. "How about telling me what's up?"

"The guy's a deputy sheriff from Texas and the broad is his girlfriend. They've been sticking their nose into some of our business in Vegas and Chicago and could cost the syndicate a lot of money if they aren't stopped. My orders are to take them out at all costs, I just need the right place and the right time."

"How you plan on doing it, Tony? This hotel is not very private, you know," Raymond warned.

"Get me three more of your men, we'll stake out their

room and when they leave in the morning we'll grab them and carry them out of town aways--maybe the Pohick campground and dump them there. I'll check into the hotel and see if I can get a room near their's so we can keep tabs on them tonight."

Tony was in luck, room 332 was available.

* * * * * *

Buster awoke and looked at his watch--two-thirty. Somebody was moving around in the hallway and making a lot of racket in the room next door and he could hear someone whispering to be quiet. Suddenly his senses became fully awake--could it be the people who had run them out of Chicago! He slipped out of bed, went into the bathroom, picked up a drinking glass and pressed it against the wall, placing his ear against the glass.

"Keep the noise down, dammit, they're in the room next door and you're going to wake them," he heard a voice say.

"Ah, stop your worrying, Tony," another answered, "These rooms are sound proof. Let's get some sleep, they aren't going to be going anywhere before morning. Besides, Nick is watching the hallway, they can't get by him."

His suspicions were correct, it was them! He couldn't believe that they had been able to trail him from Chicago and locate their exact room so quickly, but it was true, they were there next door--and they had him cornered and planned to murder both he and Jo!

Buster moved to the bed and placed his hand over Jo's

mouth as he gently shook her awake.

"Don't make a sound, Jo," he whispered. "We've got company next door and in the hall. Let's get dressed and see if we can't figure a way out."

Only one way out--through the door into the hallway and they had the exit blocked. Three of the enemy in the next room just waiting for them to open the door. Buster realized he had to have help but where could he get it at two-thirty in the morning in a city which he knew nothing about?

He paced the room, thinking--thinking!

He could call the local sheriff's department; but who's going to believe he's a deputy from Texas and needs help in Virginia, at three o'clock in the morning? Then it hit him. He was in Virginia, right across the river from Washington, D.C., headquarters of the Federal Bureau of Investigation -- Ace Belton's agency and home territory.

He looked in his billfold and searched through the business cards until he found the one that Ace had given him after arriving in Texas. It had his Texas office and motel number listed. He picked up the phone and dialed.

Please, God, he thought, let him be home. One ring, two rings, three--then a voice filled with sleep answered, "Hello, Belton here."

"Ace! Sorry to disturb you at this hour. This is Deputy Thornton. I need your help."

"Buster! Where the hell are you? Pete told me you had gone to Chicago on that murder investigation. Are you back in town?"

"No, Ace, I'm in Washington, D.C., Twin Bridges Marriott.

It's a long story how I got here but I'm in one helluva predicament. Some Chicago mobsters, who I believe were involved in Spinner's murder, followed me here and somehow found out where I'm staying. Some of them, I think three or four, are in the room next door and they've got one stationed in the hall outside our door, just waiting for us to open the door to leave. I heard them say they intend to murder us and dump our bodies somewhere in the country."

"Hold on, Buster, you been drinking or something."

"No! I'm serious, Ace--I've got information that may send a bunch of them up for life, and they don't intend for me to get back to Texas with that information."

"What you want me to do?"

"Can you get some of your people here in D.C. to come to the hotel and help me out?"

"Sure. What you want them to do, arrest the bastards?"

"No, I haven't got enough evidence yet to charge them with Spinner's murder, but I know that they were responsible. Maybe your boys could just bust in on them and hold them in the room on some kind of phony charge until Jo and I can slip out."

"O.K., Buster, that shouldn't be a problem   Here's what I'll do, I'll send out four agents. They can take the guy in the hallway, then bust in on the ones in the room.   I'll have them accuse the group of being responsible for a bank robbery over in Arlington. While my men are holding them in the room and questioning them, you can slip out. After you've had time to get away, we'll tell them it was all a case of mistaken identification and let them go."

"Sounds great, Ace, they're in room 332, I'm in 334. I've got reservations on an American flight at eight a.m. If your boys can show up at about seven and hold them, say 'till eight-thirty, we should be long gone and on our way to Texas."

"I'll take care of it, Buster. They'll be there at seven sharp. You be ready and when our boys make their move, get your ass out in a hurry."

"Thanks, Ace, I owe you one!"

At seven sharp, Buster heard a commotion in the hallway, then the door to 332 being opened, and the order to freeze! Someone yelled "what the hell!" and another voice shouting "Drop your weapons and get flat on the floor."

Buster and Jo quickly slipped out the door and headed for the stairway exit. Three flights down and they were outside. Four cabs were waiting for fares at the front of the hotel-- Buster grabbed the first and gave instructions to hurry to the American gate, National Airport!

Their plane, flight 813, was loading when they reached the gate. Eight-fifteen a.m. and they were in the air, climbing to thirty thousand feet and headed west. Buster looked at Jo, who was clutching Spinner's valise in her lap, and smiled. "Relax, Babe," he said, "We cheated death one more time."

At nine a.m. the four FBI agents apologized for mistaking the four men in room 332 for bank robbers and left. One of the mobsters, the one called Tony, rushed to the room next door where he found the door ajar and the room empty. Tony cursed and picked up the phone.

"American Airlines, I need a reservation on your next flight to Amarillo, Texas."

He dialed another number, a contact in Amarillo, and gave instructions to pick him up at the Amarillo Air Terminal at eleven p.m.

* * * * * *

The first thing Buster did, after letting Jo off at her apartment was to return to Hereford in the unmarked sheriff's Chevy, which he had left at the Amarillo Air Terminal. He then picked up his Blazer and retrieved the plastic baggie, containing the sample from the drain pipe at Murphy's Spraying Service, from the glove compartment. He had completely forgotten about the sample but now realized that it might hold a key to solving this mystery. He then drove to the courthouse to report to Sheriff Blackwell.

Carrying the valise with the one hundred thousand dollars packed inside, Buster entered the sheriff's office. Laying it on the desk, he said, "Pete, I don't know if this is clean or dirty money but there's one helluva lot of it. And those Chicago mobsters must want it back real bad, or maybe it's this journal they want."

He pulled the small, leather backed notebook from his pocket and opened it. Turning its pages, he stopped at an entry that seemed to have him puzzled. "It looks like the Corizentian Commodity, Inc. was paying him ten thousand dollars for each delivery and there were five deliveries in all," he said. "But there's an entry here that just says *fifty thousand for investment*, I can't figure that one out--investment in what and where?"

Then as if answering his own question, he continued. "Pete, I've had a lot of time to think since I left D.C. and damned if I don't believe Spinner's murder and this cattle thing are tied together."

"Now look, Buster," Pete said irritably, "I told you before, I've got enough problems without starting a rhubarb with the FBI and the CIA. They're saying that terrorists are behind this Foot and Mouth outbreak and that suits me fine. In fact, a couple of terrorist organizations have already taken responsibility for it--it's probably just a matter of time until they determine which one is telling the truth. You just keep your mind on the murder investigation and let the government solve this other mystery."

"O.K. Pete," Buster said, "But I may not be able to keep them separate. Maybe the Mafia and the terrorist groups are in cahoots. Let's just look at the evidence. Spinner was murdered about the same time this Foot and Mouth epidemic started. We're pretty certain that he was murdered by someone tied to the Mafia, because of the way he was bound and shot in the back of the head. We know he had been delivering huge sums of money from gambling casinos in Las Vegas to Chicago mobsters and that they were paying him well for his services. That makes me believe that he wasn't skimming money off the deliveries, so he must have been murdered for some other reason--maybe, because he knew too much about something and they were afraid he was going to talk. There's a couple of things that's got me puzzled, though--why in hell was Spinner's planes and premises so spick and span? That just wasn't his nature. And what was he doing flying his crop duster around in the dead of winter when there wasn't any bugs to kill?"

Throwing the plastic baggie with the dirt sample in it on the Sheriff's desk, Buster said, "Send this to the lab and see what they come up with. I've got a hunch it might answer some of our questions."

Rising from his chair, he walked to the door and placed his hand on the doorknob, then as an afterthought, he turned and said, "Pete, you know, there's going to be a ton of money lost because of this Foot and Mouth epidemic, maybe half a billion dollars, if my calculations are correct. But there's also going to be one helluva lot of money made because of it -- a lot more than has been lost, if the price of cattle and hogs continues to climb."

Pete, looking up from his messy desk, asked, "How you figure that? Even if the price of cattle doubles or triples, these cowboys aren't going to make a damned penny because they won't have any cattle to sell?"

Buster turned, and walked back to the desk, "Yeah, but what if you were on the right side of the futures' market and had bought a lot of these paper beeves for fifty cents a pound and sold them after the market peaks at about a dollar and a half a pound. Look at the profits you could make--and you wouldn't have to worry about your cattle dying, they're just a bunch of entries on a piece of paper. You wouldn't have to own a cotton-picking head of live cattle to make a fortune!"

The door slammed as Buster left the room, leaving Sheriff Pete Blackwell with a look of astonishment on his face.

Buster rubbed his chin in thought, after opening the car

door and entering his Blazer. He just couldn't figure how the gambling casino in Las Vegas and the Corizentian Commodity, Inc. were tied together, it just didn't make sense. As he fastened his seat belt it suddenly hit him--what George had been telling him the other day about the Chicago Board of Trade. *"The Chicago Board of Trade is the biggest damned gambling casino in the world, where gambling is legal and billions of dollars are gambled every day on whether grain and cattle prices are going to be higher or lower on any given day for the next two years! And that big old Chicago gambling hall is controlled by a group of commodity firms who have a monopoly on dealing the cards and throwing the dice. Just to make it more interesting, they collect bets from all over the world, even from places where it is illegal to gamble."*

He slapped the steering wheel of the Blazer as he realized the possibilities. *Maybe the same folks that own some of the gambling casinos in Vegas own some of the gambling seats on the Chicago Board of Trade!!*

If that was true, he could see the answers to a lot of his questions.

9

The sun had already set and a large, orange disc was just breaking the eastern horizon when Tony Gallento arrived in Amarillo on the American Airlines flight. As the plane circled for landing, the left wing dropped and Tony, looking out the window on the right side of the plane, was greeted by a million stars shining brightly on the cloudless black carpet which held them in the West Texas sky. Their beauty, however, was lost to this Las Vegas hoodlum whose mind was locked on plans to rid Texas, once and for all, of a meddling Deputy Sheriff from Hereford.

As he stepped out of the canopied walkway into the terminal building, he was greeted by a local hood who was waiting with an automobile.

"Glad to see you back, Tony," Giovanni 'Slick' Rosellini said, as he carried Tony's bag to the car. Slick, a short, fat man, five-four and weighing in at two hundred eighty pounds, owned one of the topless clubs on Amarillo Boulevard. He was puffing and sweating profusely, as he threw the bags into the back seat.

"Can't say I'm glad to be back, Slick," Tony replied, frowning, as he opened the car door and pulled himself in. "I thought I was done with this godforsaken place after we closed the books on that crop duster, but now we gotta take care of that damned deputy that keeps poking his nose into our business. The boss says to take him out quick before he stumbles onto something that upsets our plans. He must have found out something from that dealer in Vegas or he wouldn't have been poking around in Chicago. And no telling what kind of information Murphy had stashed in that bag that he picked up in Chicago. He's a smart bastard, got away from me in Vegas and then slipped out of Chicago in that bellhop's garb. I had him in Virginia but the damned FBI got in the way. Getting rid of him ain't going to be as easy as it was with that crop duster. He knows we're onto him and he's going to be watching his back. Looks like I'm going to need a rifle and scope so I don't have to get too close."

Slick, pulling out of the parking lot and heading downtown, interrupted. "I've already taken care of it, Tony. The boys in Chicago called and told me the plans. I got you a Ford pickup stashed at the motel and there's a thirty-ought-six, with a ten power scope, behind the seat and a three-fifty-seven just in case you need it. We know'd you couldn't carry anything on the plane."

Slick's vocabulary reflected his upbringing on the streets of New York City.

They pulled off I-40 on the ramp to the Ramada Inn

where Slick pointed out the white Ford pickup and handed Tony a set of keys. "It's hot, but we changed the plates so's in case someone spots you they won't be able to trace it to us. You can dump it here when you're finished and take a cab to the airport. I took care of the motel, you're registered as a Mr. Antonio Garcia. You're just brown enough to pass as a Mexican, and here's the key to your room."

"Where can I pick up some cowboy duds, I don't want to look too conspicuous, what with all those feds prowling a-round that hick town?"

"Take Georgia Street exit and go south about three blocks and you'll find the largest western wear store in town. Pick you up a pair of jeans, a straw hat, western shirt and a pair of boots; and they won't be able to tell you from any of those Mexican feedlot cowboys," Slick answered as he drove out of the parking lot.

Tomorrow he'd get that deputy for good, Tony promised himself as he fell into bed, totally exhausted.

* * * * * *

Buster and CIA agent Don Pope were discussing the Foot and Mouth epidemic over a cup of coffee in the Sheriff's of-fice. It was after midnight and the courthouse was empty ex-cept for a janitor who was busy waxing the hall floor. Buster mostly listened as Pope brought him up to date on the pro-gress of their investigation, even though he believed that they were on a wild goose chase. Sheriff Blackwell had given or-ders not to question the fed's evidence, so he listened without comment.

"Amarillo's Economic Development Committee has offered a million dollars to any business that will move to
Amarillo and hire as many as fifty employees on a full-time
basis," Pope said. "These two Iraqis were in town for a week
prior to the epidemic, apparently talking with the AEDC about
moving a clothing manufacturing plant to this area from Lebanon. We trailed them to Beirut and our agents there are looking into the legitimacy of their business. We believe they are
terrorists and used the AEDC meeting as a front to bring in the
Foot and Mouth virus and spread it around the different feed
yards. *If* we're right, and *if* we locate them, it's going to be
hard, maybe impossible, to get them extradited out of Lebanon
or Iraq for questioning."

Buster nodded, then asked. "What's this I hear about the
USDA people thinking that one of the northern feedlots in
Kansas or Nebraska could be behind this whole thing. Killing a bunch of cattle down here and causing the price to
jump, so they can make a mint out of the cattle they have
ready for market--has that aspect been investigated?"

"The FBI has looked into it," Pope replied, "And I suppose
it's possible but I just can't believe it's true. Cattle people are
just not the type that would harm any kind of livestock, especially to the extent that a couple million head of cattle were
exposed to a deadly virus, which causes so much pain and
sickness and death-- no, I don't buy that theory. What with all
the bombings taking place; Oklahoma City, the World Trade
Building in New York City and the military barracks in Saudi
Arabia, we believe that Iraq and Iran are stepping up their ter-

rorist attacks on U.S. facilities and this cattle virus is just another one of their moves against us. Saddam is still licking his wounds from Desert Storm and the oil embargo, and he's determined to repay us for the damage we did to his country."

Taking a sip of the steaming coffee, the CIA agent asked. "How's your murder investigation coming? I understand you've been out of town running down some leads."

"Yeah," Buster replied, "But so far we haven't come up with anything concrete. We believe that Murphy may have been involved in laundering drug money and got too greedy and the mob put out a contract on him," he lied. *This was his case and he didn't want any federal agents screwing it up, and if it turned out that solving the murder might also help solve the Foot and Mouth mystery, then so be it.*

Yawning, he got up from his chair and retrieved his hat from the hat rack. "It's been a long three days, Don. I think I'll hit the sack and see if I can make up some of the sleep I've lost," he said as he opened the door and stepped out into the night.

Damn, he thought as the pungent odor of the night air hit him, how long's it going to take before that stench is gone!

* * * * * *

As the price of cattle continued to rise on the futures' markets, the CEO of the Corizentian Commodity, Inc. called a meeting of his staff who were working the floor on the CBOT. As the last of the staff took their seats around the large mahogany table in the board room, Seigle, removing the huge Havana cigar from his mouth, spoke.

"We've probably rode this horse as far as we dare and it's probably time we started dumping our contracts. The poor bastards that sold contracts back in January, thinking the market price was going to go lower are liable to start demanding an investigation by the Commodity Futures Trading Commission, as to why we're the only company which had the foresight to buy instead of sell. There's not a damn thing they can prove but if we start dumping now, it'll put a damper on the markets and everyone will be able to cover their losses. If we try to push it much further, a lot of the smaller traders will just declare bankruptcy and we won't collect a dime."

One of the younger men at the table spoke. "Sir, if we dump too much at once, it's liable to start the markets moving in the other direction, won't it?"

"That's right. That's why I had the records department draft an orderly marketing plan. Each of you will sell only a few of your contracts daily for the next three weeks. If the market gets too soft, we will just stop selling until it firms up again. You will find a copy of the plan in the folder before you. Follow the instructions precisely."

* * * * * *

Air Force One lifted smoothly off the runway at Andrews Air Force Base, carrying the President, the Secretary of Agriculture and the Administrator of the Food and Drug Administration. Reaching altitude, the pilot turned the nose of the huge plane to the west and headed for Amarillo, Texas.

At the same time, Texas Governor Rose walked up the steps of the state's Lear jet and took a seat in preparation for his trip to Amarillo where he would meet the President for a tour of the stricken area.

10

Buster left Hereford early for the two hour drive to Dalhart, passing through two check points where the National Guard was checking every vehicle to make certain they were not carrying quarantined beef.

Stopping at the check-point on I-40 at Vega, he stepped out of his Blazer and visited with the armed Military Policeman.

"How's the quarantine going?" he asked the MP.

"Pretty quiet. We had a loaded cattle truck try to slip through yesterday--guess they thought they could find a slaughter house in New Mexico that would butcher them. The cattle looked healthy enough. Said they came from one of the smaller lots just south of here."

"What you suppose will happen to them?"

"Don't know--a couple of state highway patrolmen ushered them back to the feed yard to unload the cattle. I reckon they ended up in the slammer, that's a pretty tough offense, trying to transport quarantined beef."

Buster shook his head, "Poor bastards. Can't say as I blame them. Everybody is really taking a loss in this mess. I got four hundred head in Autry's pens just about ready for market and stand to lose a ton of money, if the government don't come through with reimbursement."

"Sorry to hear it," the MP said as Buster returned to his vehicle. "What you doing out so early, trying to get ahead of the criminal element in your county?"

"You might say so," Buster responded, "We had a murder took place about a month ago and I've been running down some leads--on my way to Dalhart to check out a couple more."

As Buster closed the door he heard the MP say, "You take care, now, and I wish you luck in locating your killer."

"Thanks!"

The sun was just coming up in the East when he pulled into Dalhart and stopped at a local coffee shop. A group of farmers were gathered around a large table talking about the weather, the wind, the drought and the cattle disease which had now hit the Dalhart area feed yards; a good one hundred miles north of Hereford.

"Morning, mind if I sit here?" he asked, indicating a vacant chair.

"Help yourself," one of them replied as he moved his chair to make more room.

Buster introduced himself and listened as he waited for the waitress to bring his coffee. As if completing a sentence, one of the farmers said, "I'll betcha a ten dollar bill that it was one of them I-raqees that did it. We shoulda gone ahead and killed that goldarned Saddam and all his cutthroats when we had the chance. Next thing you know they'll be poisoning our water supply, then what we gonna do?"

"You're probably right," the one who had moved his chair replied. "This thing ain't over by a long shot. Killing all them cattle is just the beginning of our problems. What we gonna do with all our corn now, with no cattle to eat it. These feed yards are gonna be ghost towns for a long time. I heard the County Agent say yesterday that after the cattle are all killed and buried, it will take at least two years to fumigate the area, so they can put new cattle in. I'll bet grain prices hit the bottom before the year is out. I hope the President sends the bombers back over Iraq and blows it all to hell!"

"That's what I've been thinking," another farmer replied. "I've just been thinking, I may not plant any corn this year, what with all the expense of fertilizer, water and spraying; but I don't know what else to plant, I can't think of any other crops that we can grow in this sand. We're too far north to try to grow cotton."

The conversation quieted while the waitress set Buster's coffee on the table and asked for his order. As she turned to leave, Buster saw his opening to enter the conversation. "You mentioned spraying," he said to the farmer. "What kind of crops have you got that need spraying this time of year?"

"Ain't nothing that needs spraying this time of year," the farmer replied. Pointing to the man sitting next to him, he added. "Jeff could tell you more about that than I can, he's a pilot out at Jones Dusting."

Jeff replaced his coffee cup on the table before replying, "That's right. Fact is, we just about wind up the spraying business in October when we usually have to kill some Russian aphids in our early winter wheat. I ain't had my spray plane up since I sprayed Tim Mitchell's wheat back in October."

The conversation drifted back to the cattle being slaughtered because of the Foot and Mouth Disease and Buster ate his bacon and eggs in silence, picked up his ticket and left. It was only a short drive of three miles to the airport and he turned his Blazer in that direction.

West Texas weather is unpredictable, one day the wind will blow forty to fifty miles an hour, whipping up dust and sand, and the next day it can be so calm that a kid couldn't fly a kite. Oldtimers like to say that only two kinds of people ever predict the weather in the Texas Panhandle--*strangers and damn fools.*

Buster could see that today was going to be a beauty for March. March was known to be the windiest month of the year but today hardly any wind was blowing and the sun was rising in the East in a cloudless sky. The weather put him in a pleasant mood and he was enjoying the ride, especially getting away from that horrible stench caused by the dead cattle around Hereford. For a change, he began to think positively about his investigation and could almost sense a break in the case.

He flipped on the Blazer's radio just as the newscast was ending and the weather forecast was given. "A cold front is stretched across the north, reaching from Wyoming to Iowa, moving slowly south. It should reach the Texas Panhandle in the next couple of days, dropping temperatures into the low thirties and bring a chance of moisture to the Plains. A low pressure area is building in the four-corners region and bringing moisture in from the Baja area of Mexico. If the two come together at the right time, we could see some beneficial moisture in the Texas Panhandle. That moisture could fall in the form of rain, sleet or snow. It's too early to tell at this point but keep tuned to this station and we will keep you updated," the weatherman said.

The disc-jockey came back on and announced the next country and western tune--Johnny Cash singing *Ring of Fire*.

Buster smiled as he remembered an old saying that there's nothing between Amarillo and the North Pole except a barbed wire fence, and someone left the gate open. He remembered that the biggest snow storms he had ever witnessed occurred in early spring when the humidity was high and the temperature hovered around thirty degrees. *Well, rain or snow, we could use a little moisture to settle this dust,* he thought.

A small building was set off to itself from the WW II hangers and the huge concrete runways, which had serviced B-17's and B-25's during the war. A sign proclaimed it to be the flight headquarters and a Phillips 66 sign indicated that aviation fuel was available. Buster pulled up to the building and stopped.

The lone attendant, dressed in some greasy red coveralls, which indicated that he was the local airplane mechanic, smiled and spoke pleasantly. "Morning--names Jason--grab you a cup of coffee there from the pot. It's fresh. I just made it."

"Deputy Sheriff Buster Thornton," Buster said as he poured himself a cup, then added, "from Hereford." He stepped from the coffee pot to Jason and held out his hand in introduction.

"What can I do for you, Sheriff?" Jason asked as he shook Buster's hand.

"I'm doing a little foot work on a murder case we had down in Hereford and I was hoping you might shed a little light on a problem I've got."

"Be glad to if I can," Jason replied, smiling, "But I ain't much good at murder investigations--airplane mechanic's my line of business. Now if you've got any airplanes that need investigating, I'm your man."

Buster laughed and reached into his pocket and pulled out the credit card receipt showing that Spinner had fueled up his spray plane in Dalhart in February. Handing the receipt to Jason he asked, "I was just wondering if you remember servicing that spray plane?"

Looking the ticket over, Jason brightened and said, "You betcha, I remember. That was the first spray plane that stopped for gas here since way back in October--last one, too. Red and white Cessna it was, slick little plane, came in about sun down, just before I quit work, and that Murphy feller asked me to top her out with fuel. You can see from the receipt that it didn't need much gas. Six gallons was all it'd hold, just about what it'd burn flying from Hereford to here."

Buster, deep in thought, scratched his chin and asked, "What do you suppose he was doing flying a spray plane around that time of year?"

Jason, his confidence increasing as a murder investigator, replied, "You know, I wondered the same thing at the time, but figured he must just be testing her out or something. There damn sure ain't nothing to spray in February. Most all our crop dusters store their planes for winter over there in that big old hanger, excepting Albert over at Texas Dusting. Albert takes his plane down to the Rio Grande Valley and sprays fruits and vegetables until the spring crops get to growing up here. Albert ain't married and he kinda likes to spend the winter down there on the border with all them pretty senoritas."

"I bet he does," Buster answered, laughing.

Jason looked out the dirty window in deep thought, then brightened. "You know, now that I think about it, there was something mighty peculiar about that plane. While I was gassing her up I looked into the spray tank and it was full of just pure water--no chemicals, just water."

"How do you know it didn't have any chemicals in it?" Buster asked.

"A couple of reasons," Jason answered, gaining confidence in his new found position as a murder investigator, "It was perfectly clear, no discoloration at all. If it's got chemicals in it, it's going to have some color to it. And another thing, it didn't have any odor at all. Every chemical, that I've ever seen these spray boys use, has got a distinct odor. That liquid in that Cessna didn't have no odor."

"That makes sense," Buster replied, then more to himself than to Jason, he said, "No chemicals,that's strange. Why the hell would Spinner be flying around with a full tank of water in the dead of winter?"

Jason, not waiting for further questions, volunteered, "We've got an old junker car that we loan to transient pilots who need to go into town for something. This Murphy feller said he needed to meet a man in town and I loaned him our car--said he'd probably eat supper before he returned and I told him to just leave the keys in the ash tray since there wouldn't be anyone around when he returned. Next morning the car was here and the plane was gone. I guess that's about all I know."

Buster took a final sip of his coffee, set the cup down and walked to the door. Turning, he handed a business card to the mechanic and said, "Jason, you've been a big help. You might make a pretty good detective if you ever decide to give up airplane mechanics. If you remember anything else just give me a call. I'd appreciate it."

Jason smiled and answered, "Glad to be of help, Sheriff. By the way, just whose murder are you investigating?"

"Spinner Murphy, the pilot of that plane you serviced out." Buster said as he walked out the door.

"Well, I be damned!" he heard Jason say as the door closed behind him.

* * * * * *

Two hours later and after passing through two more National Guard road-blocks, Buster pulled up in the parking lot at Tradewinds Airport in Amarillo and walked to the small terminal building. A couple of pilots were busy filing flight plans and the lone attendant was engrossed in the early morning edition of the Amarillo News. A young man dressed in khakis with a billed ball cap covering a mat of red hair was putting quarters into the coke machine.

The attendant looked up from his newspaper and asked, "Can I help you?"

"I hope so," Buster responded. He introduced himself and gave him the credit card receipt showing that Spinner had fueled up his spray plane at Tradewinds back in February.

"I was wondering if you might remember anything about this pilot or his plane?" Buster asked.

"Sorry," the attendant replied, "I didn't start working here until March. Junior could probably help you, that's him over at the coke machine. He services most planes that stop over here."

He put the paper down and shouted, "Hey, Junior! See if you can help this deputy."

Junior retrieved his coke from the bottom of the machine and walked towards Buster. Once again, Buster introduced himself and shook Junior's hand, gave him the receipt and asked the same question.

Junior thought for a minute as he looked the credit card receipt over, then smiled and said, "Sure I remember, that was Spinner Murphy, the spray pilot that got murdered over at Hereford. I serviced Spinner's planes up a lot, mostly that two-ten that he used in his charter business. Can't say as I ever remember fueling up that crop duster but this once, though. He came in about sun down and asked me to top her out. I remember some guy in a big black car picked him up and I guess they went out to eat. It was late, maybe nine o'clock before they came back. I worked late that night and I was just leaving for home when I saw them return. Spinner got out and the other guy left."

"Did you happen to see the guy he was with?" Buster asked, remembering the black sedan he noticed at the Hereford airport the day he and Shep searched for drugs at Spinner's office.

"I never did see his face but I did notice that the license plate on the car was out of state. That's kinda a hobby I got, checking license plates to see how many states I can count in a day. I remember that was the last one that day, twelve. You know, that's a lot of different states for one day, especially since I got 'em all right here in Amarillo, while I was driving to and from work. Most I ever counted was twenty-two--that was the day I was driving down to Plainview and had a chance to see more cars."

Buster nodded his head in agreement, smiled and waited for Junior to get back to the subject at hand.

Junior paused, remembering that Buster had asked about the spray plane, then continued. "I remember it was kinda strange the way Spinner acted that night. He walked to his plane, opened the cap to the spray tank, dumped in something he had in his hand, couldn't have been more'n a half-pint, screwed the cap back on, got in the plane and took off. That's the last I seen of him. Next thing I know, I see his picture in the paper and read where he's been murdered."

"Any chance you might remember what state?" Buster

asked, pulling his notepad and pen out of his shirt pocket.

"You mean the license plate?"

"That's right," Buster nodded.

Deep in thought, Junior finally answered, "Yeah, it was Nevada. I remember that big old black car and thought at the time, I bet it belonged to one of them Las Vegas gamblers. Yeah, I'm certain, it was Nevada alright."

"What about the plane, Junior, you remember anything unusual about it?" Buster asked as he wrote in his notepad.

"I guess not," Junior replied, "It was just an ordinary Cessna spray plane. I did think it kinda strange that he would be flying a spray plane around that time of year and at night. There was one thing, now that you mention it. He had his spray tank full of water--no chemical, just water. I don't see very many spray planes and I was just looking it over while I fueled her up and pulled the cap off the tank and noticed it was full but didn't have any odor. Yes sir, I'd swear, it was just plain water. And you know, that wasn't more'n a week before I read in the paper about him being found murdered. Ain't that something!"

Buster smiled and allowed as how it really was something. "You've got a good memory, Junior. You've been a big help and I want you to know I appreciate it."

Junior beamed at the compliment.

Buster gave Junior one of his business cards and asked him to call if he remembered anything else, then walked to his Blazer and headed for Hereford, thinking to himself that it had been a good day. Some of the missing pieces were beginning to fall into place.

"Unit three, this is base. Have you got a copy?"

"Base, Unit three. I'm just leaving Amarillo, Irene. What have you got?"

"Buster, Pete must have come down with a stomach virus or something--got sick to his stomach awhile ago and went home. He wants you to take his place at the reception for the Governor and the President this afternoon at the airport. They're going to be making a tour of some of the yards and get acquainted with some of our problems."

"O.K. Irene, I knew they were coming and was trying to get back into town before they arrived. I should make it in plenty of time."

The country and western music program on the radio was interrupted by an updated weather bulletin. "The National Weather Service has just issued a winter storm watch for to-morrow afternoon and tomorrow night," the voice said. "Winds of forty to fifty miles an hour from the north are expected as the fast moving cold front reaches the Texas Panhandle. Warm, moist air, moving up from the south is expected to override the cold air and result in heavy snow. Stockmen are asked to take precautions."

He went through two more check-points between Amarillo and Hereford and the thought occurred to him that it was going to be rough on these MP's having to stand out in the cold, if the weatherman was right about heavy snow.

Buster remembered his dad telling him that one of the worst blizzards he had ever seen occurred on April 5, 1937. *Could be time for another April blizzard,* he thought.

* * * * * *

Meanwhile, the wheels of government had started rolling. Mayors of several West Texas towns had sent a request to
the Governor and to the President, asking that the quarantined area be declared a disaster area. Realizing the chance
for a photo opportunity and the need to let the voters know
that he was staying on top of the problem, the President had
agreed to meet the Governor in Hereford. As Buster approached the airport, he could see hundreds of citizens, and
as many media persons, lined up next to the small operations
building, waiting for the two dignitaries to arrive. Buster
pulled off Highway 60 and drove the short distance to the
runway. Flipping on his flashing lights, the crowd parted for
him and he drove up behind the group of Secret Service vehicles parked next to the building.

As he opened the door to his Blazer, he spotted Ace Belton standing next to the mayor. Before he could approach
them, however, two burly men with small hearing devices
stuck in their ears, grabbed him and asked where he thought
he was going.

Ace saw the activity, walked over and spoke to the Secret
Service agent. "Better watch it, Jones, this is his county and
if he's anything like his boss, the High Sheriff, he might just
run you in for interfering with the law."

The two agents released Buster and smiled as Belton introduced them to Deputy Thornton. Buster informed them of
the sheriff's illness and that he would be taking his place in
the reception.

The Governor's plane was the first one to land. An area was roped off, where several microphones were tied together on a makeshift podium and the mayor had even spread a small red carpet behind the podium upon which the dignitaries would stand. The Governor and his entourage deplaned and began shaking hands with local politicians while they awaited the arrival of the President.

Buster learned that Air Force One had landed at Amarillo and the President would be flown down by helicopter since the runway at Hereford *International* was much too short for the huge jet.

After shaking hands with the mayor, Governor Rose spotted Buster, smiled and grabbed his hand. "Buster, how the heck are you?" he said.

"I'm fine, Governor. It's been awhile, didn't reckon you'd remember me."

"Remember you? How on earth you suppose I could forget you. For four years you and George Autry kept stealing the heading and heeling championship away from me and Carlton Hendrix. That's been a sore spot with me ever since--letting a couple of Texas Tech cowboys beat the University's star ropers"

Buster shook the governor's hand and said with a grin, "If I'd have known you was going to be Governor some day, I might have let you win one or two."

Governor Rose laughed, then glanced upwards.

The presidential helicopter could be seen coming in low for a landing, and as Governor Rose turned to get into the welcoming line, he said, "If you've got nothing better to do, why don't you join me in my car while we tour the area. Maybe you can give me some pointers how I can improve my heeling?"

"It'd be an honor, Governor," Buster replied.

The President stepped out of the huge helicopter along with the Secretary of Agriculture, the FDA Administrator and several aids. He shook hands with Governor Rose, who in turn introduced him to Mayor Barnett and the other dignitaries waiting in line.

As the President approached, Buster watched, feeling a bit nervous. Suddenly it dawned upon him that this man put his pants on the same way all men do and that he was no better or no worse than the people who were lined up greeting him. *Probably not enjoying this any more than I am,* he thought.

"Mr. President, I'd like for you to meet my good friend, Buster Thornton--best damned steer roper that ever slung a rope," the governor said in introduction.

"Buster," the President said, as he squeezed his hand in a firm handshake, "Jim's been telling me I need to get off the golf course and onto a horse. Maybe someday I'll be able to do that and the two of you can teach me the gentle art of heading and heeling."

"I'd like that, Mr. President," Buster responded, then looking at the Governor and smiling, added, "You might ought to steer clear of them tea sippers down at Austin, though--I don't think they ever learned the difference between goat roping and calf roping."

The President laughed as he moved to the next person in

line.

After the introductions were made, Governor Rose and the President walked to the podium and the Governor made a few remarks about the terrible epidemic and how the state would do everything in its power to help the Panhandle area cope with the situation, then introduced the President.

"I am glad to be able to visit the great state of Texas," he began, "But not proud to be coming under these circumstances. What I've been hearing and what I've been seeing on television makes my heart go out to you. I am not here to determine *if* the federal government should or should not help you in this hour of need, that has already been determined. I am here, however, to see where this aid can best be utilized and to listen to your suggestions as to how the government can serve your needs tomorrow and in the days to come. Federal aid in the form of long term, low interest loans is available for areas which have been declared disaster areas. Your Mayor and Governor have requested that I declare this a national disaster--I will be making an announcement concerning that request immediately after touring some of the affected area."

The southwest wind was bringing the pungent odor of death from one of the nearby feed yards, the President pulled his handkerchief from his pocket, wiped his nose and eyes, looked up at the hundreds of buzzards circling over the area, and added, "This stink alone should qualify you for everything that the federal government can do."

Pausing, he raised his hand, fist clutched tight, and said with bitterness in his voice, "I promise you, the perpetrators of this foul deed will be caught and punished. And, if it is proven that any nation on the face of this earth has instigated the spread of this disease, that nation will suffer the full wrath of the United States Government."

He turned and followed the secret service agents to the waiting automobiles. Buster joined the Governor in a black Chevrolet Suburban, along with the driver and two body guards.

The vehicles pulled out and headed for the Autry Feed Yard, west of town.

George joined the President in his van when it reached his feed yard, and directed the driver to the back side of the yard, where huge bulldozers and payloaders were busy digging trenches and pulling the dead cattle from the pens for burial.

They passed stacks of dead animals, which had been piled, waiting for the trenches to be completed.

Pointing to the piles, George informed the President, "In the past we would have been allowed to soak the carcasses in diesel fuel and burn them but the damned EPA won't allow it today --air pollution laws. So we just have to pile them up and wait until we can get another grave dug."

"I see," the President replied, "And there is nothing I can do about that. EPA regulations even supersede the power of the presidency. I'll see that you get more equipment from the Corps of Engineers so that you can get the cattle buried faster."

George had the driver stop next to a pit where sick cattle were being driven into a completed pit, in preparation to be shot by the waiting riflemen. The entourage stepped from their vehicles and climbed to the top of the dirt embankment, surrounding the pit and watched as the riflemen began to methodically execute the cattle. Cameras rolled as some of the weaker-stomached newsmen were forced to return to the vehicles, unable to bear the sight of the slaughter. Buster and the Governor stood to one side and watched as one after the other of the cattle were hit by the high-powered rifle slugs and fell in their tracks.

Secret Service agents were all looking into the pit, unable to believe their eyes as the two cowboy executioners fired accurately into the crowded cattle.

They didn't hear, nor did any of the others, the silenced shot that came from four hundred yards away behind one of the adjoining mounds of dirt. Governor Jim Rose, a split second before the shot, leaned towards Buster to say something in his ear, placed his hand on Buster's shoulder, causing Buster to lean just a little to the left. The Governor's wrist was shattered as a bullet, meant for Buster, tore through the bone.

The governor fell against Buster, as he realized he had been shot. Buster could see the blood gushing from the severed artery and shouted at the agents for help, as he pulled his bandana from his pocket and quickly applied a tourniquet above the wound.

The President's bodyguards rushed him to his vehicle as others surrounded Buster and the Governor.

"What the hell happened?" one of them shouted as he searched the area with his eyes, seeing no one but the two riflemen in the vicinity.

"Bullet must have ricocheted off the skull of one of those animals and hit me in the wrist," the Governor said, as he walked unassisted towards the Suburban. Smiling weakly at Buster, he joked, "Looks like we'll have to wait a spell before you give me that lesson on how to throw a rope."

Everybody accepted the Governor's theory that a bullet ricocheting from one of the slaughtered animals had hit his wrist--everyone except a Mexican-looking cowboy hidden behind a pile of dirt a quarter of a mile away with a smoking scoped rifle in his hand.

"Damn!" Tony said, as he watched the entourage leave the area, lights flashing in their rush to get the Governor to the Deaf Smith County Hospital. "That deputy must have nine lives. I'd have gotten the bastard if the Governor hadn't gotten in the way."

He would wait in his hiding place until dark, then slip back to his white Ford pickup truck, that was parked at the back side of the feed yard and return to Amarillo.

* * * * * *

Upon returning to the nation's capital, President Clifford announced that ten of the West Texas counties were to be declared disaster areas and all businesses within that area would be eligible for federal economic assistance. At his news conference, he also assured the American people that all law enforcement agencies within the federal government were put on full alert to make certain that all public utilities would be protected from future terrorist acts. In addition, he stated, he had instructed the aircraft carrier *Enterprise* and two destroyers, which were on patrol in the Indian Ocean, to steam to the Persian Gulf, where they would prepare to strike targets in Iraq and Iran if any more terrorist acts were to take place. Secretary of State Shaw and National Security Adviser Kazinski were in flight to Switzerland to meet with Iraqi and Iranian representatives to try to cool the volatile situation, he said.

* * * * * *

In response to the President's announcement, the CIA and the FBI were instructed to combine their efforts in an all-out effort to investigate the possibilities of additional terrorist actions using biological warfare against the U.S. Because of the seriousness of the situation, Vice President John Lee was given the responsibility to coordinate this effort.

"If you were a terrorist," Vice President Lee asked the members of the task force, as they sat in the huge board room of the Federal Bureau of Investigation in Washington, D.C., "Where would you concentrate your efforts if you wanted to cause additional damage to the American economy?"

CIA agent Phil Adams responded by making a statement. "If I were a terrorist, under the present conditions which exist in the U.S., where all of our federal agencies as well as many state and local agencies are operating on a high priority alert against terrorism, I would pack my bags and catch the first plane out for Iran or Iraq. I think they are smart enough to realize that this is no time to accelerate their activities against our nation."

"I disagree," FBI agent Bob Campbell interjected. "There are many places and industries where they could strike with impunity, with almost absolute assurance that they would not be caught. And I am certain they would consider this a prime time to increase their activities, while the panic is going on."

"For instance," the VP asked as he took a sip of water from the glass, which had been placed next to the podium.

"For instance, that water you just drank. A fishing boat with a couple of anglers cruising on the reservoir, where that water has been stored could dump their virus, load their boat and be gone days before any ill effects would surface in the cities serviced by water from that reservoir."

Vice President Lee nervously looked at the half-empty water glass and returned it to the table.

"I disagree with that hypothesis," a young CIA agent at the rear said. "I don't know the concentration level of these viruses. But it would appear to me that to contaminate the water in a large reservoir, sufficient enough to cause an epidemic; would require such a large amount of the material, that a small fishing boat would be unable to conceal it, until it was dumped into the water. With armed guards patrolling all of the large reservoirs, it would be too dangerous for them to attempt such an activity. Also, to smuggle that amount of bacterial agents into the country would be difficult, if not impossible."

Heads around the table nodded in agreement to this statement.

"O.K., let's assume that striking against our water supply

would not be feasible. Are there other suggestions?"

"Yes, sir!" FBI Director Barney Dunlap, from the Kansas City Regional Office, answered as he stood to make a point.

"If I were a terrorist, I would have three priorities: one,easy access; two, wide distribution, and three, time delay. In the Midwest where I am stationed, we have an industry which is prime for all three of those requirements.

"Let's remember, they have already struck at one of our food chains, the beef producing industry. And I must say, it was a very successful operation. So far we have not uncovered one concrete shred of evidence as to who started this epidemic or how it was done. Their mind-set is going to be such that they will look for other related industries. The grain storage industry, which is concentrated across the nation's heartland would be a prime target.

"I can take you to dozens of grain elevators within fifty miles of Kansas City, where millions of bushels of wheat are stored and where there are no fences and no guards. Anyone could enter those premises, dump a quart of highly concentrated Anthrax or similar virus in the dump pit without detection. The virus would be scattered throughout the system as the grain is elevated and moved from one grain tank to another.

"It might be a day, week or even a month before that wheat would be loaded and transported to a flour mill, ground into flour and shipped to a bakery where it would be made into bread. Of course, our terrorists would be long gone before we realized we had a problem, and the bread would be finding its way to the tables of every consumer in the nation."

"Mr. President, give me twenty highly trained terrorists and I will contaminate fifty percent of this nation's wheat supplies in less than a week!"

Once again, heads around the table began to nod in the affirmative, agreeing with Director Dunlap's hypothesis.

Vice President Lee said nothing for a full minute, his mind absorbing the seriousness of such a scenario. When he did speak, it was nearly a whisper. "My God! They could destroy half of the population if they were successful and we would never know it was taking place until it was too late!"

"We know that it would be relatively easy to smuggle in contaminants across the Mexican border. In fact, it apparently has already happened with the Foot and Mouth virus. And we know that it is possible to spread the virus with little chance of detection--and we know that it is virtually impossible to find the perpetrators, after they have completed their mission. Barney, you know how these storage facilities operate, how do we prevent such a scenario from happening?"

Barney Dunlap, six feet four inches tall and weighing nearly two hundred and fifty pounds, remained standing. Leaned with both palms resting firmly on the polished table top, and slowly turned his head to look squarely at each of the twenty-two persons seated at the table.

Clearing his throat, he spoke. "To prevent it, we must place guards at each facility twenty-four hours a day, seven days a week. Shipments must be terminated immediately until samples of grain from each bin, in each facility, can be taken to be certain that no grain has already been contaminated."

"Most of the wheat is shipped from the elevators to the flour mills in rail cars. Guards should also be stationed on the trains to make certain that the wheat is not contaminated, in route. We are talking about a very large number of security personnel--more than our two agencies can provide. A request should be made to the President to provide army personnel for that duty.

"Security is not as lax at the flour mills, although they could also be a target and should be made as secure as possible."

Agent Campbell put forth his hand for recognition and the VP nodded to him. "I grew up on a farm just outside of Champaign, Illinois, in the middle of the corn belt. You've been talking about the problems with protecting our wheat supplies, but the same problems exist in the corn industry. It is harvested the same way, stored the same way and processed into food the same way. Contaminated corn could spread the virus to the consumers dinner table just as readily as contaminated wheat. And the farmers delivery point for corn, the storage facilities, are just as unprotected as the delivery point for wheat."

"I agree," Dunlap nodded, "Which means that if we are to be absolutely certain that our nation's food supply is protected, every facility which stores any kind of raw food products must be placed under government security. That's going to be one helluva problem!"

"No matter how difficult the problem, the seriousness of the situation warrants that we do whatever is necessary to prevent such a scenario from happening," Vice President Lee responded. "We know that whoever is behind these terrorist acts is committed to do as much damage to our nation as possible. We must be just as committed to prevent them from being successful. I will carry this information to the President and the Cabinet and see that immediate action is taken to make all of our storage facilities as secure as possible."

11

Buster left the courthouse and walked west to Main Street where the Texas Department for Contagious Disease Control had set up an office in one of the empty business buildings. Like most small towns in rural America, that are dependent on agriculture for their economic welfare, Hereford had fallen on hard times due to the low prices for farm commodities. There were many empty buildings which once had housed thriving businesses. Government agencies had taken over several of them.

He stepped into the newly decorated office and asked the receptionist to see Dr. Turner, who had temporarily set up shop in Deaf Smith County to monitor the spread of the Foot and Mouth epidemic. The receptionist, after a short intercom conversation with the head of the TDCDC, directed Buster to enter one of the offices.

"Good morning, Deputy Thornton," Dr. Turner said. "What can I do for you?"

"Good morning, Dr. Turner," Buster replied. "I've been thinking about this cattle epidemic and thought maybe you could answer a couple of questions for me."

"I'll certainly try," the veterinarian said with a smile. "However, I'm discovering every day that there's a lot more I don't know about this disease than what I do know. I may not have your answers."

Buster took the chair indicated by the animal doctor, leaned forward and spoke. "Maybe, as a start, you could educate me a little on the disease. I don't know a damned thing about it, except it causes blisters in the mouth and sore feet on the animals."

Dr. Turner thought for awhile before answering, filling his pipe and lighting it, then responded. "I'm certain that you are probably aware by now that Aphthous fever, or Foot and Mouth Disease--also known as FMD--is one of the most dreaded of the animal diseases."

"Highly contagious, it not only affects cattle but also affects all cloven-footed animals such as swine, sheep and goats. It is important to note that there are no authenticated cases where it has affected humans."

Pausing, the vet placed the stem of his pipe into his mouth and puffed, looked towards the ceiling and blew a smoke plume upwards. Remaining in that position for a few seconds as if contemplating his next statement, then returning his gaze back to Buster, pointed the stem of the pipe towards the deputy, and continued.

"My research has turned up nine different outbreaks of FMD in the United States since 1870, the last occurring in

California in 1929. In 1914 an outbreak occurred which eventually engulfed 22 states and was not declared controlled until 1916; but only after 77,200 cattle, 85,000 swine and 9,767 sheep had been destroyed. In the 1924 through 1925 outbreak in California, over 58,000 cattle, 21,000 swine and 28,000 sheep were slaughtered to control the spread of the disease. I might add that several thousand wild animals such as deer were also infected and destroyed."

"But the worst outbreak on the North American continent occurred in Mexico in 1946, when over a million cattle were slaughtered in an effort to control the epidemic. This method of control has been labeled *the stamping-out method*."

"Under this program, a complete isolation of infected premises, with prohibition of traffic, therefrom, pending disposal of animals, disinfection, and testing is required."

"Prompt slaughter and proper disposal of animals infected with or even exposed to FMD is paramount in the program to prevent the possibility of carriers."

"Slaughter and burial or cremation are done as soon as possible after the establishment of a diagnosis. And of course, quarantines are essential to make the program successful."

Pausing, Dr. Turner rummaged through some of the papers stacked on his desk, before continuing. Then, looking up and shaking his head, as if finding what he was searching for was futile, continued.

"It is my understanding that quarantines will continue in force until all premises have been disinfected and tested, to be absolutely certain that no active virus continues to exist in the soil or in materials stored on the premises."

"Indemnities are to be paid by federal and state governments to owners of animals or property destroyed in the course of eradicating FMD. That, of course, is what the law specifies, but since we have never been confronted with such a tremendous outbreak as this; it remains to be seen whether one hundred percent reimbursement to livestock owners will be made by the federal government."

"So you see, Buster, we have adequate reasons to be concerned about controlling this outbreak in the most timely manner; before it engulfs the entire cattle, hog and sheep population in the United States."

"I understand the seriousness of the situation, Dr. Turner," Buster responded. "And can see the need for stamping out the spread of the virus; but I suppose what I am trying to determine is how this epidemic started. As I understand it, the FBI and CIA are pretty certain that foreign terrorists are responsible and did it by smuggling in some Foot and Mouth virus and spreading it around the feed yards. I don't have any idea what the stuff looks like, how it is packaged or how potent it might be. If it actually was dumped on these feed yards, how much do you suppose it would take: a ton, a barrel or what?"

Pausing, he pulled a cigarette from his pocket and lit it before continuing. "You know--I was just wondering how much of the damned stuff it would take to contaminate such a large area?"

Nodding his head in understanding, Dr. Turner answered, "We've talked about this question, to some degree, in several of our meetings in Austin. Just like you, I did not know just how potent these biological compounds can be. We had a specialist come in from D.C. who has been monitoring Iraq's capability to manufacture viruses for several years. He told us that a quart of highly concentrated anthrax virus could infect all of the people in New York City with the proper distribution process. I'm assuming that Foot and Mouth virus would be comparable with cattle."

Buster whistled, then exclaimed, "If that's the case a pint of the stuff would be enough to infect all of the cattle in West Texas."

"You're right, Buster, Frightening, isn't it?"

After a short pause when neither of the two spoke, Buster asked, " O.K. Doc, the sixty-four dollar question. What would you consider a proper distribution process?"

Without hesitation, Dr. Turner replied, "To cause that much damage with such a small amount of the virus, would require contamination of the water or air supply."

"And I assume that you have tested the water supply at these contaminated feedlots."

"That's the first thing we did, all of them, and we found nothing," the vet said.

Buster scratched his head, then his chin, and said, "Well, it's your opinion then, there's only one way it could have been done --by air--is that correct?"

Dr. Turner looked at him without blinking and replied, "Yes, that's the conclusion I came to, but understand, it is *only my opinion*. You see, we have found no evidence that the air was contaminated. Of course, the air could be contaminated one minute and clear the next, with these hellacious West Texas winds blowing fifty miles an hour. We have, however, found large concentrations of the virus in the manure in the lots, which we speculated was passed through the animals in their feces. I must tell you, Buster, we are at a loss to pinpoint how this virus was spread over such a large area, in such a short period of time, but I am convinced that this is no accidental epidemic. I sincerely believe that terrorists, some way, are responsible, and that they did it to prove to us that even the U.S. food supply is not safe from their actions."

"Well, with all the government agents working on the case, we will surely know the answers before long. Maybe they'll apprehend those two Iraqis, who were in the area, and they will shed some light on the situation," Buster said as he stood and walked to the door.

"Thank you, Dr. Turner. If you learn anything new, I would certainly appreciate a call," he said as he exited the office and walked back to the courthouse parking lot, stepped into his Blazer and turned on the ignition key. His intentions were to make a run out to Autry's feed yard to see how his old friend George was holding up under the pressure, and discuss the upcoming rodeo in which they were entered for the heading and heeling competition. Before he hit the starter he heard the radio squawk.

"Unit three, this is Sheriff Blackwell , what's your 1020?"

"Unit three here, Pete. I'm just leaving the parking lot. What's up?" Buster responded.

"Better come to my office right away," Sheriff Blackwell

said, "I may have something for you."

Buster turned off the ignition, stepped out of the Blazer and walked towards the back door of the courthouse. He failed to notice the white Ford pickup, with the Mexican cowboy, parked across the street. The cowboy seemed to be reading a paper; but his eyes were following Buster as he entered the courthouse. As Buster turned his back to the pickup, the cowboy held his hand out the window, thumb up and forefinger pointed in Buster's direction as if holding a gun and said softly, "Bang! You're dead, deputy!"

Sheriff Blackwell sat behind his desk, absorbed in a report which he was holding in his hand. As Buster entered, he held up the report and said, "Take a look at this."

Buster took the lab report and noted that it was an analysis of the sample he had taken from the loading pad at Murphy's Spraying Service. He whistled as he saw that the sample indicated a large concentration of Foot and Mouth bacteria in the dirt, as well as human blood, type O, and minute amounts of human tissue.

"Where the hell did you get that sample," Pete asked.

"You know those concrete pads where the spray boys wash down their planes? Well, I dug that dirt out of the drain at Spinner's pad," Buster replied.

The look on Sheriff Blackwell's face was one of astonishment and disbelief as he got to his feet and started pacing the floor. Buster said nothing, as he waited for some kind of response, realizing that the importance of this evidence was becoming apparent to his boss.

Finally Pete stopped his pacing and spoke. "Type O,

that's the same type as Spinner's. Damned if you wasn't right, Buster, about Spinner's murder and this cattle disease being connected. It looks like Spinner may have sold out to those Iraqis and helped them infect these feedlot cattle. Then for some reason, they killed him right there on his drain pad. We better get Ace Belton in here and let him know what we've found."

"Maybe we hadn't ought to jump to conclusions here, Pete," Buster said. "I'm sure we've stumbled onto some important evidence in our murder investigation; but I'm not convinced that the FBI and the CIA are on the right track about terrorists being behind this thing. Give me a few more days before we call Ace and his boys in on this, there's a couple of loose ends I need to tie up that may answer some unanswered questions."

"What kind of questions?" Pete asked.

"Like why would Spinner be involved in such a terrible crime--if he was--and why would he be murdered after he did such an excellent job for whoever hired him. You'd think whoever was paying him would give him a bonus instead of a bullet in the back of the head. Could be he stumbled onto some information that he didn't need to know and got himself killed for it. I'm going to take another look around over at his house and out at the airport. We may have overlooked something, thinking that he was involved in drugs," Buster answered.

"O.K., a couple more days and then we're going to have to share what we've got with the feds," Pete said.

* * * * * *

The rodeo was scheduled for Saturday, just two weeks away, at the Billings roping arena, and George and Buster had been unable to practice because of the murder and the cattle epidemic. Buster pulled past the quarantine sign with his pickup and into the Autry feed yard, parked and walked into George's office.

"Thought I best check on you and see if you're ready for the nut house yet," he joked as he shook hands with his friend.

"Just about," George said, unable to smile at the pun, "But maybe I'll be able to live through this since the government has agreed to reimburse our customers for their cattle. There's still going to be one helluva loss, though, because we are having to feed those cattle remaining in the lot until we can get around to killing them. And we can only kill and bury about a thousand a day."

"Forty thousand head, that's going to take you forty days at that rate," Buster calculated, then added, "Forty days and nights, sounds like the good Lord got you mixed up with old Noah."

"Yeah, we've got another twenty thousand head to go, another twenty days of rain," George said, shaking his head and managing to smile meekly, realizing that Buster was try-ing to lift his spirits. "However, the feed bill gets less every day; because most of the cattle are showing signs of infection and the first thing that happens is, their mouths get so sore with the blisters that they can't eat or drink. One thing about

172

it, though, we're not having to shoot nearly as many, since most of them are dying from the disease. I'm afraid they're going to start dying faster than we can bury them. Can you imagine the time, the equipment and the manpower required to drag a thousand head of steers from their pens to the pits, one at a time. And we've got to do that every damned day. The Corps of Engineers has been a big help though, those big pay-loaders of theirs will move a lot of material in a hurry."

"This is about the craziest thing I've ever seen?" Buster sympathized. "I remember reading my history book, back when I was a kid, about the time when Colonel McKenzie caught all of the Plains Indians down in Palo Duro Canyon back in 1875 and captured all their horses--over a thousand head. He herded them out of the canyon and down towards Tule Creek where he corralled them and shot every last one of them so the Indians couldn't steal them back. I thought at the time I read that, it was a terrible thing to do to horses; but that was nothing compared to what we're having to do today to cattle to keep this disease from spreading."

George ran his fingers through his hair and nodded his head in agreement. "Well, we've faced some hard times in the cattle business before and have always been able to work our way out of it. I suppose we'll be able to weather this storm; but right now it looks pretty hopeless. What brought you out this way? I figured you had your hands full trying to solve that Murphy murder."

"You're right about that," Buster answered. "But I decided you and I both need some rest and relaxation. You know, we're still signed up for the rodeo and it's less than three weeks off. We probably ought to get in a little practice before the weather changes--supposed to snow tonight according to the weatherman. If we don't get the rust out of our bones we're liable to get out there and make fools of ourselves."

George pulled himself up from his chair and put on his hat before responding. "I believe that's just what the doctor ordered, Buster. I've been stuck in this damned office for over a month and it's about to drive me crazy. I need to get away from this smell of death and see if I can't get my priorities back in order. Let's get the horses and take the rest of the day off."

As they drove to the horse corrals, George asked, "Have you heard how the Governor's getting along? I certainly hated he got hurt, especially here at my pens."

"Pete had a call this morning from the Governor's press secretary. She said he was doing fine, they were able to patch the artery and set the bone. He's going to have to wear the cast a couple of months but will be as good as new after the cast is removed. Guess he was lucky, at that. He could have caught that slug in his chest instead of his arm."

"Yeah, and you could have caught the slug in the back of your head instead of it hitting the Governor's wrist. I'd say you was pretty lucky yourself!" George responded, then added. "You know, Buster, I've been thinking. The slugs from those high-powered rifles my boys were using to kill the cattle have a lot of force behind them, enough force to penetrate the toughest bones in those animals. I can't understand how one could ricochet upward out of that pit the way it did when it hit the Governor."

174

"I've been thinking the same thing, George," Buster replied, "That bullet could have come from somewhere else, but why do you suppose someone would want to shoot the Governor? It doesn't make sense."

"Maybe it wasn't the Governor they intended to shoot. That bullet didn't miss you by more'n six inches. You need to remember that someone's been after your ass ever since you started investigating Spinner's murder. That bullet could have been meant for you."

Buster didn't respond to that statement, just nodded his head in agreement as he opened the door of the truck and walked to the horse corral.

They hooked the trailer onto the Blazer, loaded the two horses and headed for Billings arena. A white Ford pickup, parked on the shoulder of the highway, pulled out and followed them, remaining a half-mile behind. The swarthy looking cowboy driving it, smiled to himself, as he contemplated his next move.

Several ropers were just finishing their practice session as Buster and George unloaded their horses. Two cowboys, employees of James Billings, were driving the roping steers back to the chute, another cowboy was ready to hold the first steer in the chute and release him for the next team. No one was paying attention to the cowboy who stepped from his white Ford pickup and took a position at the far end of the roping arena, hidden from view by the fence. He watched as Buster and George positioned their horses on either side of the holding chute, motioned for the chute operator to release the steer, and spurred their horses in hot pursuit of the excited animal.

George's loop fell around the steer's horns and Buster's loop snaked beneath the steer's belly. In less than seven seconds, the steer lay stretched between the two horses. The cowboy behind the fence watched the process intently, going over in his mind the right moment when he could pull the trigger of the thirty-ought-six and put this meddling deputy out of the picture.

Bunch of yokels, he said to himself as he returned to the pickup and left the arena. He could do it the day of the rodeo when the stands were full of spectators. No one could see him behind the fence and he should be able to get away during the confusion, as they would all be watching the deputy as he fell from his horse.

Buster and George continued to practice with several more cowboys for most of the afternoon, roping five head, relaxing and shaking some of the cobwebs out of their minds. As they opened the gate and led their horses to the trailer, the wind shifted from the southwest to the north, kicking up dust.

"Well, if we can do as well in competition as we did today, we should be in the money," George said, as his sorrel jumped into the trailer.

"Yeah," Buster agreed. "If those cowboys we roped with today are any indication of the competition, we should take top money!"

They both laughed at the thought as the Blazer headed for town. Clouds had blocked out the sun before they reached the feed yard to unload their horses and a few large, wet snowflakes had begun to fall.

"Looks like the weatherman was right for a change,"
George said as he pulled the saddle from the sorrels back. "I
wouldn't mind seeing a little moisture to settle this dust, but
we don't need a blizzard. We got enough problems trying to
keep these dead cattle buried before they start stinking."

"I hear what you're saying but it don't look good. It's not
going to take much snow with this wind to cause us a lot of
problems, drifts could block all our roads."

Leaving George at the office, Buster headed for town and
pulled his Blazer onto the driveway at Spinner's home in the
southwest part of Hereford. It was an ordinary looking house,
three bedrooms, two baths with attached garage. Buster noted
that the exterior, brick and wood trim, was freshly painted
indicating that Spinner had been proud of his home. He
made a mental note that the grass needed mowing and it was
probably the county's responsibility to get someone to do it.,
since it was still roped off as an evidence area.

He remembered that one of Spinner's close friends told
him that as soon as the home was paid for, he was going to
start looking for a wife to help him enjoy it. Maybe if things
had worked out different, Cristy would have been that woman
and they both would still be alive.

Buster walked to the door, unlocked it and entered. The
inside of the house was as neat as the outside, not cluttered, as
with many bachelor pads he had visited. Nothing had been
disturbed since he had searched it with the drug dog after the
murder. He walked slowly through the house, touching nothing but just looking, hoping that something might indicate further searching was needed. When he had gone through all

the rooms without recognizing anything unusual, he began to look in drawers, behind pictures, under and inside of books, in trash cans and clothes closets; looking for nothing in particular but hoping that something would turn up.

The thought entered his mind that the house appeared to have been cleaned and straightened the way Spinner's hanger and planes had been cleaned. There should have been something out of place--a newspaper or a pair of shoes--something!

He walked to the kitchen, opened the cabinet, removed a water glass, filled it at the kitchen sink and drank. With his back to the sink and leaning against the cabinet, he found himself unconsciously gazing at the refrigerator as he sipped the water. Setting the glass down on the cabinet top, he stepped to the refrigerator and opened the door.

Like most bachelor's refrigerators, it had little food, a package of salami, cheese which was beginning to mold, a dozen eggs, a pound of bacon, a six pack of beer and three cokes. He took out one of the cans of beer and subconsciously opened it and took a sip. As he started to close the refrigerator door, a brown prescription bottle caught his eye and he picked it up, holding it to the light so he could read the prescription---cough syrup, prescribed by one of the local physicians. Buster put it close to his ear and shook it but heard no sound of liquid.

Strange, he thought. Why would anyone want to keep cough syrup in a refrigerator? Especially an empty cough syrup bottle?

The bottle had one of those safety caps and Buster cursed,

before he finally read the directions to *push down and turn slowly*. The cap slipped off, revealing a tightly rolled piece of paper inside.

Removing the paper, he unrolled it and read, *They told me that it was only a chemical which would make all of the cattle in the feedlots sick for about three weeks but wouldn't hurt them physically. They said it would cause a panic at the Chicago Board of Trade and we could make a good profit in the futures' market. When they insisted that I wash every trace of the chemical out of my tanks and off the plane, I became suspicious. I asked them what the chemical was and they told me that I had spread a deadly virus which would kill the cattle, and that I would be the one prosecuted if the officials ever found out. When I found out the truth, I decided to go to the authorities. Maybe it's not too late, maybe an antidote is available. I'm sorry, I should not have listened to them. If they knew I am thinking of going to the authorities, they would kill me. I must be careful, they are vicious. Tomorrow I'll tell Sheriff Blackwell.*

The note was unsigned; but Buster could tell by the handwriting that it was written by a person who was very nervous and frightened, some of the words were hardly legible.

Greed, Buster thought, *that's what got Spinner killed. He just couldn't stand the temptation to make lots of money fast. And look at all the problems and hardship his greed has caused.*

He locked the house and walked to the Blazer, head down and unconsciously pulling his coat collar up as protection against the cold north wind and the heavy snow. He failed to notice the white Ford pickup down the street and the man standing by its side with what looked like a rifle in his hand.

I'm not waiting another two weeks to finish this job. This hick cop must have found something or he wouldn't be back at Murphy's house, Tony told himself. He pulled the rifle to his shoulder as Buster reached for the door of the Blazer, but before he could get a good bead on his target, a blanket of snow was blown between the two, obliterating his view. The Blazer pulled away from the curb and disappeared around the corner; while he stood cursing his luck.

"Damn," he said as he placed the rifle behind the seat and shut the door.

Snow was falling so thickly that Tony could hardly see the road as he pulled onto the highway and headed for Amarillo, angry with himself for not taking a shot. *Probably should have done it today at the arena. No telling how long I'll have to stay in this godforsaken country, before I get another chance,* he said under his breath. *We should have let those Iraqis do it their way, then I wouldn't have to be trying to cover our tracks.*

* * * * * *

Blizzard! The snow became heavier and heavier during the night and by morning the wind had drifted the snow across all the roads bringing traffic to a standstill. Interstate 40 from the Oklahoma line to Tucumcari, New Mexico, was blocked, as was Interstate 27 from the Kansas line to Lubbock, Texas. National Guardsmen and Army personnel, billeted in tents in the quarantined area shivered in their summer clothing as the winds piled snow four and five feet deep around their tents. The small propane heaters offered little comfort to the shivering men.

The National Guard Military Police, stationed at roadblocks around the area, were brought in from their positions, since it was apparent no traffic was going to be moving quarantined meat from the area until the storm let up and the roads were cleared.

All work in the feed yards was suspended and those cattle, that had not died from the virus, were left hungry and unattended because cowboys were unable to reach the yards from their homes in town. The winds continued to pile snow deeper and deeper in the yards, until drifts covered the fences and many of the healthier cattle were able to walk over the tops of the fence rails and out of the yards. With their tails to the wind, they drifted south, trying to find shelter from the wet snow and the cold. But there was no shelter on the flat prairies except for the scattered farmsteads which dotted the area. Many of them fell from exhaustion and were immediately covered by the blowing snow.

To add to the problem, thousands of head of healthy wheat pasture cattle, held inside the wheat fields by one strand of small electrified wire, pushed the wire down and drifted south, mixing with the infected feed yard cattle in their search for protection from the wind. There was nothing the cowboys could do to stop the migration until the snow let up and snowplows could open the roads.

Many of the cattle from yards and wheat fields to the north of town, invaded Hereford and found shelter behind the houses of homeowners. Yard fences were pushed over, flower beds and shrubs were trampled. Hereford, which had advertised to be the cattle feeding capital of the world, literally lived up to its advertisements and had more cattle inside the city limits than it had people.

Trains continued to run as the tracks remained clear due to the high winds. The engineers, unable to see more than fifty feet in front of the train because of the blowing snow, plowed through several herds of the migrating cattle, killing thousands which had bunched on top of the rails.

For two days the wind continued to pile the snow in huge drifts; but on the morning of the third day the wind calmed and the sun rose in a cloudless sky. By noon the temperature had risen to forty degrees, snow began to melt and traffic began to move slowly behind the snowplows. Four-wheel drive pickup trucks, dragging horse trailers, flooded the roads as cowboys began searching the snowscape for cattle and driving those that had survived the storm to the nearest holding pens. No one tried to identify ownership, that problem could be addressed after all the cattle had been rounded up. The immediate problem was to get the cattle off the roads and out of the towns.

Buster and George joined the roundup on their horses and after locating a large herd three miles south of the Autry feed yard, headed them back through the drifts towards the pens. Nearly half the herd carried brands which were unfamiliar to George.

"My grandad used to tell me about the old days when roundup time came in this country," he said as they pushed the cattle slowly northward. "Wasn't any fences then and he said all the ranchers and cowhands would meet together, spread out and round up all the cattle in a given area. They would then bring them to a central location where they were penned and divided into herds according to brands. Might be eight or ten ranches involved and it was a community project lasting several days. They even helped each other brand the newborn once the cows were identified."

Pausing, he removed a cigarette from his shirt pocket along with a Bic lighter and lit it before continuing. "Looks like we're going to be doing the same thing for the next few days, except on a much larger scale."

Buster nodded his head in agreement. "You've got that right, with a couple hundred different brands in each feed yard as well as all the different brands out here on wheat pasture, we may be until next Christmas getting them all sorted back out."

"Yeah, but the sad part of it is that once they are all sorted, we're probably going to have to kill every danged one of them, including the wheat pasture cattle. All because they've been exposed to the virus by mixing with the feedlot cattle. The good Lord must have it in for us cowboys to allow so many problems to happen all at once."

"Ain't the good Lord causing these problems, George, it's somebody's greed. Somebody that stands to make a ton of money out of your hardship. I haven't told anyone, except

Pete, that I have uncovered evidence that definitely proves this virus was intentionally spread, and the ones behind it knew what it would do to market prices. I've got a sneaking feeling that they bought long on the futures and stand to make billions before this thing is over."

"Buster, if you're right, when the sunzabitches are caught, I hope the feds will let me line them up in one of those pits and shoot every damned one of them and bury them with a bulldozer just like we've done with the cattle. To cause this much pain and suffering to livestock is as bad as murder and rape to human beings. No one should be allowed to get away with it."

"If I have my way, they're not going to get away with it, George," Buster shouted as he spurred his horse to head a steer that was trying to turn back to the south.

* * * * * *

Because of the numerous pens in the area and the thousands of mounted cowboys, in less than a week the cattle were all penned, separated and hauled back to their proper locations. TDCDC announced that the wheat pasture cattle were now quarantined and would be watched closely to see if any of them came down with the virus.

Warm, balmy weather descended on the plains, after the spring blizzard, and melted the snow. Thousands of dead cattle that had been covered in the drifts were discovered, identified and buried by the army. The feed yards once again began the slow process of destroying the sick and dying.

* * * * * *

    The U.S. Army was quick to react to the President's order to place armed guards at every facility where raw food products were stored. The nation's highways became filled with army vehicles carrying soldiers to designated locations. No mention was made by the government, to explain the reason for the troop movements, and the media speculated that it was in preparation for a strike against the Iraqis.

12

"Tony, the boys in Vegas have located the identity of the broad who was with that deputy in Las Vegas. They found a cocktail waitress at the Frontier who fingered the room where she was registered. Name's Jo Willman and she lives in Amarillo. We can't take any chances, since she was with him when he visited that Gale girl's room, she probably knows everything he knows about Murphy's association with us. She needs to be taken out of the picture just as soon as you take the deputy down," the brusque voice said impatiently over the telephone.

"Sure, boss," Tony replied as he lay on the bed in the motel, "But how am I going to locate her?"

"I don't want you doing anything," Seigle said. "You stay on that deputy's tail until you find the right time to finish that job. There's an Iranian in Boston I can hire to do the job and if he fouls up, the feds will suspect him to be one of the terrorists they're looking for. I don't want you to have any contact with him whatsoever."

"Why tell me this if you don't want me involved?" Tony asked puzzled.

"I want you to contact Rosellini, tell him to locate the Willman girl and tail her. We need to know everything she does, where she works, where she eats, what her daily schedule is. So our man can pick the best time and the best place to make it look like an accident."

"O.K., boss, but Slick ain't too dependable, he spends too much time with those girls that work for him," Tony replied.

"You tell him if he fouls up on this one, we *foreclose*, and not just on his business."

The next morning Tony showered and shaved, dressed in his cowboy duds and drove across town to Slick's strip joint on Amarillo Boulevard. Even early, there were a few night workers from the nearby packing plant who were starting their day with a few beers and ogling the lone, scantily clad stripper as she performed lazily before their greedy eyes. Tony watched as he slowly walked across the room and entered the office at the back.

Slick, lying on the couch and nearly nude was being rubbed down by a tall black girl with even less apparel covering her curvaceous body. He pushed her aside and pulled his round torso up from the couch and reached for his trousers as he spoke angrily, "Don't they teach you how to knock in Las Vegas before entering someone's private room?"

"Didn't realize it was all that private, Slick. At ten o'clock in the morning you'd think you had better things to do."

Glancing longingly at the black girl who was pulling a robe over her shoulders, Slick replied, "Just what better thing would you suggest for anytime during the day--or night?"

"You've got me there," Tony laughed, then added, "Get rid of her, we need to talk."

Slick motioned for the girl to leave, pulled his shirt from the chair and began dressing. "Must be something important to bring you across town this time of day."

"The boss called from Chicago, said they had located the trail of that deputy's girl friend. Name's Jo Willman and she lives here in Amarillo. The boss is afraid that she knows what was in that envelope that the Gale broad slipped them in Vegas, and whatever information was in that valise they picked up in Chicago. He's sending a guy down from Boston to take care of her, but wants you to locate where she lives, where she works and what she does with her spare time before he gets here."

Slick grumbled as he stuffed his shirt inside his trousers and buckled his belt around his size fifty midriff. "I ain't no good at that kind of job, Tony. Look at me, I'd stand out like a fox in a chicken house trying to tail a good looking broad a-round this town."

"The boss didn't ask if you was any good at it, just said for you to do it. You know how rough he can get if you cross him so I'd suggest you figure a way to get it done. It shouldn't be too hard. She ain't going to be suspecting nothing and you can just keep an eye on her from your car."

Reaching for the phone book on Slick's desk, Tony flipped the pages to the *W's* and followed his finger down the column to *Willman, Jo.*

"Here she is, lives in an apartment over on the west side of town. Just park out front and wait till she comes home from work, get a few pictures and follow her around for a few days. When the guy from Boston gets here, hand over the information and pictures and your job will be done. Shouldn't be no problem."

"That's going to be boring as hell, Tony," Slick whined. "I got a business to run."

"Well, take along one of your strippers, she should be able to keep it from getting too boring," Tony said, smiling, as he opened the door and left.

Slick opened the top desk drawer and found a pad and pen, looked at the open phone book and found Jo's name and address and wrote the information on the pad. *I hope Tony's right,* he told himself, *I can't afford to get into trouble with the law. I've got three strikes against me in Chicago and being an accomplice to murder could certainly spell trouble for me.*

The next morning he was parked a half-block down the street from Jo's apartment, with a copy of the Amarillo News resting on the steering wheel. He had just about covered all the news items and was ready to start on the classifieds when the door to Jo's apartment opened and a beautiful blonde haired lady stepped out and walked quickly to her automobile.

Slick whistled under his breath as he watched Jo open the car door and slide in, her skirt rising to show a lot of flesh before closing the door.

Damn, he said to himself, *the boss wants a hit made on that! If I had her dancing at my joint I'd hafta beat the trade away with a ball bat.*

As Jo drove by the parked white Lincoln, the thought entered her mind that she hadn't seen such a car in the neighborhood before. *If you see any thing suspicious, anything out of the ordinary, call me immediately,* she remembered Buster's instructions. She noted that there was someone sitting in the car, someone very short because she could only see his head and neck through the window--and that was quickly covered by the newspaper as she passed.

Probably someone waiting for a passenger, she told herself and drove on by. Slick waited until she had reached the end of the block and turned onto the busy thoroughfare before speeding after her.

The office of the oil company where she worked was located in one of the new business complexes on the north side of the city, a ten minute drive through the early morning traffic.

As Jo slowed to turn into the parking lot, she noticed a white Lincoln, very similar to the one she had seen near her apartment, stop and park a half block to her rear. She paused before entering her office and looked closely at the vehicle. *There's lots of Lincolns in this part of town,* she told herself, *probably belongs to one of the oil tycoons who have offices here in this building.*

As she settled down to her desk in preparation for a busy day at the computer, she noticed a short, fat man walk by her office door, pause, glance at her, then walk on down the hall.

Anything out of the ordinary, she heard Buster say as her mind remembered their parting the day they returned from Las Vegas.

Curious, she walked from behind her desk to the door and looked down the hallway but the short, fat man had disappeared.

A busy day cleared her mind of any suspicions she might have had and by the end of the work day, she had completely forgotten the incidents of the morning. She left the office and walked to her car in the parking lot, unlocked the door and pulled herself in. As she circled the parking lot and headed for the exit ramp, she noticed the white Lincoln, or one similar, parked next to the ramp. Subconsciously, her mind made note of the license number.

Jo always kept a small note pad and pen in one of the coke holders which rested in the middle of the seat next to her right arm, for jotting down things, such as grocery lists, as she drove to and from work. As she turned onto the busy street, she removed the pen and wrote, JRT-543 Texas, the license number of the white Lincoln. She failed to notice that the short, fat man at the wheel of the Lincoln immediately pulled into the traffic and followed her home.

As she parked her car in the driveway next to her apartment, she noticed the Lincoln stop and park in the same space where she had seen it when she left for work. Her heart raced, this was no coincidence, someone had been following her.

Opening the door, she let herself in and immediately locked the door and pushed the dead-bolt into place. Without removing her coat, she rushed to the telephone and dialed Buster's number at the Deaf Smith County Sheriff's office.

"Sheriff's office," a female voice responded. "How may I help you?"

"I need to speak to Deputy Thornton," Jo replied.

"I'm sorry, ma'am, but Deputy Thornton is not in his office at this time. May I take a message?"

"No, it's very important that I speak to him personally. Do you suppose you could reach him on his radio and have him call me?"

"I'll try, ma'am," the friendly voice answered. "Could I have your name and number?"

"Jo Willman, and I'm in Amarillo at 382-7779. Please hurry!"

Jo replaced the phone and began to pace the floor, becoming more anxious by the minute. She walked to the window and peeked through the blinds. The white Lincoln was still parked down the street but she couldn't tell if anyone was in it from this distance. As she looked, the phone rang and she screamed, quickly placing her hand over her mouth, realizing that she had lost control of her nerves. A vision of the headlines of the Las Vegas newspaper flashed before her eyes, *Twenty-one Dealer Leaps to Her Death*.

She rushed to the phone, picked it up and heard Buster's calm voice, "What is it Jo, Irene said you sounded upset?"

"Buster! Oh, Buster! I think someone has been following me!" she cried.

Buster's heart pounded, but he kept his voice calm as he asked, "Are you sure? Tell me what happened."

Hearing Buster's reassuring voice, Jo regained her composure and began relating the day's events.

"Is the Lincoln still there?" Buster asked when she had finished her story.

"It was a few minutes ago-- hold on and let me look."

"No," she said after peeking once again through the blinds. "It's gone."

"O.K.," Buster said, "Here's what I want you to do. Pack your bags and wait for me. Don't open the door for anyone. Stay close to the phone and if anyone tries to break in, call 911 immediately. It will take me close to an hour to get there. I'll be coming in an unmarked sheriff's car, you remember the one I was driving when I picked you up the day we flew to Chicago. I'm going to change into civilian clothes. If someone is watching your apartment, we don't want to alert them that we are aware of what they are doing. Do you have a gun?"

"Yes, my father gave me his twenty-two pistol when I moved to Amarillo, he was concerned about my safety."

"Do you know how to use it?"

"Certainly, Buster! Remember, I'm a farm girl!"

"O.K.,get it, make certain it's loaded and stay by the phone. If you have to use it, aim for the crotch. A twenty-two slug is not very big but it can cause a hell of a lot of damage to a person's manly parts!"

Even as frightened as she was, Jo had to laugh at that statement. "Alright, Buster, I'll be O.K. Get here as soon as possible."

Buster pulled his Blazer into the Sheriff's parking lot, ran into his office and changed into street clothes which he kept in his office for just such an emergency as this. Within three minutes, he was back in the parking lot, climbing into the unmarked sheriff's Chevy and speeding out of Hereford towards Amarillo.

Once again he dialed Jo's number on his cell phone. "I'm on my way, Hon," he said. "How you doing."

"A little nervous but I'll be alright. Hurry!"

Buster closed the cell phone and squeezed another ten miles an hour out of the Chevy. Thirty five minutes later he was pulling into Jo's driveway.

Jo, watching through the blinds, rushed to unlock the door and let him in. Buster took her into his arms and held her tight as she let her emotions get the best of her--sobbing and trying to talk at the same time.

"I was so scared," she finally blurted through her tears. "I couldn't think of anything except what they did to Cristy, after we left her that night in Las Vegas. Do you think they would do the same thing to me?"

Buster didn't want to upset her any more than necessary but felt he should be honest with her. "I'm certain it's me they are after. Probably believe they can get to me through you, but we can't take any chances. I gave it a lot of thought on the way over from Hereford and we need to find a safe place for you to hide for a few days. I think I've figured out what they are all about, and if I am right, they won't be able to harm either of us after a few days."

Jo relaxed in his arms and Buster held her close for a few minutes then pushed her away, looked into her eyes and asked, "Did you get a good look at the guy--good enough to identify him?"

Shaking her head no, Jo replied, "I'm afraid not, about all I can tell you is that he was pretty bald and kinda short and fat." In deep thought, she added, "I did get the license number of his car, though."

"Good girl!" Buster almost shouted. "That's using your head! Where is it?"

"On a pad in the front seat of my car. I'll go get it."

"No! I'll get it, I don't want you outside until we decide what we're going to do."

With that, he slowly opened the door, looked both directions up and down the street and seeing no one, stepped quickly to the car and retrieved the notepad. Returning inside, he locked the door and stepped to the telephone.

"Irene, I need you to run a make with the DPS in Austin on a license number--late model Lincoln Towncar," pausing and looking at the note pad he read, "license number JRT-543, Texas. Call me back just as soon as you get the information. I'm at Jo's, her telephone number..."

Irene interrupted, "I have it, she gave it to me when she called. Shouldn't take but a minute, I'll call you right back."

While they waited, Jo put on a pot of coffee and listened while Buster explained his plan.

"You remember I told you about the Tinsley's, my wife's cousins who live on the farm where Spinner's body was found?"

Jo nodded in the affirmative.

"After dark, we're going to slip out and leave in my car.

We'll leave your's setting out front and whoever is tailing you will think you are still here. I'll take you to Wes's place, they'll never think to look for you there."

Jo interrupted, "I'd rather just go stay with my folks in Nazareth, I don't want to be a burden on your family and maybe cause them some trouble."

"No, that would be the first place they would look for you. If they were able to find out who you are, they could certainly find out who your parents are. Wes and Clariss will be glad to have you. And I know Wes and the boys, if I tell them to protect you, they won't let anyone within a country mile of that farm!"

"What about work, I can't just disappear without telling my boss where I'm going," Jo said, as she poured two cups of coffee.

"You can't tell anyone where you are. In the morning just call in sick, stomach virus or flu or something of the sort. Tell them you may be off for a few days. If you get in trouble with your boss, we'll take care of it after we clean this thing up. Right now, your safety is the number one priority."

Taking a sip of the hot coffee, Buster stared into the steaming cup for a few seconds, turned to Jo and said, "Hon, you've got to know, these people have billions of dollars at stake in this show. They wouldn't hesitate to murder me or you just as quickly as they murdered Spinner and Cristy. They have already tried to kill me once and they'll try again. I know what they are up to, how they spread that virus to kill all the cattle just so they could make billions on the futures market, but I can't prove it. I need a witness and maybe this bird that's been tailing you will lead me to one."

The sound of the phone startled them, and Buster rushed to answer it.

"Buster, Irene here. I got the information you wanted. The Lincoln is registered to a Giovanni Rosellini in Amarillo--owns the French Quarter strip joint on the Boulevard. Been in Amarillo about five years. He's been clean since he came to Texas but has a record a foot long in Chicago; prostitution, extortion, assault with a deadly weapon and a dozen other charges."

"That's great Irene. I'll be here until dark, then Jo and I will head for Hereford. I can't tell you what's going on but I'll bring you up to date when we get back."

* * * * * *

"Wes, I'd like for you to meet Jo Willman, a good friend of mine. Jo, this is Wes and his wife Clariss. And these two hooligans standing bashfully in the corner are Joey and Cody, my team roping buddies," Buster said in introduction as they entered the living room of the neat farm house.

"Howdy, Jo," Wes said, "Welcome to the Tinsley farm. Any friend of Buster's is a friend of ours."

Clariss nodded and took Jo's hand and squeezed it warmly. Joey and Cody both spoke at once, "Howdy, Miss Willman."

Wes led the way into the kitchen, speaking as he went, "Come on in and sit at the table, Clariss keeps a pot of coffee on and she just made a fresh batch of her cinnamon cookies today. What brings you out this time of night, Buster?"

"I need a favor, Wes, and it has to do with the murder of Spinner Murphy. It's a pretty long story so you may as well take a seat and get comfortable."

Wes drew up a chair to the table as Clariss set four coffee cups on the table and poured them full of the dark brew. The boys stood on each side of Buster's chair, with a hand on each of his shoulders. Buster reached around each of their waists and gave them a hug.

"Boys," Wes said, "get a couple more chairs out of the den, Buster don't want you hanging on him. Now, Buster, I 'spect you better get started on that long story."

* * * * * *

An hour later, Buster finished his story, having told Wes, Clariss and the boys everything that had happened since Joey and Cody had found Spinner's body in the weeds.

"As you can see, Jo's life ain't worth a plugged nickel if those mobsters find her. I'd like for you to let her stay here with you for a week or so or until I put the wraps on this case," he said.

"You know she's more than welcome, Buster," Wes said, "And I've got a thirty-thirty in the broom closet that's just itching to go skunk hunting. If they show up here they'll get more than they bargained for."

"We got our twenty-two's, Uncle Wes," Joey said. "Me and Cody will look out for her. Nobody better come messing around here while we're on watch."

Buster smiled and winked at Wes. "I knew I could count on you folks to help. I've got an idea, and if it works, you won't have to wait long. Boys, why don't you run out to the car and bring in Jo's bags. I need to get back to town and let Pete know what's going on."

The boys were back quickly, each carrying one of Jo's bags and took them to the spare bedroom. Buster got up from the chair, shook Wes's hand and thanked him one more time then took Jo in his arm's and kissed her.

"Things are going to be fine, Hon. Don't worry yourself about anything. I'll keep in touch by phone." Once again, turning to Wes, Buster said, "Why don't you get that ole thirty-thirty out and oil her up, just in case you need it in a hurry. I'll try to see you in a day or two."

* * * * * *

Pete, Buster and Johnny were sitting in the sheriff's office going over the plans.

"Johnny's about Jo's size," Buster said. "It shouldn't be too difficult to dress him up like a woman, put a blonde wig on him and make them think he's her. I'll take him to Jo's apartment tonight and tomorrow morning, if Rosellini is still on the stakeout, Johnny can leave in her car as if nothing has happened. I'll be parked just around the corner. When Johnny pulls up to the stop sign, before pulling out on the thoroughfare, he needs to turn her car sideways in the middle of the street and block the exit. I'll pull around the corner behind the Lincoln and we'll have the bastard boxed in."

199

"Sounds good," Pete said, "but we need to let the Amarillo police know what we're going to do."

"O.K., but be sure you tell them that we don't want any news of this arrest hitting the press. We'll slip him out of Amarillo and lock him up here in Hereford, until we find out what he's up to. We'll charge him with harassment until we get a statement out of him. That shouldn't be too difficult with the *three-strikes-you're-out* law in force. He knows if he is caught breaking the law again he'll be sent up for life."

While Sheriff Blackwell made contact with the Chief of Police in Amarillo, Buster dressed Johnny in a sexy looking dress and blonde wig, which he had secured from the under-cover wardrobe, and helped the young Mexican cover his brown face with powder, lipstick and rouge.

Johnny balled his fist and threatened to hit Buster when Buster pretended he was going to kiss him after the makeup was finished. At a distance, no one would be able to tell that this sexy looking object wasn't Jo.

It was well after midnight when they finally arrived at Jo's apartment. As Johnny opened the door of the Chevy to leave, he said, "Man, don't let me down, when I block that street, you better be backing me up."

"Don't worry, I'll be there with bells on, Johnny," Buster responded.

* * * * * *

Precisely at seven-thirty the next morning, the Lincoln Towncar turned the corner and parked in the space where Jo had seen it the previous day. Johnny watched through the blinds and at eight o'clock opened the door and walked to Jo's car.

From the distance, Slick thought it was the same good looking chick he had ogled the day before. He pulled his newspaper in front of his face as Johnny passed. As he pulled out to follow, he failed to notice a white Chevy turn the corner behind him and slowly approach from the rear.

"What the hell!" Slick shouted as the blonde chick turned her car sideways and blocked the road. He braked, threw the gearshift into reverse and started to turn around. Then he saw the Chevy in his rearview mirror. It too, had turned sideways and a man was exiting from the back side. Too late, Slick realized he was boxed in, and as he watched, the blonde chick was walking towards the Lincoln with arms outstretched and holding a .38 pointed in his direction.

The man behind his Lincoln was also walking towards him with a .357 pointed in his direction.

"What the hell's going on?" he demanded. "I ain't done nothing wrong."

"Get out and place your hands on the hood," Buster said calmly without arguing. "You're under arrest. After shaking him down and removing a small .32 caliber revolver from his coat pocket, Buster pulled Slick's hands behind his back and snapped on a set of handcuffs while reading his Miranda rights.

With Johnny on one side and Buster on the other, they quickly guided him to Buster's Chevy, pushed him into the back seat and closed the door. Johnny returned to the Lincoln and parked it, correctly, next to the curb, got out, locked it and walked to Jo's car. He turned it around and drove back to her apartment and parked it in the driveway, then walked to the street where Buster was waiting.

Johnny opened the front door, stepped in and Buster pulled away--the entire episode had taken less than five minutes. And, luckily no one had observed the action.

"I want to call my lawyer," Slick whined. "You guys are in trouble, I ain't done nothing."

"It's you that's in trouble, Mr. Rosellini," Buster said. "We know a lot about you. We know that you were involved in the cattle poisoning, a murder in Hereford and another in Las Vegas. We also know that you were tailing Miss Willman for the purpose of murdering her. We also know about your record in Chicago. It looks like you may be going to Huntsville for an extended stay as a guest of the State of Texas."

Buster suspected that Slick was just a peon in the conspiracy but figured that he might slip some information, if he thought he was going to be charged with murder.

"You got it all wrong, Mister," Slick said, as he sat forward on the seat behind Buster. "I didn't have anything to do with that pilot's murder, and I didn't have nothing to do with the murder of that card dealer out in Vegas."

"I didn't say who was murdered in Hereford or Vegas. If you didn't have anything to do with it, how did you know that's who I was talking about?"

Slick's face turned white and his breath came in great gasps as he stuttered and stammered, knowing that he had made a mistake. "I a-a-admit I knew about it but I d-d-didn't have anything to do with it."

"We'll let a jury decide how much you had to do with it," Buster said, smiling at Slick's nervousness.

"Look, Sheriff," Slick whined, "I ain't done nothing wrong. If I tell you what I know, will you try to help me get out of this jam?"

"If you haven't done anything wrong, you've got nothing to worry about," Buster answered.

Then, as if to himself, Slick started babbling, "I knowed I shouldn't ever have gotten mixed up in this mess. I couldn't help it, there's a guy in Chicago that I owe money and he's got a mortgage on my club. Said if I didn't do a few favors for him he would foreclose. I couldn't see no harm in tailing that girl and finding out her schedule and where she goes. I don't know what he wanted that information for but he told me if I would do it he would forget about that money I owe him. That's what I did and that's all I know."

"Come on, Slick, that's not all you know. Why did he want you tailing Miss Willman and what do you know about those two murders?"

"I just heard about them through the grapevine," Slick answered. Knowing that if the mob found out he had ratted on them his life wouldn't be worth a plugged nickel, either in or out of jail.

"Who else was involved," Buster asked as he pulled onto the Interstate and headed towards Canyon.

"Wasn't anyone that I know. The guy in Chicago said he was sending someone from Boston to pick up the information I was to get on the Willman girl, but didn't tell me who it was. Said he was a foreigner of some kind."

"You certain there was no one else in Amarillo involved?" Buster asked.

"I'm certain. All I know is that I was to get this information for them. I don't know what they wanted it for." Slick knew that the worse thing he could do now was to tell about Tony being in the area and his part in the conspiracy. If he was forced, to save his own hide, he would, but for now Tony's involvement was safe with him.

Buster knew he was lying, but thought by playing along with him, he might slip some more information.

"O.K., Mr. Rosellini, I'll do what I can to help you, but you're going to have to cool your heels for a few days in the Deaf Smith County jail. Until we can find out why Chicago is interested in Miss Willman," he said as he pulled into the parking lot at the Deaf Smith County Courthouse.

While Johnny guided Slick to the jail entrance, Buster walked to the Sheriff's office and told Pete what had happened.

"Charge him with harassment and carrying a concealed weapon for the time being, Pete. If it looks like he's going to get bonded out, we'll increase the charges to murder and ask the judge to set his bond so high that he'll be stuck here for a few days. I think we may be able to wrap this whole thing up in two or three more days. In the meantime, see if you can get Amarillo P.D. to keep an eye on the airport and follow anyone that might come in from Boston or New York that looks like he might be from the Middle East."

Turning to leave, he added, "Tomorrow's Saturday and

George and I are entered in the roping out at Billings Arena. Unless something develops I think I'll go ahead with those plans. Maybe by Monday, after spending the weekend in a cell, Rosellini will be ready to quit his lying and tell us all he knows about this whole affair. If you need me, I'll be out at Wes Tinsley's place."

* * * * * *

Pickups and trailers, driven by feed yard cowboys, began arriving at Billings Arena early on Saturday morning, the day of the roping competition. Many of the cowboys were warming up their horses by riding around the outside of the arena. Most had their lariats in hand, twirling them and now and again throwing them at imaginary steers. Wives and children were beginning to fill the seats in the bleachers surrounding the arena. A large truck with a double-decker cattle trailer was backed up to the chute and was unloading fifty head of Corienti Mexican roping steers. The steers, weighing nearly seven hundred pounds each, were sporting short, stout horns, which were wrapped with tape to keep rope burns to a minimum. Cowboys were herding the steers into a pen next to the roping chute and judges mounted on two beautiful bay horses were riding slowly around the inside of the arena, talking and laughing as they waited for the roping to begin. The PA system was crackling as the announcer tested and adjusted the volume.

"Testing, testing, one - two - three. Testing."

A white Ford pickup was parked well away from the other vehicles, in an open spot at the rear of the arena. A lone cowboy sat in the vehicle sipping a beer and watching the activities as the preparations were taking place.

Buster and George jumped their horses out of their trailer and began saddling the animals. They were careful to pull the cinches extra tight; because once a seven hundred pound steer was roped, his weight and momentum could jerk a saddle right off a horses back. After the horses were saddled, they walked to the judges stand and were told that they had drawn tenth place in the roping schedule in a field of thirty teams. That gave them plenty of time to ride the nervousness out of their mounts. They pulled themselves into the saddle and walked their horses slowly around the outside of the arena. As they rode by the white Ford pickup, which was parked well away from the other vehicles, Buster noticed the swarthy-looking cowboy with his hat tipped below his eyes who appeared to be napping. *Probably drew number thirty, and is going to catch a few winks before his number is called,* Buster thought to himself.

The cowboy, looking out under his hat brim, watched as Buster and George rode by. *Better enjoy your ride, deputy,* he thought, *it's going to be your last!*

As they walked their horses back towards the arena, they heard the announcer on the loudspeaker call for the number one team to get their horses in the box. The roping was about to begin. Buster and George tied their horses to the fence and took a seat in the bleachers to watch their competition. The Tinsley boys, Joey and Cody, who had come to the roping with Buster, threaded their way through the crowd and sat down beside them.

The first team, nervous, received no time because the header missed the horns of his steer and the steer ran head high to the back end of the arena. The next team caught their steer in record time but the heeler's rope caught only one leg, giving them a five second penalty. Out of the first nine teams, only three were able to get good clean times, with the top team registering seven seconds flat. The announcer called for team number ten, Buster and George, to enter the box.

"The next team up, folks, is George Autry and Buster Thornton. George, as you know, is owner and manager of Autry Feed Yard and Buster is the guy who keeps crime off the streets in Deaf Smith County. These two cowboys have been a roping team for many years, having won the National Collegiate Team Roping championship during their senior year at Texas Tech. Want to tell us how many years ago that was, Buster?" the announcer joked.

"Been so long ago, I clean forgot," Buster responded from the back of his horse. "All I remember is that it was a long time after you began ridiculing cowboys from that microphone. Looks like they'd have retired you forty years ago!"

The crowd laughed their approval at this good-natured bantering between two old friends.

Waiting inside the arena, along the side of the fence next to the roping box, Buster and George backed their horses in and shook out their loops.

The door to the white Ford pickup opened and the cowboy stepped out with a long, narrow cardboard box in hand. He walked to the back end of the roping arena, unnoticed, and leaned against a large fence post, almost hidden from view. Opening the box, he pulled out a scoped rifle with a silencer on the end of the barrel, keeping it hidden between himself and the fence. Shoving the barrel through the fence, he sighted down on Buster as he positioned his horse, ready to spur him after the steer when it was released from the chute. George backed his horse into the left-hand box and the judge pulled the barrier ribbon in place. Suddenly, the wind whipped a large empty paper sack under the feet of Buster's horse and he bolted. The crowd, with their eyes glued on the two riders ready to charge after the released steer, screamed their disappointment at the unexpected interruption and their screams drowned out the muted sound of the rifle shot.

Buster felt a sharp pain in his left arm as the bullet grazed his skin, heart high. The sudden movement of his horse had saved his life. At the same time he felt the pain, he saw a small puff of smoke at the end of the arena and the barrel of a rifle being pulled out of view through the fence rails.

George, setting his horse on the other side of the chute that was holding their roping steer, saw the sudden tear in Buster's shirt sleeve and the blood immediately stain his white shirt. His eyes locked on Buster's, who nodded towards the far end of the arena as he spurred his horse in that direction. George followed his lead and dug his spurs into the sorrels side. They both raced towards the end of the arena, shouting at the cowboy holding the gate to swing it open. The cowboy obliged and as the gate swung open, the two horses raced from the arena with the riders twirling their ropes over their heads.

A hush fell over the crowd, still unaware that Buster had been shot and wondering why the two cowboys were breaking the roping rules by leaving the roping box. Suddenly they could see why, a person carrying a rifle, running towards a white Ford pickup parked a good two hundred yards away from the arena. The crowd watched in silence as George rushed past the running cowboy and threw his lariat. As it settled around the gunman's neck, the shooter pulled the rifle to his shoulder with the barrel pointed in George's direction; but before he could pull the trigger, Buster's loop settled around his running feet. Buster's horse slid to a stop and began backing as George's horse spun around facing the gunman. Both horses began to back until their ropes were tight. The assassin dropped the rifle, fell to the ground and began to claw at the rope around his neck which had cut off his air.

Buster quickly dismounted and rushed down the rope to the prostrate gunman, one rope around his neck and one around his feet. Buster motioned for George to move his horse forward just enough that the rope around his neck was not choking. He then grabbed the gunman by the hair of the head and pulled his face out of the dirt.

Looking him square in the eyes, he said angrily, "Alright, you dry-gulching bastard, start talking or I give the horses orders to start backing and I can assure you that they will pull your damned head clean from your body."

The cowboy tried to get his fingers under the rope which was squeezing his neck and choking him. He managed to say weakly, "Can't breathe!"

Buster motioned to George who released his dally around the saddle horn a couple of inches and the gunman gasped as fresh air hit his lungs.

"Talk!" Buster ordered, "You've got about ten seconds!"

"Don't pull, don't pull," the gunman cried, "I'll talk!"

Buster pulled his bandana from around his neck and tied it tightly around his arm, which was bleeding profusely and dripping blood on the gunman's face, as the frightened Las Vegas hood began to babble.

"You should never have come to Vegas looking for clues to Murphy's murder. Murphy got what he deserved. He was paid well to do a job but his conscience wouldn't let him keep quiet. He was fixing to..."

Buster interrupted, "Well I'll be damned, you ain't no cowboy, you're that Vegas hood that's been chasing me all over hell and half of Texas! I got a mind to back these horses up until your head pops off!"

"No! No!" Tony screamed. "I'll tell you everything, just keep those horses still. You got to promise to keep me locked up safe away from the mob, cause my life ain't going to be worth a plugged nickel once they find out I squealed."

"I'm not promising anything other than keeping those horses from pulling you limb from limb if you tell me who murdered Spinner and why he was murdered," Buster said.

"I'm telling you," Tony shouted nervously, looking at the two horses which were holding him stretched out on the ground. "He intended to go to the authorities and tell about spraying that Foot and Mouth virus on all them feed yards. The boss paid him fifty thousand to do the job, told him the virus would just make the cattle sick for awhile. That all he had to do was dump a little of the bacteria into his spray plane, get up about five thousand feet at night, go into a glide with his motor cut and sail over the west side of those feed pens. Then turn on his spray nozzles and let the wind do the rest. After he sailed about a half mile away from the pens, he just turned his engine back on and flew to the next nearest feed yard and did it all over again. Close as those yards are together, he picked up six or eight each night with just one filling, and no one ever knew there was a plane anywhere a- round. Didn't take but about a week and he had 'em all doctored."

The first of the spectators and cowboys were rushing up to where George and Buster had Tony stretched out between their horses. Buster felt that what Tony was confessing was something that needed to be kept quiet for awhile. He inter- rupted Tony and said, "O.K., butt-head, I'm going to let you up and we're going to the courthouse, but I guarandamntee you, that you either spill your guts or we'll bring you back and let these horses spill them for you!"

George released his dally and Buster pulled the rope from around Tony's neck, then pulled the other rope from around his feet. Picking up the rifle, he jabbed it into Tony's back and walked him to his Blazer where he retrieved a pair of handcuffs, cuffed Tony's hands behind his back and pushed him into the rear seat.

Cody and Joey, who had been watching from the bleach- ers, rushed up as Buster shoved the gunman into the Blazer. Seeing the blood on Buster's shirt, they both shouted as one,

"Gol-dang, Uncle Buster, you've been shot!"

"It's O.K., boys," Buster answered, "just a flesh wound. I'll be alright. How about taking our horses to the trailer and loading them. Me an George are going to take this coyote into the Sheriff's office and find out why he wanted me dead."

The boys took the bridle reins from George and watched as the Blazer pulled out and headed for town. While George drove, Buster picked up the mike to his radio and called in.

"Base, this is unit three," he said into the mike.

"Unit three, this is base, go ahead," the female voice replied.

"Irene, I'm bringing in a prisoner. He's O.K. but I've got a little problem, not bad but see if you can get ahold of Doc Wilson and have him meet me at the sheriff's office," Buster said, painfully, then added. "We'll be there in about ten minutes."

The arm was bleeding again by the time George pulled into the courthouse parking lot. He helped Buster from the Blazer then dragged Tony from the rear seat. Buster, weakened from the loss of blood, staggered as he walked up the courthouse steps.

"Better let me take you to the hospital," George volunteered, as he held to his right arm and kept him from falling.

"No way!" Buster replied, "I'll be alright soon as I sit down. I want to be present when we present this murderer to the Feds."

Pete was in his office when they walked in and helped Buster to a chair. "You look like hell," he said to his deputy,

"What happened and who is this *hombre*?"

"This *hombre* ain't no *hombre*," Buster answered, smiling weakly. "More than likely, he's an Iraqi. He's the Las Vegas hood that I told you was trying to kill me and Jo in Vegas, Chicago and Virginia. He took a potshot at me out at the roping arena. Nicked my arm but me and George took care of him. He's got some things he wants to tell us, now that we made him an offer he can't refuse."

Sheriff Blackwell looked closely at Buster's arm, then said, "That'll wait, right now we're going to get you to the hospital and get that arm taken care of."

Before Buster could protest, the door flew open and Doc Wilson rushed in carrying a large black medical bag.

"Who's hurt," he asked with much concern in his voice before he noticed the blood on Buster's shirt?

"Just a nick, Doc," Buster said, pointing to his arm. "Bone's O.K. Probably needs cleaning up and a bandage. We're going to listen to this bird sing while you take care of it."

Doc Wilson opened his bag, took out an antiseptic solution, scissors and bandages and began to work on Buster's wound. Pete stepped in front of the handcuffed would-be assassin, flipped on a tape recorder, and read the Miranda rights and asked if he wanted a lawyer present. Gallento answered "No."

"O.K., punk, we're listening, what's your name and why did you try to kill my deputy?"

"Tony Gallento," Tony replied almost in a whisper, "And you got to promise, sheriff, that you'll keep me safe from the mob. They find out I ratted and they'll kill me, sure as hell!"

"I'll promise you nothing," Pete replied with fire in his eyes, "And if you don't start talking pronto, the mob won't have to do it, I'll stomp you to death myself!"

Tony realized that there was only one way out for him now, tell the sheriff everything and hope that he could make a deal later.

"The boss sent me and Benny to Texas back in January to help Murphy doctor up these feed yards with Foot and Mouth virus," he said.

Buster groaned when Doc Wilson's probe got a little too deep, then interrupted Tony. "We need to know who your boss is and where you got the virus, it's a cinch that you didn't make it yourself."

"The boss is Frankie Seigle at the Corizentian Commodity, Inc. I don't know for certain where we got the virus, but I heard some of the boys say that the boss paid some Iraqis a half a million bucks for it and they smuggled it in through Mexico." Tony replied, almost in a whisper.

Pete adjusted the tape recorder a little closer to Tony's mouth to make certain he was getting a good recording, then asked how Spinner had gotten involved.

"Murphy had been doing some legal flying for the syndicate and the boss convinced him he could make a lot of money, if he helped us make a bunch of cattle sick. Said the cattle would get over it after a month or so but it would make the futures' markets go wild. We gave Murphy fifty G's to invest in cattle futures, but he got cold feet and never did invest it--hid the money, somewhere. Then when he found out this

virus was killing cattle, he told me and Benny that he was going to tell the authorities so that maybe an antidote could be
spread to stop the virus. We forced him out to his hanger, tied
his hands and feet and Benny shot him. Then we carried
him out north of town and dumped him in some weeds. We'd
of gotten away with it if it hadn't been for them two kids. His
body would have rotted out there in that lake bottom or the
coyotes would have taken care of it for us."

Pete interrupted, "Who's this Benny you keep mention-
ing?"

"Benny Carruso," Tony answered. "He's a guy I work
with out in Vegas--Sicilian--crazy as hell. He'd kill his own
grandmother just to see her bleed. Someone needs bumping
off, Benny's the man the boss calls on."

"I suppose he's the one who threw Cristy Gale out the
window, too," Buster said, "And you had nothing to do with it.
He was probably the one who took a shot at me today and you
just happened to be standing there with the rifle in your
hands. Don't give me that crap, Tony! Benny might have
helped, but you're the one that pulled the trigger."

Tony dropped his head in defeat but said nothing.

"O.K., Tony, why was Spinner carrying all that cash to
Chicago from Vegas, and why deliver it to a commodity trading company?" Buster asked.

"The Syndicate owns the casino in Las Vegas and also
owns the Corizentian Commodity, Inc. in Chicago, with a seat
on the Chicago Board of Trade. The money was gambling
profits, which were not reported to the IRS, and the boss
came up with this scheme to clean it up by investing it in cat-

tle and hog futures while the market price was low, then do something to cause the markets to go up in a hurry. While every other investor was betting the futures' markets would go even lower, we bought every contract we could get our hands on, knowing that soon as the cattle started dying, the market would go wild."

"Well, you was right about that," Pete said, "In less than two months, the price of beef has tripled and everyone in the cattle feeding business in this part of the country has lost their asses, while you crooks have made billions. Hanging's not good enough for you. "

Picking up the telephone, he pressed the intercom and said, "Irene, see if Ace is in his office and ask him to come down, I've got some important information for him."

In less than five minutes the door opened and Chief FBI agent Ace Belton stepped in. Seeing Doc Wilson putting the final wrap on the bandage around Buster's arm, he ignored the others in the room and asked, "What the hell happened to you, Buster?"

"Just a little nick, Ace," Buster replied. Nodding towards Tony, he added, "That goon's one of the mob that your boys helped me with in Virginia. He can't shoot worth a damn or I'd be pushing up daisies instead of letting this old sawbones dig around on me."

Doc Wilson smiled and pulled the bandage a little tighter just to hear Buster groan.

Ace looked at Tony then at Pete, "What's going on, Sheriff? I haven't got time to be involved in any small time murder investigation. I was just on the phone to CIA Director Al-

216

len and he says that we've about got this Foot and Mouth mystery solved. They've arrested two Iraqi terrorists in Beirut and charged them with spreading the virus. I need to call him back and get more details."

"Better cool it, Ace," Pete said. "You're going to be a helluva lot more interested in listening to what's on this tape than listening to some bad information from a Washington bureaucrat -- terrorists didn't do it, mobsters did."

Pete picked up the tape recorder, rewound it and set it in front of the FBI agent and flipped the switch to *Play*.

Ace Belton, Chief FBI agent in charge of chemical and biological investigations, listened unbelievingly, as he heard the mobster's story replayed.

13

"I have been instructed by the President of the United States to inform you that if the two terrorists, we have in custody in Beirut, are not extradited within twenty-four hours, missiles will be fired from our ships in the Persian Gulf at targets in Baghdad, and planes from our aircraft carriers will attack all military facilities within your country," Secretary of State Shaw said to his Iraqi counterpart across the huge table.

The meeting, taking place in Geneva, Switzerland, had been arranged by the Swiss delegation to the United Nations in an effort to cool the volatile situation which had developed as a result of the Foot and Mouth epidemic in the Texas Panhandle. All evidence pointed to the Iraqis as the source of the virus and Moslem militants had even announced their involvement.

"You must understand, Mr. Secretary, that my country had nothing to do with the unfortunate situation that exists in your cattle feeding industry. We offer our sincere sympathies to your nation; however, we are extremely disappointed that you would even consider that we would perpetrate such a foul deed, when there is not one shred of evidence of our involvement," the Iraqi responded.

"Oh, but you are mistaken, Mr. Aboud," Shaw replied, "We do have evidence, enough to satisfy us that your country is behind this entire act of terror. We know that the virus was manufactured in your country; we know that two of your people smuggled the virus into our country; and we have those people under arrest in our embassy in Beirut. We also know that a word from Mr. Hussein to the Lebanese government to issue extradition papers will be needed before Lebanon will grant us permission to take those two terrorists back to the U.S. for trial."

"You misunderstand our influence in Lebanon, Mr. Secretary," the Iraqi responded. "The Lebanese do as the Lebanese please, and we do not meddle in their internal affairs. You are asking me to do the impossible."

"And you misunderstand, Mr. Aboud. I did not come here to barter, nor did I come here to argue. I came to carry a message that your country will feel the complete wrath of our nation. Even greater than that suffered by your people during the Desert War; if you have not used your influence to see that those two terrorists are on a plane headed for the United States within seventy-two hours--three days. This is not an idle threat, this is an ultimatum. You must understand that we will not tolerate terrorist acts by Iraq or any other nation within the borders of our nation. The clock is ticking! I advise you to contact your Prime Minister, immediately, in order that we will not be required to do something regrettable to both sides on this issue."

With that statement, Shaw stood and walked out of the room as both the Swiss intermediary and Aboud protested loudly.

* * * * * *

The cattle futures' market had jumped from fifty cents a pound to nearly two dollars a pound, since the news of the Foot and Mouth epidemic hit the wires. The market wire service was reporting that every commodity house, but one, had believed that the market price of cattle and hogs was headed for new lows and had sold thousands of contracts at the fifty cent level. Corizentian Commodity, Inc., the report said, had believed that the market would rise. And for six months prior to the cattle epidemic had been buying every contract available. Now they were cashing in those contracts at huge profits, and it was strange--or lucky--the report continued, that Corizentian Commodity, Inc. had read the markets correctly and had purchased such a large number of futures contracts at the low price. It did not, however, speculate that Corizentian Commodity, Inc. may have had prior knowledge that a Foot and Mouth epidemic was imminent. The Commodity Futures Trading Commission, the CFTC, had taken no action to investigate nor to stop trading cattle futures; as they had done when the Hunt boys had cornered the silver market and when the Ferruzi company had cornered the soybean market. Corizentian Commodity, Inc. continued to liquidate its holdings at profits never before seen at the Chicago Board of Trade.

* * * * * *

After listening to the tape of Gallento's confession, FBI agent Ace Belton sat dumbfounded in Sheriff Blackwell's office. It was absolutely impossible for him to believe that the FBI and the CIA could have been so wrong in their investigations. It was also very embarrassing for him to accept the fact that an inconspicuous sheriff's deputy had been able to singlehandedly solve, what all the agencies of the federal government had been unable to solve.

Finally, he spoke, almost as if he were disappointed. "Well, I guess I had better get back to the CIA and tell them to release those Iraqis. Looks like we were wrong and you guys have wrapped up this thing and tied it with a ribbon."

"I wouldn't be too hasty, Ace," Pete said. "These mobsters had to get that virus somewhere, and your two Iraqi terrorists may be the culprits who smuggled it into the country. They may have been in collusion from the very beginning. I'm sure the President is going to want to know if they acted alone or if old Saddam put them up to it. Also, I'd think we need to keep this information quiet until the top dogs are brought to bay. Once the news hits the press, you can bet your hat that those Chicago mobsters are going to take their winnings and head for tall timber. We've got our murderer, but you've still got to corral the people who were the brains behind this conspiracy."

"O.K., Pete, you're in the driver's seat. What do you suggest?"

Pete walked around the room, pushing his unruly white hair out of his eyes, thinking seriously before replying. "Well, Ace," he said, "We can hold this goon for a few days on a charge of attempted murder, for trying to kill Buster, before we charge him with Murphy's murder. I'm just a little ole county sheriff, but if I was in your *federal* shoes I'd keep this quiet for a couple of days until I had a team of my agents knocking on Corizentian Commodity, Inc.'s door with a search warrant and records subpoena. You could arrest the whole damned bunch for: illegally smuggling in the virus; spreading the virus; contaminating the environment; killing a half million head of cattle; rigging the Chicago Board of Trade, and complicity in the murder of Spinner Murphy and Cristy Gale --among other things!"

Buster interrupted, "And don't forget the Las Vegas bunch, Pete. That's where the money came from in the first place. I wouldn't be surprised if the IRS wouldn't be real interested in that five million dollars that they failed to report. And apparently, this Benny Carruso was involved in Cristy's murder and I personally want to see him burned. If we work it right, we could round up the whole bunch in one sweep."

"I wouldn't be surprised if, when we arrest the people at the top, we get a lot of finger pointing, and some of those fingers might be pointing at your Iraqis--maybe even at old Saddam, himself," Pete said.

"You're right, Pete, I wasn't thinking straight," Ace said, shaking his head. "We need to pull the noose on all these bastards at once and we certainly don't want the national media involved until they are all under lock and key. How about you, Buster, looks like this is your show, do you want to be in on winding it up?"

"You danged right!" Buster replied. "This bunch tried their best to murder me and Jo and it's going to be a pleasure to see all of them pay for what they've done!"

"How about it, Doc, is that arm going to be O.K., or do we need to confine him to bed?" Pete asked.

Smiling, Doc Wilson replied, "I wouldn't suggest any barroom brawls, but I'm sure it'll be O.K. for traveling. Just make certain you keep it away from any more powder and lead."

"Alright," Ace said. "It's agreed. We've got an agency Lear setting out at the airport. Pack your bags and we'll leave for Chicago in a couple of hours. In the meantime, I'll notify the Director and put plans together for a coordinated raid on the Corizentian Commodity, Inc. and the Las Vegas Casino for Monday morning. Remember, for this to be successful, none of us can breathe a word of this outside this room until we make our move, understand?"

Everyone in the room nodded their head in agreement as George Autry spoke. "Pete, these mobster's have made my life miserable and destroyed my business. How about deputizing me and letting me take part in this show. Buster might know how to catch 'em by the heels, but he might need me along to slip a rope over their horns. I'd really appreciate it."

Pete laughed and replied,"I've got no problem with that, if it's alright with Ace. How about it, Ace, can you use another good man?"

"No problem," the FBI agent answered as he looked at George. "Welcome aboard."

Pete motioned to Buster and they both stepped to the back of the room out of earshot of the others. "Buster, I know these federal agents, they'll do everything they can to take credit for solving this case. Keep your cellular phone with you at all times and call me the minute you get inside the building to make the raid on the Corizentian Commodity, Inc. office. I'll see that we get the credit for busting this case."

Buster, smiling, nodded his head in agreement as he turned and headed for the door.

Buster and George met Agent Belton at the airport and the sleek jet thundered into the West Texas sky and headed for Chicago. Sheriff Blackwell had other plans that did not require the help of the FBI. He picked up the phone and dialed CBS news in New York City and asked to speak with Don Prather.

"I'm sorry, sir," the female voice said, "Mr. Prather is in a meeting and is unable to take your call at this time."

"You tell Mr. Prather that Sheriff Blackwell of Deaf Smith County, Texas, has some very important news and if he is not interested I'll call ABC and give them the scoop," Pete said.

"Concerning what subject, Sheriff Blackwell?"

"Just tell him what I said, he'll know what subject."

After a short wait, the familiar voice of Don Prather came on the line, "Sheriff Blackwell, thanks for calling. What have you got for me?"

"Don, listen closely. If you will be in my office Monday morning at nine o'clock, I'll give you a story that I guarantee will blow your mind."

"Sheriff," Prather responded, "My schedule is full, I can't do that. Just tell me what it is, and I promise not to release it until Monday."

"Look, Don, when this cattle epidemic broke, you had your crew in Hereford in less than eight hours, don't tell me you can't be here."

"O.K., Sheriff, I can't make it, but I'll send a crew down. They can take the story."

"In person, Don, at nine Monday. No other way. If you're not interested, I'm certain Hennings will be," Pete replied.

A long pause, then Prather asked, "Why me, Sheriff?"

Pete smiled to himself and answered, "You were the only one who seemed to give my department any credit for looking for answers to this Foot and Mouth epidemic. I just thought I'd repay you for your kindness."

"Do you know who is behind it," Prather asked. "Have they caught the terrorists?"

"Monday morning at nine, Don--in person!"

Another long pause, "O.K. Sheriff, I'll be there but you damned well better have some worthwhile information or

I'll have..."

Pete interrupted, "It's worthwhile, Don, see you Monday," and hung up the phone.

* * * * * *

At nine A.M., two days later, the FBI SWAT team and the two Texas sheriff's deputies slipped into the freight dock of the building, housing the offices of Corizentian Commodities, Inc. and quietly climbed the stairs to the fifteenth floor. Agents, disguised as janitors, had already infiltrated the building and reported that approximately twenty of Chicago's known mob members were conducting a meeting in Frankie Seigle's office. As they climbed the stairs, Buster pulled his cellular phone from his pocket and punched Sheriff Blackwell's number.

"It's on, Pete," he whispered, "We are in the building. I'm going to leave the line open, maybe you can hear what takes place."

Sheriff Blackwell looked at Don Prather and winked as he switched on the speaker phone, then quickly told the newsman what was taking place in Chicago, as they listened to the activity coming across the open line.

With clockwork precision, the team rushed through the outer door of the office. The receptionist screamed as the group burst through the door, not knowing what was taking place. One of the group grabbed her and placed a firm hand over her mouth to stop her screams, while the others headed for the door to Seigle's office. As they burst through the office door, several of the mobsters pulled weapons and started firing, believing they were being raided by rival gang members.

Buster and George, with guns already in their hands, fell to the floor, rolled behind a sofa and began firing at the nearest members of the gang. Three of them were knocked from their chairs with blood pouring from shoulder wounds. Buster observed Seigle on the floor, crawling towards a side door. As he slipped from the room, Buster followed, keeping the padded furniture between him and the gunmen. As he crawled through the open door, he could hear the shouts of the FBI, "FBI! FBI! drop your weapons and get face down on the floor."

In Texas, the speaker phone on Sheriff Pete Blackwell's desk relayed the action through Buster's mobile phone. Don Prather was dumbfounded at the action that he was hearing take place in Chicago.

Sporadic gunfire continued, until the gang members realized that it actually was FBI and they didn't have a chance to resist. Several of the mobsters were wounded, none seriously, but the FBI, with their bulletproof vests came through the skirmish unscathed.

Seigle ran down the long hallway towards the stairs with Buster close on his tail. Just before reaching the door to the stairway, Buster made a flying tackle and grabbed the crime boss by the legs and pulled him to the floor. He could see the small, chrome plated pistol in Seigle's hand as he swung it around in his direction. Buster's reflexes, however, reacted quickly, grabbing the wrist of the gun hand with his left, held it firmly as he came around with a roundhouse right and caught the gangster with a bone crushing blow to the temple. Seigle's body went limp and the small revolver fell from his grasp.

Buster pulled himself from the floor, removed the handcuffs from his belt, rolled Seigle over on his stomach and cuffed his hands to his back, as the gangster began to regain consciousness. Pulling Seigle to his feet, Buster herded him back down the hallway to the room where the FBI and George were making their arrests and shoved him through the door."

Removing his cellular phone from his pocket, he asked, "Pete, you still there?"

"Damned right, I'm here, Buster, along with Don Prather and his T.V. crew. I had the speaker phone on and we heard everything, loud and clear. What's it look like now."

"We've got eighteen or twenty of Chicago's criminal elite, who were behind this conspiracy. They put up a pretty good battle, pulled their weapons and started firing before they realized it was an FBI raid. Seigle almost got away but I corralled him in the hallway. George and I are O.K. and it looks like all of the FBI boys are fine. Two or three of the hoodlums are bleeding pretty bad but they'll live."

Pausing to get his breath, Buster asked, "What you mean, Pete, Prather and his T.V. crew heard it all?"

CBS news anchorman Don Prather listened transfixed to the conversation and could hear the commotion in the background as the FBI herded the handcuffed mobsters out the door. "Deputy Thornton, this is Don Prather, how about telling me *what the hell* is going on. I flew down here last night, at Sheriff Blackwell's request, but he wouldn't tell me a damn thing. Said I'd have to wait and talk to you."

Pete interrupted Prather and said, "Buster, start at the beginning, from the time Spinner was murdered 'till now, and tell him how you solved this whole thing."

Don Prather could not believe his ears as he listened to the story being told by Buster. When he had finished, he said, "Deputy Thornton, would you meet me in New York City and join me on this evening's news segment? The nation needs to hear your story!"

"That's alright with me, Don, if Pete's willing to pay the airfare," Buster replied, laughing.

"Don't worry about that, Buster," Prather replied, "I'll have a CBS jet pick you up and we'll take care of everything."

"One more condition, Don," Buster said, "The young lady I was telling you about, Jo Willman, is holed up on a farm north of Hereford because this bunch intended to murder her. She had her vacation ruined, lost half her wardrobe and almost got herself killed on account of these bastards and was as big a part of this thing as me. I'll agree to an exclusive interview on your program if you will bring her up and let her tell her story. Also, George Autry has been involved in this from the beginning. In fact, he was the first to put me on the right trail. I want him along, also."

Don Prather smiled at Pete and said, "You drive a hard bargain, Buster, but it's a deal, and why don't the three of you plan on spending a week in the *"Big Apple"* at my expense. You deserve it!"

Sheriff Blackwell hung up the phone, turned to Prather and said, "You remember your first visit to Hereford when you insinuated I didn't know what I was talking about when I said there was no evidence that foreign terrorists were behind this conspiracy?"

"I remember," Prather replied.

"I've got a confession on tape made by Spinner's killer, and he spilled his guts--confessed everything, including the names of the people at the top, and he isn't a foreign terrorist. I'll let you listen to it if you'll give your word that you'll keep his name confidential. It will corroborate everything that Buster told you."

"You've got my word," Prather replied.

After playing the tape, Pete said, "Well, now that we've proven that I was right, how about setting the record straight and let your listeners know that the law west of the Potomac is still pretty capable of taking care of crime in its own home territory. It might get me a few more votes in the upcoming election."

Prather smiled and said, "No problem, Pete. I'll even come down on election day and vote for you, if that will help."

Immediately after herding the mobsters into the waiting FBI vans, Agent Belton called the Washington office. He asked to speak to Director Friedman and was informed that the Director and other top law enforcement officers were meeting with the President and Cabinet members in anticipation of an imminent air strike against Iraq.

"It's imperative that I speak to the Director, immediately," he informed the Assistant Director. "The President must not be allowed to give that order!"

He quickly explained about the raid on the Corizentian Commodity, Inc. office and how they were responsible for spreading the Foot and Mouth virus. The Assistant Director transferred his call to the Cabinet Room and Agent Belton explained on the speaker phone, to those who were meeting with the President, that it was not a foreign government behind the terrorist act but was an act perpetrated by Chicago mobsters in an effort to disrupt cattle market prices.

The President's face turned deathly pale when he realized that the air strike was scheduled to begin in five minutes. He quickly ordered Admiral Kelly, Chairman of the Joint Chiefs of Staff to contact Admiral Johnson on the carrier *Enterprise* to abort the strike.

With only one minute before the first missile was to be fired, Admiral Johnson gave the command to abort!

* * * * * *

Fifteen minutes of CBS evening news was devoted to the breaking story of the raid on Corizentian Commodity, Inc. by the FBI and the Deaf Smith County Sheriff's department. It was complete with live interviews with Deputy Buster Thornton, Jo Willman and George Autry. Don Prather commended Deputy Sheriff Buster Thornton for solving the case and apologized to Sheriff Pete Blackwell for taking his statement out of context that *it was possible that foreign terror-*

ists were responsible for starting the Foot and Mouth epidemic.

Prather also had a representative of the White House on the program who confirmed that all cattlemen who lost money as a result of the quarantine would be reimbursed one hundred percent for their losses. And that the federal government would finance a complete program for disinfecting all facilities where FMD had been found. The quarantine would continue for six months while decontamination proceeded.

* * * * * *

Special Agent Ace Belton received a commendation and promotion from FBI Director Friedman and the record showed that agent Belton and his team were totally responsible for "solving the worst act of terrorism to ever take place in the United States of America!"

That was alright with Deputy Sheriff Buster Thornton, he was going to laugh all the way to the bank; because three national book publishing companies were bidding for his story and movie rights. The bids were already up to five million dollars!

ABOUT THE AUTHOR

Gerald McCathern, a native of the Texas Panhandle, has been writing most of his adult life, having published his own nationally circulated newsletter, *The Agriculture Watchdog*. He has written a syndicated column for several newspapers and has authored several books, including *From the White House to the Hoosegow, Gentle Rebels, To Kill the Goose, Line of Succession,* and *Horns.*

Gerald has had an exciting life, having served in the Aviation Engineers during WWII, working as a roustabout, roughneck and graduate geologist in the oil fields of West Texas, and farming, ranching and cattle feeding in the Texas Panhandle.

As the National Wagonmaster during the agriculture protest movement of 1977-1979, he led over 5,000 tractors and 50,000 farmers across the nation to Washington, D.C. in their effort to carry their economic problems to Congress and the American people. During the three year period of the protest, he became very respected in the political realm, having met and worked with most of the leading political figures of that time, including President's Carter and Reagan; Senators Dole and Harkins; and Speakers of the House, Wright and O'Neil.

As a spokesman for the farmers, he appeared on *Good Morning America* and *The Donahue Show*, as well as on many radio talk shows, and met with the editorial board of *The Washington Post*. In 1981 President Reagan appointed him as Special Assistant to Secretary of Agriculture John Block in Washington, D.C., where he worked on many high level programs including a top secret effort to prevent Castro from taking over Jamaica.

The tractor which Gerald drove from Texas to Washington, D.C. the winter of 1979, a 1486 IHC, is now enshrined in the Smithsonian Museum in Washington, D.C.

Gerald met and married his wife, Bonnie Traweek while attending Texas Tech in 1947. They have three children and eight grandchildren and reside at their home in Hereford, Texas.